Film Style in Indonesian Cinema, 1998–2018

Film Style in Indonesian Cinema, 1998–2018

Lighting, Production Design and Camera Movement

Ari Purnama

EDINBURGH
University Press

Edinburgh University Press is one of the leading university presses in the UK. We publish academic books and journals in our selected subject areas across the humanities and social sciences, combining cutting-edge scholarship with high editorial and production values to produce academic works of lasting importance. For more information visit our website: edinburghuniversitypress.com

© Ari Purnama, 2023

Grateful acknowledgement is made to the sources listed in the List of Illustrations for permission to reproduce material previously published elsewhere. Every effort has been made to trace the copyright holders, but if any have been inadvertently overlooked, the publisher will be pleased to make the necessary arrangements at the first opportunity.

Edinburgh University Press Ltd
13 Infirmary Street, Edinburgh, EH1 1LT

Typeset in Garamond MT Pro by
Cheshire Typesetting Ltd, Cuddington, Cheshire

A CIP record for this book is available from the British Library

ISBN 978-1-4744-9661-2 (hardback)
ISBN 978-1-4744-9662-9 (paperback)
ISBN 978-1-4744-9663-6 (webready PDF)
ISBN 978-1-4744-9664-3 (epub)

The right of Ari Purnama to be identified as the author of this work has been asserted in accordance with the Copyright, Designs and Patents Act 1988, and the Copyright and Related Rights Regulations 2003 (SI No. 2498).

Contents

List of Illustrations	vi
Acknowledgements	ix

Part 1: Exposition: What the Book Sets Out to Do and Accomplish

1. Introduction	3
2. Towards a Stylistics of Indonesian Film	29
3. What Can Film Style Do in Narrative Cinema?	47

Part 2: Rising Action: How Indonesian Cinema Has Evolved Aesthetically

4. Evolution by Means of Stylistic Suppression	79

Part 3: Climax: The Analyses, or: How Lighting, Production Design and Camera Movement Have Transformed Indonesian Cinema into a Stylistically Complex Cinema

5. Lighting and Visual Opacity	121
6. Production Design and Diegetic Detail	149
7. Camera Movement and Textural Reflexivity	179

Part 4: Resolution: Wrapping Up and Looking Ahead

8. Concluding Notes: All the Stylistic Pieces Matter	203
Bibliography	208
Filmography	219
Index	225

Figures

2.1	*Duduk bersila* as a staging device in *Sang Pencerah*	30
2.2	*Duduk bersila* in *Sunan Kalijaga dan Syech Siti Jenar*	31
2.3	Screengrabs of Indonesian films uploaded to Adobe Lightroom for visual observation and analyses	42
3.1	A decorative lighting pattern in *Kuldesak*	51
3.2	The *effect lighting* convention simulates the sunlight in *Soekarno: Indonesia Merdeka*	53
3.3	Translucent curtains patterned as a visual motif in *Sang Pencerah*	58
4.1	Low-key lighting in *Tjitra*	81
4.2	Low-key lighting in *Darah dan Doa*	83
4.3	Low-key lighting in *Bernapas Dalam Lumpur*	86
4.4	High-key lighting applied to scenes of pathos in *Bernapas Dalam Lumpur*	87
4.5	As the ghost appears to avenge her death, the intensity of the key light gets reduced to create a sinister atmosphere in *Sundel Bolong*	88
4.6	A flashlight and a candelabrum act merely as props than practical light sources in *Malam Jum'at Kliwon*	90
4.7	The masked vigilante 'The Black Wolf' leaps onto the sacred *beringin* tree during a chase scene in *Srigala Item*	93
4.8	The *tedak siten* ceremony in *Sunan Kalijaga*	99
4.9	The *tedak siten* ceremony in *R.A. Kartini*	101
4.10	Macroscopic details in the production design of *R.A. Kartini*	102
4.11	A pan shot tracks the peeping tom's movement in *Gagak Item*	103
4.12	A pan shot elicits a comic effect in *Harta Karun*	104
4.13	A walk-and-talk shot visualises a pivotal moment between the main characters in *Darah dan Doa*	107
4.14	An aggressive zoom-in technique inflects the parents' surprised reaction at their son's superpower in *Samson Betawi*	111
5.1	Intensified visual darkness in *Darah Garuda*	122
5.2	Intensified visual darkness in *Siti*	123

5.3	High-key lighting applied to a scene of apparition in the 1980 *Pengabdi Setan*	126
5.4	A medium long shot opens the climactic sequence in *Sang Pencerah*	129
5.5	Intensified visual darkness obscures the facial expressions of the two most central characters in the climatic scene of *Sang Pencerah*	130
5.6	Intensified visual darkness blankets a crucial shot even though narratively pivotal lines are being uttered by the two main characters in *Sang Pencerah*	131
5.7	As the two opposing figures finally reconciling their differences, visual darkness is pushed to the limits in the climax of *Sang Pencerah*	132
5.8	Intensified visual darkness permeates the opening shot of a critical scene in *Cerita Cibinong*	136
5.9	A single source lighting technique helps intensifying visual darkness in the most violent scene in *Cerita Cibinong*	137
5.10	A striking silhouette effect created by the single source lighting technique as the violent scene reaches its crescendo in *Cerita Cibinong*	138
6.1	Typical Indonesian household appliances denote the interior of a *toko kelontongan* in *Laskar Pelangi*	154
6.2	Smaller objects specify the time period of *Laskar Pelangi*, most notably the 1970s Rheumason box	155
6.3	A replica of the Sekolah Muhammadiyah, a central setting for *Laskar Pelangi*, built and designed on location in Gentong, Belitong	157
6.4	A poster of 1970s *dangdut* star Rhoma Irama (top) and 1970s-style paper folders (bottom) add micro details to *Laskar Pelangi*'s visual style	158
6.5	Photos of New Order-era President Suharto and Vice President Adam Malik authenticate *Laskar Pelangi*'s period specificity	159
6.6	Electronic calculators (top) and bundled wooden sticks (bottom) visualise a socio-economic contrast between two elementary schools in *Laskar Pelangi*	160
6.7	Offerings as part of the Javanese *tedak siten* ceremony are visualised in microscopic details in *Sang Pencerah*	164
6.8	*Rantaian sedap malam* (strings of tuberoses) on the rooster's cage provides an essential layer of microscopic detail in *Sang Pencerah*	165
6.9	A hard-boiled egg rendered with a hand-painted graphic illustration displaying a *wayang* character in *Soekarno: Indonesia Merdeka*	165

6.10 A copy of the Cairo-based Islamic political magazine *Al Manār* in *Sang Pencerah* 166
6.11 Javanese, Indonesian, Dutch and Arabic taught by Ahmad Dahlan at the *kweekschool* in *Sang Pencerah* 167
6.12 A piece of *batik* cloth hunged on a bamboo structure as a visual motif with symbolic significance in *Sang Pencerah* 168
6.13 Window frames and steel bars function as *aperture framing* devices in the cinematography of *Sang Pencerah* 169
6.14 An angry mob destroys Ahmad Dahlan's *langgar* in *Sang Pencerah* 170
7.1 A highly stylised shot involving a camera movement that follows a flying cigarette in *Kala* 182
7.2 A free-ranging camera movement takes viewers into the interior and exterior spaces of the setting in one unbroken shot in *Catatan Akhir Sekolah* 183
7.3 The Hole Drop shot in *The Raid: Redemption* in which the camera descends into and travels through a hole 184
7.4 The car-to-car flyover shot in *The Raid 2: Berandal* in which the camera exits the first car, floats on the highway and then enters the second car 185
7.5 A roaming camera hovers over the different types of moviegoers in *Janji Joni*: the sexually aroused couple; the movie pirate; the film critics; and the 'perfectionist' 188

Acknowledgements

My motivation to write this book is that it's the book I've wanted to read since I entered my postgraduate training in film studies: a book that discussed Indonesian films from an aesthetic angle. But as I examined the published works on Indonesian cinema, I couldn't find one. So, I undertook the task myself: studying Indonesian cinema with one eye on its aesthetic dimension and the other eye on its makers and their artistry – not only film directors but also cinematographers, production designers, art directors and other craft practitioners – to demonstrate that Indonesian film has a lot to offer artistically to enrich the traditions of world cinema. Throughout the process, I was frequently reminded of this indelible line that Detective Lester Freamon (Clarke Peters) uttered in David Simon's HBO series, *The Wire*: 'We're building something here, detective. We're *building it from scratch*. All the pieces matter.' Because this type of research and monograph had never been done on Indonesian films before (at least to my knowledge), like Freamon's approach to solving a case, I had to 'build it from scratch'. Closely watching more than two hundred Indonesian films from 1939 to 2018, taking thousands of screen grabs, uploading them to Adobe Lightroom (which holds my entire visual database), categorising these screengrabs into several headings, interviewing the film practitioners and engaging with secondary sources – all of this was part of the research efforts to build this study that the book presents. Like Lester Freamon, however, I couldn't have done it alone. I was also surrounded by people who were instrumental in helping me build this work 'from scratch' – directly and indirectly. So, I want to thank them here wholeheartedly.

My appreciation goes first to the Indonesian filmmakers, audiences, critics and scholars I've talked to – formally and informally – over the years. In particular, I'd like to thank Faozan 'Pao' Rizal, Angie Halim, David Hanan, Dag Yngvesson, Ben Murtagh, Ekky Imanjaya, Eric Sasono, Sheila 'Lala' Timothy and the folks at Cine Crib who continue discussing and reviewing Indonesian films on YouTube. My immense gratitude goes to BASE Entertainment, Shanty Harmayn and Joko Anwar for permission to use one of the most evocative images from *Perempuan Tanah Jahanam/Impetigore* for the book's cover. It's truly an honour! I thank my colleagues at the Department of Cinema Studies, the University of Oregon, particularly Priscilla Peña Ovalle, Daniel Steinhart, Michael Aronson, Michael Allan, Dong Hoon Kim, HyeRyoung Ok, Peter Alilunas, Erin Hanna and Sangita Gopal. I am indebted to the support my colleagues and mentors gave me during my doctoral years at the University of Groningen, particularly Barend van Heusden, Liesbeth Korthals Altes, Julian Hanich, Susan Aasman, Martin Rossouw and Kim Middel. I'd be remiss not to thank these incredible film scholars who have shown me what an amazing field the study of film style is at the University of Wisconsin-Madison, who also made my stay as a visiting researcher in the fall semester of 2014–15 an inspiring one: David Bordwell, Kristin Thompson, Jeff Smith, Vance Kepley and Kelley Conway. I also feel that the film scholars whose works have inspired me deserve the credit for showing me the excitement of investigating the art of cinematography in great detail: Patrick Keating, Jakob Isak Nielsen, Frances Guerin, Daisuke Miyao and Christopher Beach. I am tremendously thankful for the book publication grant provided by the Oregon Humanities Center (OHC) and the College of Arts and Sciences (CAS) of the University of Oregon. My gratitude especially goes to Paul Peppis and Jena Turner of OHC for their phenomenal support. Of course, I cannot be more grateful for the incredible assistance, kindness and generosity that Gillian Leslie and Sam Johnson gave me from day one at Edinburgh University Press. I'd also like to thank Sean Martin-Iverson, Masdian Diasto, Frans Ari Prasetyo, Klaas Fleischmann, Paul Schuchhard and Roland Kok sincerely for their friendship and attentiveness. I feel tremendously grateful for the support my mother, Ipa Iis, and brother Andri Suryo have given me over the years. Lastly, I want to acknowledge the indispensable role of my beloved best friend, partner, comrade – you name it – Coosje Oldenhuis, in every step of the way to making this book come to fruition. Now that the book is finished, I promise I will climb the Martini Tower of Groningen with you this time.

Part 1: Exposition

What the Book Sets Out to Do and Accomplish

CHAPTER 1

Introduction

This is a book about film style, how instrumental it is to the rebirth of Indonesian cinema in the twenty years after the collapse of Suharto's authoritarian regime (1998–2018) and why it matters to the study of Indonesian films. Though its nuances will come later in this chapter, my central argument in the book is fairly straightforward: film style matters to the renewal of Indonesian cinema because it has significantly revitalised Indonesian films aesthetically. In what way? The short answer is that film style matters because post-Suharto-era filmmakers have refurbished the visual aesthetic of Indonesian films by foregrounding visual stylisation with three chief devices in cinematography and mise en scène: lighting, production design and camera movement. In doing so, they have helped make Indonesian films visually appealing to the local audiences who have been accustomed to watching international films – whether Hollywood, European or East Asian products – thanks to the access provided by the cinema chains, online film communities, pirated VCD (video compact discs) and DVD markets, social media (YouTube and Vimeo) and transnational streaming services in the 2000s and 2010s. But this foregrounding of visual stylisation isn't pursued simply to coat a cosmetic layer over the films' themes and narratives. Rather than merely producing a set of surface features, the foregrounding of visual stylisation yields a multitude of aesthetic functions, rendering Indonesian cinema in the post-Suharto era stylistically complex, with a pronounced degree of visual sophistication. That's the short answer. The long answer will fill the rest of the book's content.

The book's goal is twofold: first, to show that contemporary Indonesian cinema is artistically rich and innovative, therefore worthy of systematic analyses; second, to demonstrate that Indonesian film can be studied from an aesthetic angle productively. Thus, my agenda with this book is a transformative one: I want to usher in a different way of thinking about Indonesian film; one that's anchored in the conviction that Indonesian film is not only interesting politically, socially and culturally – as most academic works in the field have shown so far – but also aesthetically. Before we launch into going over the terrain we'll be venturing into in this book, let's backtrack and trace a few pivotal moments that set the scene for the book's inception.

SETTING THE SCENE

On 24 April 2012, I planned to see *The Hunger Games* (Gary Ross, 2012) at Blitz Megaplex, an upscale cinema chain located inside a swanky mall in downtown Jakarta. When I arrived at the location, I saw a sea of local moviegoers storming the cineplex to buy tickets for an Indonesian feature film that was being shown at the same screening time. It didn't take long for me to notice that this Indonesian film began to attract a long line of people. As I was walking toward the ticket counter, senior high school students in their school uniforms, hip-looking couples in their early twenties and *hijab*[1]-wearing middle-aged Muslim mothers with their teenage children were all standing in line to buy the tickets for *Serbuan Maut* (*The Raid: Redemption*, Gareth Evans, 2011). *Serbuan Maut* – known more popularly as *The Raid* – is a high-octane action film whose main feature of onscreen action is grounded in the indigenous martial art *pencak silat*, packaged and delivered in run-and-gun documentary-style cinematography. To be completely frank, I wasn't aware at the time that *The Raid* had garnered a substantial buzz among local movie audiences.[2] This enthusiasm for *The Raid* took me by surprise because I had assumed that these people were queuing to watch the latest Hollywood blockbusters – not a *filem lokal* (local film). I was so intrigued and eager to find out what the hype was all about. So, I dropped *The Hunger Games* plan and joined the collective excitement to see the locally made film: *The Raid*.

Flash-forward to 2016, at the Metropolitan Mall in the centre of Bekasi, a city in the West Java province, the *bioskop* (movie theatre) located inside this mall was packed with high school and university students wanting to watch *Siti* (Eddie Cahyono, 2015) – a low-budget dramatic feature film made in the student city of Yogyakarta. This independent film had recently won the Citra Award for Best Film at Festival Film Indonesia (FFI) – an Indonesian equivalent of the Oscars. With a budget of merely Rp150 million (US$12,500),[3] *Siti* became a high watermark for the local filmmaking scene because it was the first indie film made outside Jakarta – the country's centre of film production – to receive high recognition from the Indonesian motion picture industry. Almost all of the audience members remained seated for the post-screening Q&A session, even when there were no leading stars on the panel. When the host invited them to ask questions, many raised their hands and stood up, firing questions at the film's director Eddie Cahyono and producer Ifa Isfansyah – co-founders of Fourcolour Films, one of the pioneering independent film production companies in Indonesia. The questions they asked primarily revolved around the film's striking and unconventional visual style for Indonesian film: *Siti* features a high contrast black and white cinematography presented in the 1:33 Academy aspect ratio, and a heavy reliance on the *long-take* technique with which many of its scenes are presented in a series of lengthy unbroken shots. This idiosyncratic visual style garnered *Siti* so much attention that the Q&A session lasted for sixty minutes – thirty minutes longer than the initial schedule.

Several months later, precisely between 17 and 20 November 2016, in Utrecht, The Netherlands, the Indonesian Embassy to the Kingdom of the Netherlands organised an Indonesian Film Festival held at Wolff Catharijne Bioscoop. The festival organiser asked me to host the Q&A session with the Indonesian film director Riri Riza. His latest feature film *Ada Apa Dengan Cinta? 2* (*What's Up with Cinta? 2*), premiered at the festival. The film festival had a good turnout, but the number of visitors increased dramatically on the day this film premiered. The screening of this anticipated sequel to the successful romantic teen drama *Ada Apa Dengan Cinta?* (*What's Up with Cinta?*, Rudi Soejarwo, 2002) played to a full house. Some visitors who had already bought tickets even had to sit on the steps inside the screening space because there were no available seats left.

The sheer enthusiasm for Indonesian movies permeates the online world, too. Young movie fans are now reviewing Indonesian films on their blogs and social media channels. In the late 2010s, I witnessed the mushrooming of Indonesian YouTube channels that are dedicated to films. For example, the channel Cine Crib[4] – run by a couple of university students and working professionals in Bandung – publishes weekly reviews on the latest Indonesian film releases. They regularly evaluate the local films they watch and periodically share their 'Best & Worst Indonesian Movies' list with their subscribers. As of July 2022, their channel has garnered 51 million views and 239,000 subscribers. They are not the only ones actively assessing Indonesian films, though. We can find many similar movie-reviewing channels on YouTube, as well as podcast episodes available for streaming and download.[5] What binds these social media entities together is the genuine interest in viewing, discussing, critiquing and assessing Indonesian films as fans, really. I find this phenomenon fascinating.

But, what's the big deal? These developments are fascinating to me because when I grew up in Indonesia in the late 1990s, it was uncommon to find many Indonesians enthusiastic about *filem lokal* – let alone openly claiming to be fans. What I remember about the state of Indonesian cinema during that time is that it was acutely depressing. During my junior high school years between 1997 and 2000, I hardly saw any Indonesian film shown in cinemas in the centre of my hometown, Bandung. From what I recall, local films were mostly screened in third-class movie theatres in the city's periphery – marginalised in the literal sense. For Bandung, this peripheral space was located, among others, in the margins of the Bandung Metropolitan Area:

Cimahi, Soreang, Banjaran, Cicalengka and Ujung Berung. In these satellite towns and districts, one could still find Indonesian films being screened at *bioskop pinggiran* (third-class cinemas).

The state of Indonesian film wasn't always like that, though. Filmmaking on the Indonesian archipelago has a long but uneven history. Motion pictures were introduced in the Netherlands Indies as early as 1897 in the period generally known by historians of Indonesia as the 'late colonial state' (1880–1942) or during the transition from the Old Colonial Age to the New Colonial Age.[6] In just a few years after the first motion pictures screening held by the French photographer and travelling showman Albert Talbott, the distribution and exhibition of moving pictures took off rapidly in the Netherlands Indies.[7] After Indonesia became independent in 1949, the national film industry began to take shape in the 1950s during the era of President Sukarno. It wasn't until the Suharto era (1966–98) that local film production reached its zenith. Indonesian films were popular among local audiences in the 1970s and '80s – at the height of Suharto's New Order regime. Even though Indonesian films struggled to compete with Hollywood, Chinese and Indian movies during this period, local audiences still regularly viewed Indonesian films in cinemas proper and at open-air mobile screening events traditionally known as *layar tancap* – literally meaning 'moveable screen pegged into the ground'.

I would be remiss not to mention that in the mid- to late 1980s, the Betamax videocassette players and the mushrooming of video rental places also helped boost the viewership of local films. And if your family could not afford to own a Betamax player (like mine), you could go to a neighbour's house that had one and pay a small fee to watch a movie with other kids in the *kampung* (urban village). I know this because I experienced it first-hand as a kid who loved watching the Indonesian *silat*[8] films (martial arts) of the time. However, I was too little to be able to see them in the movie theatre as the minimum age for anyone to see a film in the cinemas was seventeen years old ('*17 tahun ke atas*'). In the early 1990s, commercial television stations such as TPI (Televisi Pendidikan Indonesia/Indonesian Educational Television) equally helped introduce many classic Indonesian films to younger viewers through their daytime movie programming. Through this programming, I was introduced to the films of Benyamin S, Rhoma Irama, Rano Karno, Sjuman Djaya, Teguh Karya, Warkop DKI, Suzanna and other well-known figures of Indonesian cinema history.

By the mid-1990s, however, the popularity of Indonesian films waned. At the time, it seemed as though Indonesians were embarrassed to watch Indonesian films or even to acknowledge their existence. But there is a good reason for this: the local film industry was mainly producing cheaply-made softcore pornographic films known as *film esek-esek* (sex films), featuring a slew of *artis panas* (erotic actresses).⁹ Consequently, for the majority of the urban population, it was considered much cooler socially and more acceptable culturally to watch the latest of Steven Spielberg's or James Cameron's movies than to watch Indonesian feature films like *Ecstasy & Pengaruh Sex* (*Ecstasy and Sexual Influence*, Yonky Souhoka, 1996) or *Sentuhan Erotik* (*Erotic Touch*, Norman Benny, 1997). Indonesians often refer to this period of decline in Indonesian cinema history as the period of *mati suri* (suspended animation) – it was far from being alive, but it wasn't entirely dead either. What's sad was that Indonesian films became the butt of many jokes among local movie fans – including my high school friends with whom I often went to see Hollywood movies after school.

By contrast, in the 2010s, local audiences were again eager to watch Indonesian films. Also, the dubious reputation of Indonesian film as cheap, unsavoury, low taste and vulgar seemed to dissipate. Remarkably, the tenor surrounding the reception of local films had changed radically compared to when I was in middle school.

As good as this new development sounds, it doesn't mean that the post-Suharto Indonesian film world is free of problems. One of the significant challenges the Indonesian film industry faces today is that Hollywood products still dominate the exhibition sector. Firstly, the quantity of imported films against locally made films is staggeringly imbalanced; the latter is outnumbered. In 2016, for instance, 158 locally made films were screened, compared to 331 American films.¹⁰ Even in 2010, during a turbulent period in which film imports were subjected to higher tariffs, 180 imported films passed the censors and were screened, compared to 87 local films.¹¹ Secondly, the amount of screening time that Hollywood films get is much higher than Indonesian films. Although on paper, film exhibitors are required by law (Film Regulation No. 33, 2009) to screen Indonesian films for 60% of their screening time every six months, the reality shows otherwise. According to film journalist Adrian Jonathan Pasaribu of the Indonesian film website and database *FilmIndonesia.or.id*, Indonesian films get, on average, up to six weeks of exhibition time.¹² Hollywood films, by contrast, can be shown in cinemas for up to three months or more.¹³

Nevertheless, it's still fascinating to witness the revival of Indonesian cinema as indicated by the activities carried out by *penggiat sinema* (cinema activists) described above. What has happened? And what is it about these locally-made films and the specific features that compel people to see and talk about them, online and offline?

These intriguing questions have prompted me to embark on this study. Above all, though, it is the questions about how film as an artform works that perpetually engage my curiosity. More specifically, it is my interest in the ways in which the arrangement of cinematic techniques in cinematography (lighting and camera movement) or production design (location choice, set designing, props and so on) function in a narrative filmic artwork and the creative choices that filmmakers make that motivates my desire to study films. This book is a manifestation of that interest as I endeavour to answer those overarching questions by analysing the visual techniques of Indonesian film, using a perspective that approaches and treats it as a creative artistic product: the poetics of cinema. We will return to this aspect of the book in Chapter 2; for now, let's unpack the book's essential properties.

THE SCOPE, GUIDING QUESTIONS AND LAYERS TO THE ARGUMENT

Indonesian cinema has undergone substantial transformations in the twenty years since the country transitioned from an ironclad authoritarian rule under General Suharto to an electoral democracy (1998–). But reform in politics and the economy has not trickled down entirely to the cultural sectors.[14] The continuing presence of Suharto's authoritarian cultural policy on the one hand and the powerful influence of religious fundamentalism on the other, continue to curtail artists, musicians and filmmakers to exercise their creative expression by imposing formal and informal censorship, even punitive actions.[15] One of the shocking events in this period that demonstrated the increasing religious fundamentalism was the arrest of teenage punk rockers in the city of Banda Aceh. On 14 December 2011, 59 male and five female punk music fans were arrested at a local punk rock concert without any lawful reason other than being musicians with colourful spiky hair. The Indonesian sharia police of Banda Aceh then shaved the heads of these detained punk fans, made them bathe in a lake and forced them into a 'moral rehabilitation' programme.[16] Yet, against this backdrop of fundamentalist cultural politics in the post-Suharto era – also known as the *Reformasi* (reform) era – the Indonesian film world has changed in many ways. For instance, we see greater diversity in production modes, gender representation and the social background of filmmakers – there are more women and self-taught filmmakers now than before.[17]

Apart from those industrial changes, we can also identify changes in the aesthetic dimension of Indonesian cinema. In particular, the visual style of Indonesian films has undergone significant transformation in the post-1998 period. It is this visual stylistic dimension of contemporary Indonesian film that we will be focusing on in this book.

I take visual style to be the systematic organisation of film techniques that shapes the look and feel of a film, resulting from the filmmakers' creative choices.[18] Style is understood differently here from how it is traditionally conceived in the discipline of film studies; that is, as a taxonomic system ('group style') or as a manifestation of a single director's distinctive artistic vision ('directorial style').[19] Rather, style is conceptualised as an organising system that any individual film possesses because, one way or another, every film is put together by the filmmaker(s) using techniques made possible by the filmmaking technology available to them at the time.

The book's central idea is this: contemporary Indonesian filmmakers have been able to leverage visual techniques that were repressed or underexplored in the previous era of Indonesian cinema history, thereby rendering post-1998 Indonesian cinema a *stylistically complex cinema*. Let me clarify from the outset that complexity has nothing to do with the evaluative quality of the films. In fact, I don't make any qualitative judgements on any of the films in this book at all. We can consider visual-stylistic complexity as a distinct mode of cinematic presentation wherein the systematic deployment of film techniques such as cinematography and mise en scène yields multiple aesthetic functions and effects beyond serving storytelling imperatives. I believe it's much more productive to view complexity here as a design feature rather than a quality marker. Just because a film demonstrates a complex visual style, it doesn't guarantee that the film is good. Conversely, a film that doesn't show a stylistic complexity doesn't automatically make it a bad film. Therefore, by arguing that post-Suharto Indonesian cinema can be characterised as stylistically complex cinema, I am not suggesting that the previous eras' films are poorer in quality or not as aesthetically sophisticated as contemporary films. I am suggesting that in the pre-1998 Indonesian film aesthetics, visual stylistic techniques such as cinematography and production design have more restricted roles in shaping cinematic storytelling and viewers' experiences. In other words, they're taking the backseat, whereas acting, dialogue and music are in the driver's seat, guiding viewers' attention and eliciting their emotions.'

Several research questions guide my inquiry and shape the book's content. As a start, knowing that visual stylisation significantly contributes to rendering Indonesian cinema a stylistically complex cinema, how does this work? What are the visual techniques central to the stylistic transformation of Indonesian cinema? What are the functions of these chief visual techniques? What circumstances have facilitated these changes? And finally, what is the broader significance of visual style in contemporary Indonesian film culture?

In answering those questions, let me elaborate on the core argument I provided earlier in this chapter by peeling off its layers. The first layer: the visual stylistic transformation of contemporary Indonesian cinema has been driven primarily by the filmmakers' reinvigoration of three stylistic devices belonging to the domains of mise en scène and cinematography:[20] lighting, production design and camera movement.

The second layer: visual style in post-Suharto cinema performs a multitude of functions. Rather than merely beautifying the cinematic images displayed on the screen or simply transmitting pertinent story information, those primary stylistic devices are significantly involved in producing art mood or atmosphere, suggesting action or event through eliciting imagination, reflecting on the medium of film and particularising the specific features of Indonesian culture and society. Thus, the role of visual style in contemporary Indonesian cinema is complex as it engages in denotative, expressive, symbolic, decorative, suggestive, reflexive and local-regional culture-specifying functions.

The third layer: this visual stylistic transformation has been enabled by several key factors, including technological development in filmmaking, the filmmakers' educational and artistic backgrounds, the reorganisation of the film profession in Indonesia and the fluidity of creative workers in the film industry, and the influence of the aesthetics of world cinema and other arts, particularly the visual arts.

The fourth layer: the larger significance of visual style in the contemporary Indonesian film ecosystem resides in the fact that it provides a creative outlet for filmmakers to represent the diverse local and regional cultures within Indonesia that have long been repressed and underrepresented during the Suharto era.[21] In this case, the transformation of cinematic visual style is not isolated from the broader transformation of cultural fields in post-Suharto Indonesia, whereby 'various kinds of cultural practice' communicate 'new ideas about nation and citizenship', as Intan Paramaditha suggests.[22]

Apart from those analyses-based arguments, I also put forward a conceptual argument in this book, which goes as follows. Based on a close analysis of the use of those three visual stylistic devices by contemporary Indonesian filmmakers, I have found that to understand the diverse and shifting functions of such techniques requires the interpretation of meaning alongside and as part of such a stylistic analysis. Thus, stylistic analysis cannot be divorced totally from meaning making. Employing and expanding upon a poetics of cinema approach to contemporary Indonesian fiction films, I seek to challenge the dichotomy between style and content in film art.

As I have stated above, the particular stylistic devices I am examining in this book relate to lighting, production design and camera movement. We need to define these terms for us to be on the same page. Lighting is understood as the arrangement of lights or illumination of the space, figures and objects in a scene. Production design is defined as the construction of the overall pictorial design of the film, which includes location choices, set design and the selection of props. Next to these analogue ones, contemporary production design also includes digitally-created environments enabled by computer-generated imagery (CGI). Camera movement in this book is used as an umbrella term to encompass a broad range of moving shots or any kind of onscreen moving effects – from the ones produced manually by moving the physical camera or by altering the lens' focal length (the zoom technique) to those created digitally.[23]

Within each of these stylistic devices, specific techniques have played a significant role in revamping the visual style of Indonesian cinema: low-key lighting and intensified visual darkness; location shooting combined with location designing in production design; and free-ranging or prowling camerawork in camera movement.

A final point I'd like to mention as part of my overall argument is that these cinematographic and production design techniques didn't just appear suddenly in the post-1998 era. These techniques, in fact, have a history in Indonesian filmmaking. Still, before the 2000s, these cinematographic and production design tactics were underutilised due to many factors, including technological limitations, prevailing aesthetic norms, the socio-political-cultural paradigm that governed the film industry and the degree of creative freedom that craft practitioners like cinematographers and art directors possessed in previous eras. In the 2000s and 2010s, filmmakers leveraged these techniques and reinvigorated their forms and functions, making them much more salient to the visual aesthetics of Indonesian film.

WHY STUDYING CINEMATIC VISUAL STYLE MATTERS

Examining cinematic visual style is far from trivial. It is significant to the study of film in general and the study of Indonesian cinema more specifically. Most fundamentally, film is an audio-visual medium, so the systematic arrangement of images and sounds gives us access to the world of the story from which we can attain comprehension and understanding of a film's narrative and meanings. Without stylistic elements such as acting, camera movement, art direction, editing, sound, music and so on, we wouldn't have any access to the film's plot in the first place. As David Bordwell contends:

> Film style matters because what people call content comes to us in and through the patterned use of the medium's techniques ... Style is the tangible texture of a film, the perceptual surface we encounter as we watch and listen, and that surface is our point of departure in moving to plot, theme, feeling – everything else that matters to us.[24]

Bordwell isn't the first to argue against the prevalent assumption that style is an inferior dimension of artwork with much less value than the supposedly superior content or substance – represented by the aphorism 'Substance over style'. Outside of film studies, writer and philosopher Susan Sontag, in her essay "On Style", has similarly proposed that the overvaluing of content over style is problematic, so it needs to be re-examined more critically. Sontag even goes so far as to contend that the antithesis of style versus content is a ludicrous dichotomy.[25] Literary scholar Francis-Noël Thomas and cognitive scientist Mark Turner propose a similar idea in their award-winning book on writing style, *Clear and Simple as the Truth: Writing Classic Prose*.[26]

Given that film style is 'our point of departure in moving to plot, theme, feeling' and other things that are meaningful to us, we can safely believe that the systematic handling of stylistic devices shapes viewers' experience and enjoyment of watching Indonesian films. As such, issues of film style are relevant, not only to film academics but to audiences and participants of the film communities, who discuss, critique, judge and appreciate Indonesian movies generally. I'll give you an example. In the reception of the Indonesian box office hit *Dilan 1990* (Pidi Baiq and Fajar Bustomi, 2018), the film has been criticised mainly for its production design. The film is an adaptation of a novel whose story is set in Bandung in the early 1990s. But local viewers find the depiction of this postcolonial city and the period in which the film is set contrived and inauthentic. Despite the film's success in generating a widespread buzz across Indonesia as the most entertaining teen drama of the 2010s, it is, however, considered to fail in representing its setting and period authentically.[27] In this respect, the execution of mise en scène in this period movie matters tremendously to the local viewers, and it shouldn't be taken for granted.

Analysing cinematography and production design as components of visual style furthermore matters because these stylistic components are essential to the engineering of the cinematic experience. Lighting (or lack thereof), location choice and set design are just a few components of cinematography and production design that contribute immensely to the production of filmic atmosphere. As Julian Hanich argues, in cinematic arts, the evocation of atmosphere depends on 'the persistent use of specific settings, seasons, daytimes, and types of weather, music, etc.'[28] Likewise, this also applies to lighting and camera movement techniques. However, Hanich points out that these stylistic devices are also indispensable instruments for achieving a different kind of aesthetic effect that relies heavily on suggestion rather than direct presentation. In horror and thriller films, for instance, these stylistic elements help filmmakers to suggest rather than explicitly show violent, terrifying and repulsive events or actions such that they can elicit the viewers' imaginations. By examining Indonesian cinematic visual style, we shall gain insight into how this aesthetic of suggestion manifests in Indonesian filmmaking and whether there are any distinctive creative twists that make this style different from how Western filmmakers have pursued it. So, analysing lighting, production design and use of camera mobility within contemporary Indonesian cinema will enrich the scholarship on filmic mise en scène and cinematography more generally.

Lastly, examining film style in contemporary Indonesian cinema gives us a thumbnail sketch of the aesthetic evolution of Indonesian film. Through this effort, we will not only obtain a modest aesthetic history of Indonesian cinema, but also ideas about the dynamics of creativity, constraints, innovation and collaboration that have contributed to the transformation of Indonesian films over the years. A filmic artwork, as much as it is a product of culture and commerce, is a creative product put together by a band of practitioners working collaboratively – epitomising what Keith Sawyer has conceptualised as artistic group creativity.[29] When it comes to cinematic mise en scène, for instance, as Frank Kessler rightly notes, this dimension of collective effort cannot be underestimated in the study of film style:

> In practice, and even though the director may have the right to take all final decisions, mise en scène is thus the result of the collaborative efforts of (at least), alongside the director, the set and costume designers, the make-up artists, the cinematographer and the sound technicians, and maybe even the scriptwriter. Their combined efforts aim at telling the film's story audio-visually or, to use a more evocative term, cinematically.[30]

By examining film style in Indonesian cinema, I wish to shed light on the craft and creative artistry of Indonesian filmmakers, particularly those who have played crucial roles in developing the visual style of many Indonesian contemporary films: the producers, directors, cinematographers, production designers and art directors.

SCHOLARSHIP ON INDONESIAN CINEMA AND THE PAUCITY OF AESTHETIC INQUIRY

Given the significance of cinematography and production design in the transformation of Indonesian cinematic visual style and the more general importance of contemporary Indonesian film aesthetics, one would expect this to be a prominent topic in the recent scholarship on Indonesian cinema. But this is not the case. By and large, the scholarly literature produced by both Indonesian and international scholars has not adequately addressed and examined the aesthetic dimension of Indonesian film. Let's survey the most recent academic works so we'll have a concrete picture of this situation.

In his book *Indonesian Cinema after the New Order: Going Mainstream*, Thomas Barker argues that Indonesian films in the post-Suharto years are more accepted by local audiences because, unlike those produced in the Suharto era, contemporary film production has become inextricably entangled with wider pop culture. Barker claims that Suharto-era films were assembled under the parochial nationalist framework labelled *film nasional* and consequently were made under tight state control. By contrast, post-Suharto films are made under the logic of pop culture, with young middle-class Indonesians as their primary target audiences.[31] By operating under this pop culture logic, Indonesian filmmakers in the twenty years after the fall of the Suharto regime have launched Indonesian films to become part of the mainstream culture, hence his book's subtitle: *Going Mainstream*. Barker maintains that although Indonesian film has gone mainstream, the current industry remains controlled by the encroaching 'hands of the past', with the past being the authoritarian cultural policies and institutions established during the Suharto era that carried over to present-day 'reformed' Indonesia.

Like Barker, Katinka van Heeren in *Contemporary Indonesian Film: The Spirit of Reform and the Ghosts from the Past* similarly claims that despite the changes in how films are made and distributed contemporarily in Indonesia, 'the ghost' of the Suharto-era film policies continues to haunt the post-1998 film industry.[32] For example, thanks to new media technologies like the video compact disc and digital video camera, independent filmmakers in the post-Suharto period have bypassed the conventional system to make, distribute and show their films. Through this 'side-stream' filmmaking approach, filmmakers can release their works straight to video compact discs, alleviating restrictions applied typically to theatrical releases.[33] At the same time, though, censorship practices have become worse than during the Suharto era, according to her. At one end, filmmakers still face the formal censorship exercised by the state-run censorship board LSF (Lembaga Sensor Film). At the other end, they now face the informal or 'street censorship' carried out by interest groups such as right-wing organisations that often threaten filmmakers' creative autonomy and even physical safety. For instance, they often ban or halt filmmakers from making or screening films that explore politically sensitive subject matters. One of these hot button issues is the 1965–6 anti-communist purge in Java, Bali and other parts of Indonesia, orchestrated by Suharto's military force and state apparatus.[34] However, van Heeren claims that apart from censorship, another equally powerful force shapes film texts: commerce. Thus, how certain social realities and collective identities are represented in Indonesian films depends upon the necessity to comply with the film laws (censorship) on the one hand and the pressure to satisfy market forces (commerce) on the other. Van Heeren, thus, concludes that Indonesian film in the post-Suharto era is an ideological battleground where various groups fight to express their values, identities and imaginations of how Indonesia should be.

Another book that seeks to explain the dynamics of contemporary Indonesian film is *Menjegal Film Indonesia* ('Tackling Indonesian Film'), put together by Eric Sasono and his colleagues Ekky Imanjaya, Hikmat Darmawan and Ifan Adriansyah Ismail.[35] Approaching Indonesian cinema from a political economy perspective, they aim to understand the intricate contours of the Indonesian film industry from the Sukarno until the post-Suharto era. Their research cuts deep into the mechanics of the Indonesian film industry as a cultural business, with discussions ranging from the economics of production and exhibition to national film policy. Their study provides the most comprehensive industrial account of Indonesian film to date. They argue that the film industry in Indonesia has not yet achieved an optimal state of development. Like Barker and van Heeren, Sasono et al. contend that the powers that ruled the industry during the Suharto presidency have preserved and continue to exert their influence in the current period. But in the post-Suharto era, these powers are accompanied by other societal elements that seek to gain influence in the film industry. For instance, when it comes to censorship, the state-run LSF is the official institution authorised to cut films. And yet, *dai* (Muslim preachers) and religious interest groups like the Islamic MUI (Majelis Ulama Indonesia/Indonesian Clerics Assembly) and FPI (Front Pembela Islam/Islam Defenders Front) often exercise their 'street censorship' over Indonesian films by pressuring the government to ban films or holding street protests against filmmakers.[36]

Sasono et al. also show that post-Suharto-era filmmakers are more diverse in their backgrounds than in the previous eras. Filmmakers from other disciplines outside of film or who have studied outside of the state-run film academy IKJ (Institut Kesenian Jakarta/Jakarta Arts Institute) are now actively making films alongside those who are formally trained. These autodidact filmmakers have mostly learned the craft through informal training such as filmmaking workshops at a local cinema club.[37] Moreover, there are more women filmmakers now than there have been in previous eras of Indonesian film history.[38] In their view, while some notable changes have occurred, many significant aspects of the industry remain unchanged. In this sense, Sasono et al.'s conclusions are not too far from Barker's and van Heeren's regarding the industrial dynamics of Indonesian cinema in the post-Suharto era.

No doubt, these academic books from Barker, van Heeren and Sasono et al. have made substantial contributions to the growing body of scholarship on contemporary Indonesian cinema, insofar as the influence of politics, government policy, capital and religion on the Indonesian film world is concerned. But there's something important missing in these studies: rigorous analysis of the films. While they provide a detailed picture of institutional change in the Jakarta-based Indonesian film industry, they hardly show us how the films' 'internal dynamics',[39] to use Bordwell's phrase, are at work as a result of those industrial changes. These internal dynamics include narrative design and storytelling strategy, stylistic patterning and thematic undertaking. As such, while the first question I posed earlier in the introduction (What has happened to Indonesian cinema since the fall of Suharto?) is well-explored in the literature, the second question remains unanswered: What is it about the films themselves that has made Indonesian audiences eager to watch locally made films again?

If we take Barker's pop culture thesis to be accurate, how does pop culture translate into a set of formal and stylistic strategies filmmakers use systematically to entice and engage young Indonesian audiences to watch Indonesian films? Unfortunately, Barker doesn't give us the answer to this valid question in his book. The same goes for van Heeren's work. As much as she manages to shed light on the role of discourse in shaping contemporary Indonesian film practices, her analysis of film narrative practices is problematic, partly due to insufficient attention to the aesthetic and narrative strategies employed by Indonesian filmmakers. She argues that censorship and commerce 'define the film texts produced',[40] but this places too much emphasis on extra-textual forces like the ongoing debates on Islam, sex, violence, and the anti-communist massacre while positioning the filmmakers as powerless pawns caught between these social struggles for ideological dominance. As a result, her discussion of contemporary film narrative practices overlooks how contemporary filmmakers have also harnessed their creativity to alleviate censorship using particular formal and stylistic tactics. As David Hanan has shown in his article "A Tradition of Political Allegory and Political Satire in Indonesian Cinema", Indonesian filmmakers are well-versed in using allegory and political satire to critique the status quo in an oblique way, sustaining the local tradition of criticism known as *sindiran*.[41] In this regard, van Heeren fails to recognise – or at least to properly take into account – the filmmakers' agency and inventiveness in crafting their films to evade censorship or to express criticism of the governing institutions through creative and subtle means like *sindiran* and other forms of satire. Growing religious fundamentalism, on the one hand, and the embrace of economic neoliberalism, on the other, have certainly characterised post-Suharto Indonesia. But we shouldn't take wholesale the influence of these social, political and market mechanisms. Rather, we must question whether these 'hidden hands' are the most determining factors shaping the filmic works.

Looking beyond the most recent academic works, I maintain that, overall, aesthetic matters have received little attention in the scholarship of

Indonesian film. The canonical works in the field, so far, have dealt mainly with the social, cultural and political dimensions of Indonesian cinema. Salim Said's pioneering *Shadows on the Silver Screen* chronicled the social history of Indonesian film, while Karl G. Heider's *Indonesian Cinema: National Culture on Screen* analysed the films from the New Order era through a cultural-anthropological lens. Through the framework of media politics, Krishna Sen's *Indonesian Cinema: Framing the New Order* unravelled the ideological underpinnings of New Order era cinema, anchored in Suharto's parochial philosophy of governance. Besides these monographs, Misbach Yusa Biran's *Sejarah Film 1900–1950: Bikin Film Di Jawa*[42] also contributes significantly to the historical study of film production in Java during the colonial era – a research topic hardly explored before the publication of his book. As much as these books cut deep into Indonesian cinema's social, cultural and political dimensions, they do not scrutinise the films very closely. Scrupulous film analysis, supported by visual evidence (shots or screen grabs) taken from film scenes, is scarce in the body of scholarship produced so far.

I say 'scarce' because there are published works that prove to be some exception, but they are in the minority. I can single out the works of David Hanan and Ben Murtagh here. In *Cultural Specificity in Indonesian Film: Diversity in Unity*, Hanan dissects canonical Indonesian films and analyses particular moments in the films to support his overarching thesis about the depiction of regional cultural specificity in Indonesian films. Hanan examines scenes from feature films such as *Roro Mendut* (Ami Priyono, 1982), *November 1828* (Teguh Karya, 1979), *Ada Apa Dengan Cinta?* and experimental films like Gotot Prakosa's *Meta Ekologi* (1979). Hanan also includes film stills – supplied mostly by Sinematek Indonesia (the Indonesian Film Archive) – making his descriptions and arguments visually concrete. From a film semiotics tradition, Hanan treats Indonesian films as textual units, part of a larger sign system influenced by culture. In *Moments in Indonesian Cinema History*, Hanan sustains his detailed engagement with specific Indonesian films as case studies, from Usmar Ismail's *Darah dan Doa* (*The Long March*, 1950) to the films made by the new generation of women filmmakers in the 2010s, such as *Sekala Niskala* (*The Seen and Unseen*, Kamila Andini, 2017) and *Marlina si Pembunuh dalam Empat Babak* (*Marlina the Murderer in Four Acts*, Mouly Surya, 2017).[43] Different from Hanan's works, Murtagh's monograph *Gender and Sexualities in Indonesian Cinema* discusses specific Indonesian films in how they represent gay, lesbian and transgender individuals onscreen and how it has developed over time.[44] Commendably, each chapter in his book gives adequate attention to particular films considered critical for portraying the lives of gay, lesbian and transgender Indonesians (whether negative, positive or ambiguous), such as *Istana Kecantikan* (*Palace of Beauty*, Wahyu Sihombing, 1988), *Catatan Si Boy*

(*Boy's Diary*, Nasri Cheppy, 1987), *Arisan! (The Gathering*, Nia Dinata, 2003), *Realita Cinta dan Rock N' Roll (The Reality of Love and Rock N' Roll*, Upi Avianto, 2006) and *Coklat Stroberi (Chocolate Strawberry*, Ardy Octaviand, 2007).

Still, Hanan and Murtagh's books are not concerned with the visual aesthetic evolution of Indonesian film and how film style in contemporary Indonesian cinema functions because they have different research questions from mine that they seek to answer. From surveying all these works, though, we can see that visual style remains unexamined in the existing literature on Indonesian film.[45] One may ask, why is this the case? Here's my proposed explanation.

At least two historical-institutional reasons explain why Indonesian cinematography and production design, or visual aesthetic in general, have received little attention from scholars in the field. First, less information is available on the works and careers of Indonesian cinematographers and production designers than on directors, producers and actors, both in Indonesian and English.[46] The absence of truly professional associations and media outlets through which they could disseminate their discourse of artistry exacerbates the lack of exposure to their works. Unlike in the United States, where the American Society of Cinematographers (ASC) with their *American Cinematographer* magazine has been providing working cinematographers with a space to express their approaches to the art and craft of cinematography, in Indonesia, professional cinematographers have never had such an established outlet. In the Suharto era, cinematographers were obliged to join the KFT (Ikatan Karyawan Film dan Televisi Indonesia/Indonesian Film and Television Workers League) to be able to work legally in the film industry. But the KFT, in practice, was more of a government-controlled body, established to ferret out communist sympathisers in the film production sector rather than to support filmmakers professionally.[47] It is only in the post-Suharto era that cinematographers and production designers have been able to form professional associations: the IPD (Indonesia Production Designer) and SI (Sinematografi Indonesia)/ICS (Indonesian Cinematographers Society). Even then, the nature of these young associations (founded in 2013 and 2014, respectively) and their activities are unclear. It is uncertain whether they will publish their media outlet analogous to *American Cinematographer* magazine, which has been crucial to sound the working cinematographers' voices in Hollywood since 1920. So, to unearth information about their works, the researcher needs to do a good deal of data gathering first-hand. This information gathering can be done by interviewing them or digging into what John Thornton Caldwell calls the *industrial craft reflexivity*.[48] This refers to documentation in the form of behind-the-scenes documentaries or making-of testimonials, whether online or in print, in which cinematographers and production designers share their insights into the creative choices that they have made that contribute to the film's visual style.

A second factor that seriously contributed to the lack of film aesthetic studies is the field's historical development since the 1990s. The academic study of Indonesian film did not arise from film studies proper. Instead, it came out of several disciplinary origins, among which is area studies (i.e., Southeast Asian Studies) that hosted a myriad of social scientific and cultural studies approaches, except a film-as-art approach. Consequently, Indonesian film has been regarded as a significant social phenomenon, but not as an artistic field or artform that produces works of substantial artistry, meaning and value. The amount of literature published in English on Indonesian cinema that centres on identity politics, using theoretical approaches derived from postmodernism, feminism, critical theory, queer theory and cultural studies, provides substantial evidence of the field's commitment to cultural and identity politics as a research agenda. Thus, we can find more published works that uncover how gender and sexuality, race, religion (Islam) and nationhood are represented in Indonesian films than in examining film techniques and filmmaking artistry.[49] While we can find academic studies (in English) on the formal and stylistic aspects of the Indonesian traditional arts,[50] whether examining *wayang golek* (the Sundanese rod-puppet theatre of West Java), *wayang kulit* (the Javanese shadow play), *batik* (waxed and dyed textile art), *gamelan* (the indigenous orchestra), or *Bedaya-Serimpi* dances (the Javanese court dance drama), we have yet to see the equivalent of those works in the field of Indonesian cinema studies.[51]

By examining the visual stylistic dynamics of contemporary Indonesian cinema, I wish to lay the groundwork for building an aesthetic history of Indonesian cinema, which is sorely needed. But this is not all. With this book, I also want to remedy the lack of attention to Southeast Asian cinema in the English-language scholarship on film style. Although film style research has undergone a revival in the 2000s and 2010s,[52] American and European films and filmmakers still gain the biggest attention in the academic output on this subject. Moreover, these works tend to sustain the belief that a film director is the film's author and, by default, the creative genius behind the film's expression of visual style – a symptom known as 'entrenched auteurism' to use C. Paul Sellors's phrase.[53]

The good news is that in the 2010s, we've seen the emergence of scholarly works that focus on film style in a transnational context and zoom in on specific domains of craft in film production – from cinematography to costume design. Even more promising is that these books bring to light the 'hidden' contributions of other above-the-line and below-the-line creatives and workers to the production of filmic images, including cinematographers, gaffer and lighting designers, camera operators, production designers, art directors, costume designers, visual effects supervisors and editors.[54] By doing so, the scholars behind these invigorating books bring closer the interaction and connection between academic film studies and practical film production. By taking Indonesian film as its subject of analysis, this book adds to this new wave of film stylistics a study of a non-Western cinematic context embedded in a developing economy with diverse cultural composition and artistic expressions.

THE ARC OF THE BOOK IN FOUR ACTS

Propelling the first act (Part 1: Exposition) forward, Chapter 2 provides an analytical sneak preview that foreshadows what the stylistic analyses will look like in the central part of the book (Chapters 5–7). In this chapter, I also lay out the poetics of cinema as the book's operating system for studying Indonesian film. The poetics of cinema as an approach comes with an analytical tool that I use to examine visual style in contemporary Indonesian cinema: analytic stylistics. Analytic stylistics is grounded in the presumption that style serves one or more functions or effects to the end of a filmic work. Now, to understand analytic stylistics, we must precisely define these functions of style in film art. So, in Chapter 3, I wrap up the first act of the book with an exposition of the theoretical ideas that film theorists, film historians and film philosophers have articulated about the functions of film style. These ideas are essential to outline in this chapter because they function as the book's theoretical backbone that supports my analyses of visual style in contemporary Indonesian cinema.

The second act (Part 2: Rising Action) launches into the historical stylistics of Indonesian cinema. The purpose of this chapter is to trace the evolution of visual style in Indonesian cinema history. This chapter is essential because therein, I will show the continuity and changes of visual style in Indonesian cinema pertaining to the three stylistic devices that I argue to be salient in the post-Suharto era: lighting, production design and camera movement.

The book's third act (Part 3: Climax) is my favourite part of the book because it contains the flesh of the work: the stylistic analyses on which the book's arguments are based. Chapter 5 is the first of the three analytical chapters that excitingly animate this third act in which I analyse a key stylistic device in the visual transformation of post-Suharto Indonesian films: lighting. In this chapter, I will devote most of the pages to describing and explaining the emergence of a specific lighting tendency that valorises extreme visual darkness. This lighting mode is a reinvigorated form of the low-key lighting technique, which has already existed in Indonesian cinema since the colonial era. But a notable difference is that the low-key lighting technique is now pushed toward creating underexposed images, rendering the Indonesian cinematic images visually opaque.

In Chapter 6, I examine the exploration of production design as another salient visual stylistic device in post-Suharto Indonesian cinema. The purpose of this chapter is to describe and analyse how contemporary filmmakers are exploring the craft of production design to revamp the look of Indonesian film, and how this exploration differs from the way it was pursued in the earlier periods of Indonesian cinema history. I claim that, in the post-Suharto era, filmmakers have reinvigorated production design by accumulating macroscopic and microscopic visual details through their integration of location shooting with location designing for exterior and interior shots. Therefore, not only do they go to existing locations to shoot the film's scenes, they also design these locations by decorating and dressing them or by building an entirely new set in the chosen locations. By interlocking these two production design tactics together (location shooting and location designing), filmmakers in the post-Suharto period have bathed the visuals of their films in *diegetic details*. The accumulation of these minute details in post-New Order production design fulfils multiple functions. But not all of these functions will be equally salient. Contingent upon genre, mode of production, theme and the artistic motivation of the filmmakers, some aesthetic purposes are prioritised while others are de-emphasised – I call this the aesthetic phenomenon of *bounded multifunctionalism*.

In Chapter 7, I analyse the third indispensable stylistic device in post-Suharto cinema: camera movement. I argue that there is an intense exploration of free-ranging camerawork in post-Suharto Indonesian cinematic visual style. Like any other type of camera movement, this free-ranging camerawork is multifunctional. But my claim is that reflexivity as an aesthetic feature has gained more presence in post-Suharto films than in films from the previous eras. As such, it is a significant effect pertinent to the increased complexity in the functions of visual style in contemporary Indonesian film aesthetics. In short, camera movement not only contributes to making the visual texture of Indonesian films more dynamic but also reflexive – calling attention to the artifice of the medium and offering viewers a different kind of engagement that values the artifice in its own right.

In the fourth act (Part 4: Resolution), the book wraps everything up and looks ahead by offering some concluding thoughts. So, in the book's last chapter, I conclude by first addressing the broader significance of visual style in contemporary Indonesian film culture. Beneath the fold, I will then suggest the implications of this research for the study of Indonesian arts and culture.

Finally, I will point to future research that could be done to advance and enrich this poetics approach to studying Indonesian cinema.

To help you navigate the book seamlessly, let me share a few notes about how I cite Indonesian words and phrases, names and film titles, abbreviations and the specifically-Indonesian terminologies used to indicate the different periods covered in the book. Every Indonesian word or phrase I introduce in this book will be italicised and provided with the English translation next to it in parenthesis. For words or phrases derived from local languages in Indonesia, such as Javanese, Sundanese or Balinese, I will explicitly mention them. For example, *pareh* (Sundanese for rice). Regarding naming practices, unlike Westerners, most Indonesians do not have surnames, and many have only a single given name (e.g., Sukarno, Suharto, Edwin). When they do have first and last names, people refer to them according to the name by which the person is commonly known. This convention also applies to written works. So, in this book, to avoid confusion, I will mention any Indonesian filmmaker with a complete first and last name, and the name by which this filmmaker is commonly known will be italicised. In the subsequent mention of this filmmaker within a chapter, I will mention the italicised name – for instance, *Usmar* Ismail (first mention), and then Usmar (subsequent mention). For film titles, I will use the Indonesian titles and provide the official English titles or the translations of them in parenthesis and italicised because not all Indonesian films have official English titles. The book's filmography includes film titles cited in the text, plus those that I consulted in the course of my research. The names of Indonesian organisations will be abbreviated, and the English translation of them will be provided in parenthesis. In many cases, I will use abbreviations such as d.p. (director of photography) and prod. des. (production designer) to specifically mention the creative collaborators of the film's director. Lastly, I will refer to the Indonesian historical periods discussed in this book as follows: the colonial era (before 1949), the Sukarno era (1950–65) and the Suharto or the New Order era (1966–98). I will refer to the period after the collapse of Suharto and his New Order regime mainly as the post-Suharto era, but I will also use the following designations: the contemporary period, the post-1998 era and the post-New Order era.

Notes

1. The *hijab* is a veil worn by Muslim women when in public or in the presence of any male outside of their immediate family.
2. After premiering at the Toronto International Film Festival (TIFF) on 8 September 2011, *The Raid* was then screened as the closing film at the

Indonesia International Fantastic Film Festival (iNAFFF) in Jakarta on 20 November 2011. According to Rusli Eddy – the director of iNAFFF – the tickets for this screening were sold out within ten minutes. See 'Film "The Raid" Tayang di Indonesia', *Viva.co.id*, November 2 2011, https://www.viva.co.id/showbiz/260949-film-the-raid-tayang-di-indonesia.

3. 'Siti – Production & Contact Info', *IMDbPro*, accessed 8 August 2022, https://pro.imdb.com/title/tt4186170/.
4. Cine Crib's YouTube channel is available here: https://www.youtube.com/channel/UCrMqntY4lAQu0JHYFl8Z0nw/featured.
5. See, for example, the following YouTube and podcast channels: Hans Tau Film; KINCIR Cinema Club; Kripik Film; Moovvie; Casscapade; and Podluck Podcast: Cinema Paradisco.
6. 'The late colonial state' is from R. B. Cribb, *The Late Colonial State in Indonesia: Political and Economic Foundations of the Netherlands Indies, 1880–1942* (Leiden: KITLV Press, 1994). Meanwhile, 'New Colonial Age' is from Merle C. Ricklefs, *A History of Modern Indonesia Since c. 1200* (Basingstoke, Hampshire & New York: Palgrave Macmillan, 2008), p. 183.
7. For more discussion on Albert Talbott's Scenimatograph and his role in the early travelling shows in the Netherlands Indies, see Chapter 1 ('Trials and Tribulations of Early Travelling Shows: 1896–1898') of Dafna Ruppin's PhD dissertation: 'The Komedi Bioscoop: The Emergence of Movie-Going in Colonial Indonesia (1896–1914)' (PhD Thesis, Utrecht University, 2015).
8. Silat films or *filem silat* in Indonesian is a genre of Indonesian film that features the *pencak silat* martial art as its main attraction. But Indonesian audiences also use *filem silat* or *film laga* to refer to action films in general.
9. J. B. Kristanto, 'Sepuluh Tahun Terakhir Perfilman Indonesia', in *Katalog Film Indonesia 1926–2007* (Jakarta: Nalar, 2007), xxi–xxix.
10. Muhammad Hafil, 'Film Impor Masih Mendominasi', *Republika Online*, 21 February 2017, https://republika.co.id/berita/senggang/film/17/02/21/olpu5w326-film-impor-masih-mendominasi.
11. Lisabona Rahman, 'Apa Kabar Film Impor?', *Film Indonesia*, 8 May 2011, http://filmindonesia.or.id/article/apa-kabar-film-impor; 'Daftar Judul Film Indonesia Berdasarkan Tahun "2010"', *Film Indonesia*, accessed 3 October 2018, http://filmindonesia.or.id/movie/title/list/year/2010.
12. Adrian Jonathan Pasaribu, 'Box Office Terus Menurun, Waktunya Mengambil Risiko?', *Film Indonesia*, 26 July 2012, http://filmindonesia.or.id/article/box-office-terus-menurun-waktunya-mengambil-risiko.
13. J. B. Kristanto and Adrian Jonathan Pasaribu, 'Catatan 2011: Menonton Penonton', *Film Indonesia*, 30 December 2011, http://filmindonesia.or.id/article/catatan-2011-menonton-penonton.
14. See, for example, Ariel Heryanto and Vedi Hadiz, 'Post-Authoritarian Indonesia', *Critical Asian Studies* 37, no. 2 (2005), pp. 251–75; and Vedi Hadiz, 'Indonesia: Order and Terror in a Time of Empire', in *Empire and Neoliberalism in Asia*, ed. Vedi Hadiz (London and New York: Routledge, 2006), pp. 123–38.

15. Tod Jones, 'Indonesian Cultural Policy in the Reform Era', *Indonesia* 93, no. April (2012), pp. 147–76.
16. See 'Police Arrest Punks in Indonesia – in Pictures', *The Guardian*, 14 December 2011, http://www.theguardian.com/world/gallery/2011/dec/14/police-arrest-punks-indonesia.
17. For accounts that specifically discuss these aspects of the post-Suharto Indonesian film industry, see: Yvonne L. Michalik, ed., *Indonesian Women Filmmakers* (Berlin: RegioSpectra, 2013) and Eric Sasono et al., *Menjegal Film Indonesia: Pemetaan Ekonomi Politik Industri Film Indonesia* (Jakarta: Rumah Film, 2011).
18. This alternative conceptualisation of film style has been developed, among others, by David Bordwell, Kristin Thompson and Noël Carroll in several publications, such as: David Bordwell, *Poetics of Cinema* (New York, NY: Routledge, 2008); David Bordwell and Kristin Thompson, *Film Art: An Introduction*, 8th Edition (Boston, MA: McGraw Hill, 2008); David Bordwell, *Figures Traced in Light: On Cinematic Staging* (Berkeley, CA: University of California Press, 2005); David Bordwell, *Visual Style in Cinema* (Frankfurt am Main: Verlag der Autoren, 2001); David Bordwell, *On the History of Film Style* (Cambridge, MA: Harvard University Press, 1997); David Bordwell, 'Visual Style in Japanese Cinema', *Film History* 7, no. 1 (Spring 1995), pp. 5–31; Noël Carroll, 'Film Form: An Argument for a Functional Theory of Style in the Individual Film', *Style*, Literature Online, 32, no. 3 (1998), pp. 385–401; and Noël Carroll, 'Film Form: An Argument for a Functional Theory of Style in the Individual Film', in *Engaging the Moving Image* (New Haven, CT: Yale University Press, 2003), pp. 127–46.
19. For an explanation regarding the differences between the concept of style in an individual film and the concepts of style as a taxonomic system ('group style') and a personal signature ('directorial style'), see Noël Carroll, 'Style', in *The Routledge Companion to Philosophy and Film*, eds Paisley Livingston and Carl Plantinga (London and New York: Routledge, 2009), pp. 268–78; Carroll, 'Film Form: An Argument for a Functional Theory of Style in the Individual Film'. For an account on how film style has been theorised prior to the advent of the poetics of cinema approach, see Chapters III, IV and V of Jeremy G. Butler, *Toward a Theory of Cinematic Style: The Remake*, Electronic Edition (Morrisville, NC: Lulu, 2003).
20. Frank Kessler in his illuminating book about the origin and evolution of mise en scène as a concept and practice in the cinematic arts contends that one of the most fundamental functions of mise en scène in a narrative fiction film is 'to shape and give body to the diegesis, the world in which the story occurs'. In this regard, production design, which encompasses location choice, set design and arrangement of props, actively contributes to achieving that function of mise en scène for it 'endows the diegetic universe with specific qualities'. Frank Kessler, *Mise en scène* (Montréal: caboose, 2014), pp. 33–5.
21. Following David Hanan's definition, a local-regional culture or society in the Indonesian context is identified as 'an entity that exists and conceives of itself as existing at a sub-national level'. On the Indonesian archipelago, most of these entities 'stem from pre-national times and, furthermore, many existed in pre-

colonial times, as pre-state communities, often with their own different languages'. David Hanan, *Cultural Specificity in Indonesian Film: Diversity in Unity* (Cham: Palgrave Macmillan Imprint, Springer International Publishing, 2017), p. 225.

22. Intan Paramaditha, 'Film Studies in Indonesia: An Experiment of a New Generation', *Bijdragen Tot de Taal-, Land- En Volkenkunde/Journal of the Humanities and Social Sciences of Southeast Asia* 173, nos 2–3 (January 1, 2017), p. 359, https://doi.org/10.1163/22134379-17302006.
23. Some film scholars like Bordwell and Thompson prefer to use the term 'the mobile frame' over camera movement (see Bordwell and Thompson, *Film Art*, p. 479) to be inclusive of those moving effects that are achieved digitally as well. But I believe the term camera movement is more established both within the fields of filmmaking, cinematography and film scholarship, and it connotes a wider set of onscreen moving effects (even including those that are created in the absence of moving the physical camera). That's why, in this book, I will primarily use the term camera movement to refer to this cinematographic device.
24. Bordwell, *Figures Traced in Light*, p. 32.
25. Susan Sontag, *Against Interpretation and Other Essays* (New York, NY: Farrar, Straus & Giroux, 1966). Reprint, *Against Interpretation and Other Essays* (London: Penguin, 2009).
26. Thomas and Turner, *Clear and Simple as the Truth*.
27. This criticism is voiced by various Indonesian film reviewers online including Cine Crib and Kupas Film.
28. Julian Hanich, *Cinematic Emotion in Horror Films and Thrillers: The Aesthetic Paradox of Pleasurable Fear* (New York, NY: Routledge, 2010), p. 171 (emphasis added).
29. R. Keith Sawyer, *Group Creativity: Music, Theater, Collaboration* (New York & London: Routledge, 2003).
30. Kessler, *Mise en scène*, p. 33.
31. Thomas Barker, *Indonesian Cinema After the New Order: Going Mainstream* (Hong Kong: Hong Kong University Press, 2019).
32. Katinka van Heeren, *Contemporary Indonesian Film: Spirits of Reform and Ghosts from the Past* (Leiden: KITLV Press, 2012).
33. *Film pinggiran* ('side-stream' filmmaking) has its roots in the underground experimental film scene that emerged in Jakarta in the 1980s. It was the avant-garde filmmaker and film lecturer Gotot Prakosa who coined the term 'side-stream' filmmaking. See Gotot Prakosa, *Film Pinggiran* (Jakarta: FFTV-IKJ and YLP Fatma Press, 1997), cited in Katinka van Heeren, 'Indonesian Side-Stream Film,' in *Asian Hot Shots: Indonesian Cinema* (Marburg: Schüren, 2009), pp. 71–97. For an inquiry into the significant values of video compact discs (VCDs) in contemporary Indonesian film culture, see Ari Purnama, 'The Video Compact Disc and the Digital Preservation of Indonesian Cinema', in *Exposing the Film Apparatus: The Film Archive as a Research Laboratory*, eds Giovanna Fossati and Annie van den Oever, Framing Film (Amsterdam: EYE Filmmuseum/ Amsterdam University Press, 2016), pp. 141–50.

34. The documentary films *Jagal* (*The Act of Killing*, 2012) and *Senyap* (*The Look of Silence*, 2014) – directed by Joshua Oppenheimer – explore the lingering impact of this atrocity on contemporary Indonesian societies from the perspectives of the perpetrators and victims.
35. Sasono et al., *Menjegal Film Indonesia*.
36. A prime example of this 'street censorship' is the ban of the teen film *Buruan Cium Gue!* (*Kiss Me Quick!* Findo Purwono, 2004). The censorship board had approved this film to be screened in cinemas. However, after its release, the influential Muslim preacher Abdullah Gymnastiar, known publicly as Aa Gym, voiced his protest against the screening of this film in mainstream media. He had never seen the film himself, so he based his normative judgement and criticism simply on the film's title, particularly on the word *cium* (kiss). He believed that it would encourage Indonesian teenagers to engage in premarital sex. He managed to gather support from Islamic governmental and mass organisations. After two weeks of protests from these groups, the film was withdrawn from cinemas on 21 August 2004.
37. Sasono et al., *Menjegal Film Indonesia*, pp. 123–7.
38. Ibid., p. 118.
39. Ari Purnama, *A Conversation with David Bordwell: Poetics of Cinema, Film Stylistics and Research Valorization*, Vimeo, 23 October 2013, video, 53:28, https://vimeo.com/77626940.
40. van Heeren, *Contemporary Indonesian Film*, p. 15.
41. The tradition of *sindiran* using teasing allusion and indirect parallelism harks back to colonial times and can be found in traditional arts such as the Javanese *wayang kulit* and the Sundanese *wayang golek* (puppet plays) as well as in indigenous theatre. For more discussion on the tradition of allegory and satire in Indonesian cinema and other traditional arts, see David Hanan, 'A Tradition of Political Allegory and Political Satire in Indonesian Cinema', in *Asian Hot Shots: Indonesian Cinema*, eds Yvonne Michalik and Laura Coppens (Marburg: Schüren, 2009), pp. 14–45; Barbara Hartley, *Javanese Performances on an Indonesian Stage* (Honolulu: University of Hawaii Press, 2008); and Andrew N. Weintraub, *Power Plays: Wayang Golek Puppet Theater of West Java* (Athens, OH: Ohio University Press, 2004).
42. Misbach Yusa Biran, *Sejarah Film 1900–1950: Bikin Film Di Jawa*, 2nd edn (Jakarta: Komunitas Bambu dan Dewan Kesenian Jakarta, 2009).
43. David Hanan, *Moments in Indonesian Film History: Film and Popular Culture in a Developing Society 1950–2020* (Cham: Springer International Publishing AG, 2021).
44. Ben Murtagh, *Genders and Sexualities in Indonesian Cinema: Constructing Gay, Lesbi and Waria Identities on Screen* (New York, NY: Routledge, 2013).
45. The other building block of film art is, of course, *sound*. Although in this book I focus on the visual dimension, I don't want to suggest that sound is unimportant to the stylistic revitalisation of Indonesian cinema. But because my expertise is limited to visual aesthetics, I will leave the research on sound aesthetics in Indonesian cinema to scholars who have a far better understanding of sound

recording and reproduction – including music scoring – and who possess erudite knowledge on the theories of sound in cinema. Ultimately, I am hopeful that someday we shall arrive at a stylistics of Indonesian film that also delves into the analysis of sound-image relations.

46. Books on Indonesian film directors and producers (i.e., biographies and memoirs) include: Usmar Ismail, *Usmar Ismail Mengupas Film* (Jakarta: Penerbit Sinar Harapan, 1983); David Hanan, 'Gotot Prakosa and Independent Indonesian Cinema', *Cantrills Filmnotes* 63/64 (1990), pp. 23–4; Nano Riantiarno, *Teguh Karya Dan Teater Populer 1968–1993* (Jakarta: Penerbit Sinar Harapan, 1993); Satyagraha Hoerip, *Dua Dunia Dalam Djadoeg Djajakoesoema* (Jakarta: Dinas Kebudayaan DKI Jakarta & Institut Kesenian Jakarta, 1995); Ramadhan K. H. Hadimaja and Nina Pane Budiarto, *Pengusaha, Politikus, Pelopor Industri Film: Djamaludin Malik, Melekat di Hati Banyak Orang* (Jakarta: Kata Hasta Pustaka, 2006). Books on Indonesian film actors include: S. M. Ardan, *Jejak Seorang Aktor: Sukarno M. Noor Dalam Film Indonesia* (Jakarta: Aksara Karunia, 2004); Ludhy Cahyana and Muhlis Suhaeri, *Benyamin S: Muka Kampung Rezeki Kota* (Jakarta: Yayasan H. Benjamin Sueb, 2005); and Rano Karno, *Rano Karno: Si Doel*, ed. Mirna Yulistianti (Jakarta: PT Gramedia Pustaka Utama, 2016).

47. Krishna Sen, *Indonesian Cinema: Framing the New Order* (London; Atlantic Highlands, NJ: Zed Books, 1994), pp. 55–6.

48. John Thornton Caldwell, *Production Culture: Industrial Reflexivity and Critical Practice in Film and Television* (Durham, NC: Duke University Press, 2008).

49. See, for instance, the following publications: Marshall Clark, 'Men, Masculinities and Symbolic Violence in Recent Indonesian Cinema', *Journal of Southeast Asian Studies* 35, no. 1 (February 2004), pp. 113–31; Laura Coppens, 'Films of Desire: Queer(ing) Indonesian Cinema', in *Asian Hot Shots: Indonesian Cinema*, eds Yvonne Michalik and Laura Coppens (Marburg: Schüren, 2009), pp. 177–99; Charlotte Setijadi-Dunn and Thomas Barker, 'Imagining "Indonesia": Ethnic Chinese Film Producers in Pre-Independence Cinema', *Asian Cinema* 21, no. 2 (2010), pp. 25–47; Alicia Izharuddin, *Gender and Islam in Indonesian Cinema* (Singapore: Palgrave Macmillan, 2017); and Dag Yngvesson, 'Non-Aligned Features: The Coincidence of Modernity and the Screen in Indonesia' (PhD Thesis, University of Minnesota, 2016).

50. Two notable works here are: Claire Holt, *Art in Indonesia: Continuities and Change* (Ithaca, NY: Cornell University Press, 1967); and Stephanie Morgan and Laurie Jo Sears, eds, *Aesthetic Tradition and Cultural Transition in Java and Bali*, Monograph/University of Wisconsin, Center for Southeast Asian Studies 2 (Madison, WI: University of Wisconsin, Center for Southeast Asian Studies, 1984).

51. See, for instance, the following works: Kathy Foley, 'The Sundanese Wayang Golek, the Rod Puppet Theatre of West Java' (PhD Thesis, University of Hawaii, 1979); Ward Keeler, *Javanese Shadow Plays, Javanese Selves* (Baltimore, MD: Princeton University Press, 1987); Sylvia Fraser-Lu, *Indonesian Batik: Processes, Patterns, and Places* (Singapore: Oxford University Press, 1986); R. Anderson Sutton, *Traditions of Gamelan Music in Java: Musical Pluralism and Regional Identity* (Cambridge:

Cambridge University Press, 1991); and Miriam J. Morrison, 'The Bedaya-Serimpi Dances of Java', *Dance Chronicle* 2, no. 3 (January 1978), pp. 188–212.

52. See, for example, the following books: John Gibbs, *Mise-en-scène: Film Style and Interpretation* (London; New York: Wallflower, 2002); John Gibbs and Douglas Pye, eds, *Style and Meaning: Studies in the Detailed Analysis of Film* (Manchester: Manchester University Press, 2005); and Adrian Martin, *Mise En Scène and Film Style: From Classical Hollywood to New Media Art* (Basingstoke [etc.]: Palgrave Macmillan, 2014).

53. C. Paul Sellors, *Film Authorship: Auteurs and Other Myths* (London: Wallflower, 2010), pp. 3 and 6, cited in Christopher Beach, *A Hidden History of Film Style: Cinematographers, Directors and the Collaborative Process* (Oakland, CA: University of California Press, 2015), p. 1.

54. See, for example, the following books: Beach, *A Hidden History of Film Style*; Daisuke Miyao, *The Aesthetics of Shadow: Lighting and Japanese Cinema* (Durham, NC; London: Duke University Press, 2013); Lindsay Coleman, Daisuke Miyao and Roberto Schaefer, eds; *Transnational Cinematography Studies* (Lanham, MD: Lexington Books, 2017); Lucy Fischer, ed., *Art Direction and Production Design: A Modern History of Filmmaking*, Behind the Silver Screen (London; New York, NY: IB Tauris, 2015); Patrick Keating, *The Dynamic Frame: Camera Movement in Classical Hollywood* (New York, NY: Columbia University Press, 2019); Patrick Keating, *Hollywood Lighting from the Silent Era to Film Noir* (New York, NY: Columbia University Press, 2010); Patrick Keating, ed., *Cinematography* (New Brunswick, NJ: Rutgers University Press, 2014); Charlie Keil and Kristen Whissel, eds, *Editing and Special/Visual Effects*, Behind the Silver Screen (New Brunswick, NJ: Rutgers University Press, 2016); and Adrienne L. McLean, ed., *Costume, Makeup, and Hair*, Behind the Silver Screen (New Brunswick, NJ: Rutgers University Press, 2016).

CHAPTER 2

Towards a Stylistics of Indonesian Film

As a preview of the analyses that I develop in Chapters 5–7, let's consider a segment from the feature film *Sang Pencerah* (*The Enlightener*, Hanung Bramantyo, d.p. Faozan Rizal, 2010). During a critical moment in this biopic of the founder of Indonesia's second-largest Islamic organisation, Muhammadiyah, Ahmad Dahlan (Lukman Hakim) and his pupils gather inside a *langgar* (small mosque). They are in the middle of a heated debate about the direction of Muhammadiyah as an organisation. As the discussion turns into a bickering session between his pupils, Dahlan quickly reminds them of Muhammadiyah's true purpose, which is to become an educational organisation with a social mission rather than an Islamic political party. Dahlan warns them: '*Hidup hidupilah Muhamadiyah! Jangan hidup dari Muhamadiyah!*' ('Enliven Muhammadiyah! Don't make a living off of Muhamadiyah!'). This prescriptive statement emblematises Dahlan's role as the revered 'enlightener' in the film and ultimately underlines the film's theme, namely the sacrifice of the individual's ambition for the collective good. Through Dahlan's prescriptive words, we could interpret the key message of the film to be: Javanese Muslims should never forget one of the core values of Islam, which is to help the *fakir miskin* (the underprivileged folks), rather than using religion to serve one's own political interests.

How this scene is presented visually reveals one facet of continuity and one of change in the visual style of Indonesian film (see Figure 2.1). As an example of continuity, the way in which the figures are positioned in this scene points to a particular body language known as *duduk bersila* in Indonesian. *Duduk bersila* is a sitting posture with both legs folded and one leg positioned on top of the other. This sitting style is common in religious practice in Southeast Asia, whether in Buddhist meditation or Islamic praying rituals such as *dzikir* or *tahlilan*.[1] But *duduk bersila* is also 'a sign of attention and respect at ceremonial gatherings in many places across the Indonesian islands', according to David Hanan.[2]

This sitting style has carried over to cinema since the early years of filmmaking on the archipelago and continues to be part of the staging vocabulary of Indonesian films until today. In a silent film from the colonial era, *Singa*

Figure 2.1 Duduk bersila *as a staging device in* Sang Pencerah

Laoet (*Sea Lion*, Tan Tjoei Hock, 1941), the characters are arranged in this *duduk bersila* manner in many of its scenes. In *Darah dan Doa* (*The Long March*, Usmar Ismail, 1950), during a pivotal scene in which the protagonists (the Republican Army) are greeted by the villagers that turn out to be insurgents planning to exterminate them, the figures are placed in the scene according to this sitting style, too. During the Suharto period, we can find *duduk bersila* in many films, but most notably in the epic *silat* films, such as *Saur Sepuh: Satria Madangkara* (*Saur Sepuh: The Madangkara Warrior*, Imam Tantowi, 1988) and Islam-themed films like *Sunan Kalijaga dan Syech Siti Jenar* (*Sunan Kalijaga and Syech Siti Jenar*, Sofyan Syarna and Ackyl Anwari, 1985) (see Figure 2.2). In the post-Suharto era, many filmmakers sustain this *duduk bersila* staging tradition in various kinds of films. One of the most commercially successful films from this era, *Ada Apa Dengan Cinta?* (*What's Up with Cinta?*, Rudi Soejarwo, 2002), for instance, features this sitting style during its most poignant scene as the all-girl characters in the story console their best friend who's had a traumatic experience. Last but not least, in *Pengabdi Setan* (*Satan's Slaves*, Joko Anwar, 2017), we can find *duduk bersila* employed throughout a *tahlilan* scene in which villagers are seen conducting a *tahlilan* ceremony for the recently deceased woman named Mawarni (Ayu Laksmi) who died after encountering paranormal activities.

The prevalence of *duduk bersila* in Indonesian cinema demonstrates Hanan's *cultural specificity* concept that he developed for understanding Indonesian film. Seen through this conceptual lens, Hanan considers *duduk bersila* as a manifestation of *cultural dominant*, which is a shared cultural norm

Figure 2.2   Duduk bersila *in* Sunan Kalijaga dan Syech Siti Jenar

found across the Indonesian archipelago that places an emphasis on group body language. We can trace this form of group body language all the way back to the pre-Islamic arts of Java, as evidenced by the wall reliefs of Borobudur – the ninth-century Mahayana Buddhist temple in Central Java. Hanan notes that the wall reliefs at Borobudur exhibit the prominent position of *duduk bersila* as the sitting style for depicting central protagonists such as the Buddha, the Mother of the Buddha, a king, gods or a bodhisattva, or their attendants, servants, Brahmins, priests, Buddhist nuns, dignitaries, warriors and merchants.[3] Curiously, the case of *duduk bersila* in Indonesian cinema reveals the 'dynamic synthesis'[4] – to borrow Karl G. Heider's concept – or the interplay between culture and artistic media that characterises Indonesian arts in general, but applies to Indonesian film as well. What I'm trying to say is: we have *duduk bersila*, which is a form of cultural dominant (group body language), transformed into a specific representational manner in traditional arts of a specific cultural group within Indonesia (the Javanese-Buddhist wall reliefs), and again transformed into a visual strategy for positioning figures in one of the most modern media forms (narrative film).

As much as the *Sang Pencerah* scene above reveals the continuity of *duduk bersila* as a persistent staging repertoire in Indonesian film aesthetics, it also demonstrates a significant change in pictorial presentation. We can see this when we compare and contrast this particular shot with the one from *Sunan Kalijaga dan Syech Siti Jenar* by describing their visual characteristics. These shots are also appropriate to compare because of their similar subject matter

(Islamic teaching in pre-twentieth century Java) and narrative contexts (Muslim clerics gather to discuss the important matter of the future of Islam in Javanese societies).

Despite these similarities, the two scenes are different cinematographically, though. Firstly, each of them is lit distinctively. The *Syech Siti Jenar* scene is lit in a *high-key lighting* mode – a technique of lighting that produces a low to no contrast between the light and dark areas of the shot. As a result, the images are optimally bright; the illumination is distributed evenly, leaving no area of the image under any shadow. By contrast, the *Sang Pencerah* scene is handled with a low-key lighting technique, in particular with a selective lighting method. Rather than illuminating the whole space and the characters in the scene evenly, the cinematographer Faozan Rizal chose to selectively illuminate a few areas in the scene such as the face of the main character Dahlan and the background wall, leaving the rest of the image in the dark. Here, the light-to-dark ratio is incredibly imbalanced, meaning darkness reigns over brightness in this scene. Another key difference lies in the sources of illumination within the diegetic environment of the film. In *Syech Siti Jenar*, lighting sources are unknown, and the oil lamp at the centre of the space acts merely as a prop that does nothing to enhance the illumination. In *Sang Pencerah*, the lighting is motivated by the *lampu minyak* (oil lamp), which contributes to illuminating the scene instead of simply being there as a decorative element of the set. Thus, the oil lamp in *Sang Pencerah* works as a *practical light* – a functioning lighting fixture placed in the scene as part of the décor.

The differences in lighting approach affect the range of functions lighting performs in each scene. In the *Syech Siti Jenar* case, the function of lighting is restricted mainly to provide maximum visual clarity. We can see the figures, décor and space in the story world clearly without any obstruction. The segment from *Sang Pencerah*, on the other hand, is visually opaque; lighting here functions much less as a tool for achieving optimal visibility. Rather, it performs at least three functions: 1) producing atmosphere; 2) articulating the film's theme; and 3) creating a painterly effect. This dark lighting style produces a particular atmosphere, which can mean two things: first, the atmosphere of conviviality and solemnity; second, the atmosphere of the period, which is early nineteenth-century pre-electricity Java. But this lighting convention also articulates another facet of the film's theme: spiritual enlightenment. There is no other moment in the film that visually expresses this theme more emblematically than this one. In this segment, Ahmad Dahlan is prominently lit, which works to single out his role in the story as 'Sang Pencerah' – literally meaning 'the enlightener'. In the film, Dahlan is portrayed as the leader who brings his pupils from a state of ignorance to a state of enlightenment. Dahlan is depicted in the film as a complex figure who, on the one hand, wants to get rid of the syncretic elements of Javanese Islam and introduce a more fundamentalist form of Islam that he learned in Saudi Arabia. On the other, he is portrayed as a Muslim leader who has a modern vision of the role of Muslims in colonial-era Indonesia, which relies on liberal education and social empowerment. Of course, in the context of Indonesian Islam, both fundamentalist and liberal Islam are regarded as 'modernist' movements, and Muhammadiyah (especially in its origins) was, above all, a modernist movement. It's no wonder that the overlapping fundamentalist and liberal tendencies of the modernist strand are embodied by the figure of Dahlan himself. Unlike the 'traditionalist' Islam – represented by the most politically active Islamic organisation in Indonesia, Nahdlatul Ulama (NU) – Muhammadiyah has stayed away from being directly involved in politics.[5]

Lastly, the lighting style here performs a pictorial function, which is to create a painterly graphic effect known as *chiaroscuro* in the visual arts. How the segment is lit alludes to the European Baroque paintings of the seventeenth century, in particular, the paintings of the *pittura tenebrosa* style. Also known in English as tenebrism, *pittura tenebrosa* was a stylistic trend characterised by the extreme contrast of light and shadow, often favouring large areas of darkness in the paintings.[6] The shot from *Sang Pencerah* could readily be compared with the iconic works of tenebrism such as the paintings of Gerrit van Honthorst and Georges de La Tour in which a single source of light is used to motivate the lighting. The light-to-dark ratio imbalance is another parallel. In this respect, the *Sang Pencerah* shot has an intertextual and intercultural trait: it alludes to a visual tradition in another artform, established in a culture outside of Indonesia, even though the subject matter and the emphasis on the group body language (*duduk bersila*) is specific to Indonesia.

In conclusion, lighting in *Sang Pencerah* has a wider range of aesthetic capabilities, which are not restricted to illuminating the space and figures in the scene per se. Thus, lighting is functionally more complex in *Sang Pencerah* than in *Sunan Kalijaga and Syech Siti Jenar*. Now, I have provided the analytical sneak preview above also as a way for me to introduce the poetics of cinema as an approach that grounds my study and the method on which this project relies. But what is it exactly?

THE POETICS OF CINEMA: A BOTTOM-UP FILM STUDIES

In simple terms, the poetics of cinema is a critical approach that treats film as an artform. It has been developed, articulated and put into practice, primarily, by David Bordwell. In a more nuanced way, Bordwell conceives the poetics of cinema as the following:

> Poetics derives from the Greek word *poiesis*, or active making. The poetics of any artistic medium studies the finished work as the result of a process of construction – a process that includes a craft component (such as rules of thumb), the more general principles according to which the work is composed, and its functions, effects, and uses. Any inquiry into the fundamental principles by which artifacts in any representational medium are constructed, and the effects that flow from those principles, can fall within the domain of poetics.[7]

Though the origin of poetics as an approach to examining the arts lies in Aristotle's *Poetics*, in the modern era, precursors to the poetics of cinema include the works of the Russian Formalists and Prague Structuralists, early film theorists like Hugo Münsterberg, classical film theorists such as Rudolf Arnheim, André Bazin, Sergei Eisenstein and contemporary film theorists like Noël Burch. Their writings have paved the way for Bordwell's poetics of cinema to emerge as a fully developed research programme in film studies.

The primary interest of poetics of cinema is to uncover two things: first, the operating system that governs the constructed film object; second, the functions, purposes or effects elicited by the application of that operating system through the arrangement of narrative events and stylistic elements. We can think of the poetics of cinema as a heuristic, that is, a hands-on problem-solving tool to tackle 'middle-level questions' about the cinematic arts.[8] In an interview with Bordwell that I conducted during the Summer Film College in 2013 in Antwerp, he explains:

> As a research programme, the poetics of cinema goes after certain questions. The broadest set of questions that it deals with is questions about the principles that underlie artistic filmmaking, and here I mean practically all filmmaking, the principles as they developed and changed in different times and places. What we are trying to do with this research programme is trying to disengage what seems to be the underlying logic of the kinds of films made in different times and places.[9]

How does this poetics of cinema approach work in practice? First, it places the analysis of the filmic work at the centre of its critical procedure. Bordwell suggests that if we do research under the poetics of cinema framework, we must begin our investigation into a film by reverse engineering it, breaking down its internal dynamics.[10] Then, we can go on to propose the functions generated by the systematic handling of those internal dynamics. At this point, the goal of the analysis is to provide functional explanations that can help us to understand why the film looks a certain way. So, for instance, if we use *Sang Pencerah* as the object of analysis, we can reverse engineer the film by asking how the film tells its story and what cinematic techniques are being used to tell the story in this way. Having followed this procedure, I have discovered that the film focuses on the development of Ahmad Dahlan, the protagonist, from studious teenager to charismatic leader who challenges the status quo. Because of this central position of Dahlan as an enlightened reformer of Islam during a 'dark period' in the history of Java, low-key lighting has been employed as one of the main stylistic devices in the film. So, we can then ask what the particular functions of these lighting techniques are in the film. As I have explained in the analytical sneak preview, low-key lighting has multiple functions in the film: it imbues the images with a touch of realism; it sets a solemn atmosphere; it creates a painterly effect; and it accompanies the representation of Dahlan as 'the enlightener'.

But the analysis doesn't stop there. We can also inspect the external dynamics that help shape the film's overall form and style. External dynamics may include the filmmaking norms of the period; the filmmaking technology available to filmmakers in a particular era; the prevailing trends in the other artistic disciplines of the time; the social and political circumstances; the infrastructure of film exhibition, distribution and consumption; and the culture within which the film is located. So, with regards to *Sang Pencerah*'s visual style, for instance, the most pertinent enabling factor, to begin with, is the production circumstance that involves the film's budget, camera and lighting technology, institutional demands (i.e., the production company MVP Pictures) and the stylistic conventions of historical/biographical films.

The goal of starting from the analysis of the internal dynamics of a specific film is to make sense of the functional logic of the film's constructed formal and stylistic properties. Meanwhile, the objective of examining the external dynamics is to seek plausible explanations for the contextual factors influencing the filmmakers' creative choices in constructing those internal dynamics.

To arrive at that point, we must gather as much information as we can about the film or audio-visual media production culture to which the filmmakers belong. In case information about this is scarce, we need to extrapolate it from the film itself, as Bordwell asserts:

> As a historian of forms, genres and styles, the poetician starts from the concrete assumptions embedded in the filmmaker's craft. Sometimes these are articulated by practitioners; sometimes they must be inferred from the product and the mode of production.[11]

Besides scrutinising the internal and external dynamics, we may also look into the intertextual dynamics at play, which refers to the interaction between the film in question and other films. The aim of this analysis is to find out whether the film directly or indirectly alludes to other films either within or outside of the same genre, period and country of origin. The visual style of Joko Anwar's *Kala* (*Dead Time*, 2007), for example, explicitly cites that of American film noir through its heavy use of high contrast shadowy lighting as well as low-angle and Dutch angle shots. The investigation, however, can also expand into other artistic fields – from literature to the performing arts – to discern any cross-disciplinary artistic inspiration, pollination or even appropriation. In *Opera Jawa* (*Requiem from Java*, Garin Nugroho, 2006), for instance, the epic Hindu tale of Ramayana is reimagined as a cinematic piece that blends traditional Javanese performing art (court dance drama) and modern installation art to depict a particular episode from the tale 'The Abduction of Sita' by the evil Rahwana.

Like any research approach, the poetics of cinema has limitations, too. One particular shortcoming has to do with its antagonistic attitude toward hermeneutics as a means of gaining a better understanding of a filmic work or film art more broadly. In several publications, Bordwell strongly repudiates film interpretation.[12] More specifically, he decries a particular kind of 'film reading' that he considers 'doctrine-driven'.[13] And the doctrine he refers to here is a mélange of different theoretical paradigms – psychoanalysis, semiotics, feminism, and Marxism – known as the Grand Theories. He disdains this tendency to 'subsume individual films to a broad baggy scheme, often cobbled together from other disciplines', as Richard Rushton and Gary Bettinson put it.[14] Arguing for the pursuit of middle-level research as a core objective of the poetics of cinema, Bordwell and his partner-in-poetics, the film and art philosopher Noël Carroll maintain:

> We do not need to understand a film by projecting onto it the semantic fields "privileged" by this or that theory. Most important, the middle-level research programs have shown that *you do not need a Big Theory of Everything to do enlightening work in a field of study.*[15]

Later on, they add that with middle-level research programmes, 'you can do a lot with films besides interpreting them'.[16]

Now, the dominance of Grand Theories-driven interpretive criticism in film studies has largely dissipated since the millennium. But Bordwell's ideal of an interpretation-free poetics of cinema persists. In *Poetics of Cinema*, published in 2008, Bordwell writes:

> Finally, and to return to a difference with the doctrine-driven methods of film studies, explanation in poetics doesn't confine itself to issues of what films mean. Of course, meaning in one (very general) sense comprises a big part of what poetics describes, analyzes, and explains. *But meaning in the narrower sense that is the product of film interpretation (a "reading") isn't necessarily the goal of the poetician.*[17]

What Bordwell refers to as 'meaning in the general sense' consists of *referential* and *explicit* meaning.[18] Meanwhile, 'meaning in the narrower sense', in his view, comprises *implicit* and *symptomatic* meaning.[19] Bordwell claims that the activity of comprehension yields referential and explicit meaning, whereas the pursuit of interpretation produces implicit and symptomatic meaning.[20] Poetics of cinema as a research programme deals with the former, but not with the latter – at least according to Bordwell's conception thereof.

But this point is where I depart from Bordwell. To begin with, Bordwell's ascription of implicit and symptomatic meaning as the outcome of an interpretive activity, and vice versa, referential and explicit meaning as the product of comprehending activity, is too narrow in itself.[21] As Ira Bhaskar contends, comprehension and interpretation are tightly overlapping in practice, 'precisely because the meanings they deal with cannot be schismatically separated from each other'.[22] The interrelationship between the referential-explicit meaning and the implicit one, for instance, is more dynamically and complexly interwoven than Bordwell has explicated. As George Wilson argues, the implicit meanings of a narrative film cannot be separated from its referential ones because 'the implicit meanings of a film are inextricable from the network of relationships that constitute a fabula portrayed in film'.[23]

Moreover, Bordwell's objection to interpreting film is anchored in his animosity toward the enterprise of interpretation as a whole. But this is problematic. Although Bordwell primarily takes issue with the products of 'Interpretation Inc.',[24] as he calls it, he goes so far as to suggest that the problem lies exactly in the act of interpretation itself, characterising it strictly as an institutionally formed critical enterprise. By attributing interpretation as merely the extractor of implicit and symptomatic meanings – processed through the institutional frames of reference that the critic maps onto the film's cues – Bordwell conceives a reductive characterisation thereof. As a result, his sharp criticisms of interpretation are 'in danger of being aimed largely at a straw man'.[25] As Bhaskar claims, 'Bad examples of any activity do not deny its inherent validity.'[26]

Besides, even if we accept Bordwell's schismatic conceptualisation, why cannot 'meaning in the narrower sense' be the goal of the poetician? If it cannot be the only goal, can it at least be *one of the goals*, or a supplementary *goal*? Can we envisage a poetics of cinema in which hermeneutics also plays a role? I believe we can, and by doing so, we can remedy the shortcoming of the poetics of cinema approach.

The principal reason why interpretation is compatible with poetics is that *interpreting* as a sense-making activity or a process through which we *deal with difference* – to evoke Barend van Heusden's theory – operates on many levels, even on the level of *description*.[27] Richard Neer even argues, 'Attention to aspect-perception reveals that *seeing is saturated with interpretation.*'[28] As John Gibbs and Douglas Pye argue in *Style and Meaning: Studies in the Detailed Analysis of Film*, even when we describe what we see and hear in a film, the outcome of that description is never completely uncontentious.[29] They stress their point further by saying:

> While we can strive for objective recognition of say the action and the spatial and temporal dimensions of a shot, no description can be exhaustive and any description of the interaction of elements that make up even a simple shot will inevitably embody a viewpoint, a way of grading the elements we observe in their relationships with each other to register what we understand their priority to be. Description is inextricably bound up with interpretation.[30]

In Bordwell's own works, we can find cases where interpretation does come into play, even when his goal isn't exactly to engage in *symptomatic interpretation* aimed at uncovering 'repressed' symptomatic meanings.[31] For example, in *Figures Traced in Light*, when discussing how European filmmakers in the 1960s and 1970s made use of stylistic techniques like the *long take*[32] to de-dramatise emotionally-charged events in their films, he singles out moments from Michelangelo Antonioni's and Miklós Jancsó's films as cases in point. On Antonioni's approach to de-dramatisation in *Il Grido* (*The Cry*, 1957) and *L'Avventura* (*The Adventure*, 1960), he writes:

> He renders acting more impassive by means of a fairly muted performance style, long-held poses, and a tendency to turn figures from the camera at moments of dramatic intensity, a "dorsality" reminiscent of Mizoguchi. The result is the "inexpressive" shot that actually *expresses lassitude, anomie, suppressed pain, or emotional distances between the characters.*[33]

Meanwhile, on Jancsó's de-dramatisation strategy in *Magyar rapszódia* (*Hungarian Rhapsody*, 1979), he notes that:

> the camera tracks, cranes, zooms, and racks focus to create a floating, plastic, constantly shrinking and swelling space. Oxymoronic as it sounds, Jancsó's version of dedramatization is florid, even "maximalist," as became evident with *Red Psalm* (1972) and the films that followed. *The contending groups have become pure emblems of social forces, playing out rituals on the bare arena of the Hungarian plains—cinematic pageantry enacting a neo-Marxist reading of history.*[34]

Some level of 'reading' must come into play to make sense of Antonioni's and Jancsó's ways of using particular cinematographic and acting styles to de-dramatise filmic events. From my perspective, although people across cultures can recognise the figures in *Il Grido*, for instance, as male and female encountering one another, it requires a specific cultural and psychological schema in order to decode the body language of the characters as a manifestation of urban 'anomie', 'suppressed pain' and 'emotional distance'.[35] Of course, the study of body language as a subcategory of non-verbal communication lies outside the purview of this book, but I hope I have made my point clear that even in our attempts to describe and analyse stylistic elements, we cannot do without some form of interpretation. As Gibbs and Pye claim, 'to understand style we must grasp how it works in its context to present and shape the film's dramatic world. To understand style is to interpret what it does.'[36]

Although Bordwell has emphasised the notion that stylistic features on their own do not contain specific meanings, there are stylistic devices which are repeatedly linked with a particular set of meaningful associations. In the domain of camera movement, for instance, Lennard Højbjerg has demonstrated that the circular moving camera style has been regularly applied to specific filmic moments, namely to convey the ecstatic feeling of falling in love. In this regard, apart from creating 'explicit narration' and 'ornamental visual patterns',[37] the circular camera movements are used in many films to 'emphasize the intoxicating and self-centered nature of love'.[38]

I aim to relax the tension between Bordwellian poetics and hermeneutics in this book by allowing thematic meaning-making to figure as one of the functions elicited by the patterning of techniques in cinematography and production design. To briefly foreshadow it here, in Chapter 6, for instance, in my analysis of production design in *Sang Pencerah,* the way in which the destruction of a particularly important piece of set design, namely Ahmad Dahlan's *langgar* (small mosque), is tied to the theme of intolerance in the religiously plural Indonesian society. The symbolic significance of this use of production design elements cannot be divorced from the political context that surrounds the film. In the late 2000s and early 2010s, the religious minorities in Indonesia, including the Ahmadiyah sect, were under attack. The Ahmadiyah followers had to endure physical attacks, including the destruction of their mosques, because many dominant religious organisations believe that they have deviated from mainstream Islam.[39] The devastation of Dahlan's *langgar* in *Sang Pencerah*, which was built on location in Yogyakarta, plays a crucial role not only to advance the story of Dahlan's trial and tribulation in the film, but also to suggest a social-political criticism against the mainstream Muslim majority in post-Suharto Indonesia. And this can only be attained by actively pursuing interpretation next to stylistic analysis.

The limitations of the poetics of cinema approach are nevertheless outweighed by its heuristic usefulness as a methodology. One of the upshots of this approach lies in its inclusiveness. Rather than privileging a certain kind of film over others, the poetics of cinema is open to examining *any* type of film, irrespective of the film's critical status, cultural standing or production context (for instance, whether it is an independent or a big budget studio film). On this aspect of the poetics of cinema, Rushton and Bettinson remark:

> The approach is not confined to typical or classical filmmaking ... A poetics is not limited to films that promote or undermine prevailing ideologies, as certain Grand Theories tend to be. Nor is it confined to a canon of *chefs-d'oeuvre*. A poetics of cinema is as much concerned to elucidate the average, ordinary film as it is the undisputed masterworks of the medium.[40]

Taking this into account, the poetics of cinema becomes a lens that is more than appropriate to examine contemporary Indonesian films, which are diverse in type, genre and production modes.

WORKING WITH ANALYTIC STYLISTICS

If the poetics of cinema is my approach, the tool with which I work to examine the visual style of Indonesian film is *analytic stylistics*. As one of the modes of inquiry belonging to the poetics of cinema (besides *thematics* and *large-scale form*), stylistics 'deals with the materials and patterning of the medium as components of the constructive process'.[41] According to Jeremy G. Butler, analytic stylistics as a method of inquiry depends on 'explicit or implicit assumptions about the purpose and function of style in the filmic text', and suggests that 'the goal of the analysis is to deconstruct how style fulfills that function'.[42] To achieve that, the analyst – or the stylistician, to use the poetics of cinema's parlance – examines the workings of style within the textual system by 'seeking patterns of stylistic elements and on a higher level, the relationships among those patterns themselves'.[43]

Analytic stylistics is different from the other kinds of stylistics in film and television studies such as *descriptive stylistics*, *evaluative stylistics* and *historical stylistics*.[44] The purpose of *descriptive stylistics* is to describe and chart out the stylistic components of a filmic or televisual text in minute detail. Meanwhile, the goal of analytic stylistics is to analyse the systematic patterning of a stylistic device such as lighting, camerawork, sound or music in a particular segment of a film, or throughout the film, to discern and decode the functions and meanings of the technique employed. We can also distinguish analytic stylistics from *evaluative stylistics*, which is geared toward evaluating the use of sound and images in a filmic or televisual text, and from *historical stylistics*, which is a method that engages in a large-scale analysis of the continuities and changes of a particular cinematic style, or the use of a technique over historical periods. The objective of historical stylistics is to explain the stylistic evolution of films made in a particular institution, for instance Hollywood, and offer causal inferences about the drivers of the change. As a note, although I will engage primarily in analytic stylistics in this book, in a small-scale fashion, I will also describe the ways in which the stylistic devices I am analysing (i.e., lighting, production design and camera movement) change over time in Indonesian cinema in Chapter 4.

In this book, I draw on extensive research that includes an engagement with secondary sources comprising scholarly literature, journalistic pieces and qualitative data such as interviews with cinematographers, art directors, production designers, film critics, *penggiat sinema* (cinema activists) and moviegoers in Indonesia.

But the strength of the book comes from its primary sources: *the Indonesian films* themselves. I focus primarily on narrative fiction films for this research. But my selection isn't restricted solely to award-winning arthouse or festival-oriented independent films. In fact, the films that constitute my corpus in this book are diverse in their genre status, mode of production, format and length (including short films) – from feature length to short films, from big-budget box office hits to exploitation movies. In total, my corpus for this study consists of 215 films made between 1939 and 2018. Surely, this amount barely scratches the surface of Indonesia's overall filmic output from the past ten decades since the first feature film was made in 1926. But as an initial set of data, these films provide a compelling portrait of visual stylistic continuities and changes in Indonesian cinema.

During each viewing of these films, I took screengrabs of the film's shots and then placed them systematically in the Adobe Lightroom software for me to observe and analyse them more closely (see Figure 2.3). Although my research focuses on contemporary, post-Suharto Indonesian films (1998–2018), I have tried to acquire films from each era of Indonesian cinema history, including silent films from the colonial period. Unfortunately, many of the colonial-era films are lost. Of the 114 fiction films produced in the Netherlands Indies between 1926 and 1949, only less than twelve titles are known to survive at Sinematek Indonesia in Jakarta.[45] However, according to David Hanan, and based on my observation at Sinematek Indonesia during my research visits, these titles mostly exist in an 'incomplete form'.[46] The ones I managed to view are those that have been digitised by Sinematek Indonesia, comprising the seven following titles: *Gagak Item* (*Black Raven/De Zwarte Raaf,* Joshua & Othniel Wong, 1939); *Srigala Item* (*Black Wolf/De Zwarte Wolf,* Tan Tjoei Hock, 1941); *Singa Laoet* (*The Sea Lion,* Tan Joei Hock, 1941); *Tengkorak Hidoep* (*The Living Skeleton,* Tan Tjoei Hock, 1941); *Harta Karun* (*The Treasure,* Usmar Ismail, 1949); *Gadis Desa* (*Village Girl,* Andjar Asmara, 1949); and *Tjitra* (*Image,* Usmar Ismail, 1949). I hope that future research in the

Figure 2.3 *Screengrabs of Indonesian films uploaded to Adobe Lightroom for visual observation and analyses*

stylistics of Indonesian film can excavate and bring to light the earlier films produced between 1926 and 1939.

By looking at Indonesian films very closely as a point of departure for the analyses, my working with analytic stylistics as a method points to the power of questions-driven observation from which any good investigation – scientific or otherwise – benefits. Here's what primatologist Frans de Waal says about this point in his compelling book *The Ape and the Sushi Master* (an excellent example of good investigation):

> I learned that the secret of observation is to *ask the right questions*, and that observation needs to be followed by speculation about *causes, functions,* and *connections* between events. The goal is to sharpen the observations to the point that one is not just watching animals for pleasure and general information, but because one wants *specific answers to specific questions*.[47]

If we replace the word 'animals' in his passage with the word 'films' – even more precisely 'Indonesian films' – what we will end up with is an accurate description of two things that this book relies upon, as delineated in the preceding pages: analytic stylistics and the poetics of cinema.

There's one thing missing in de Waal's statement, though, and that is *theory*. We need a theory or a set of theories to ask the right questions and determine what it is we're precisely examining. So, in the next chapter, we'll survey some of the pertinent theories that underpin the book's argument.

Notes

1. *Dzikir* or *dhikr* is a devotional practice in Islam in which short prayers are recited repetitively, silently or aloud. The repetition is counted using *tasbeh* (prayer beads). *Tahlilan* is a praying ritual practised by Indonesian and Malaysian Muslims, especially by those belonging to the 'traditionalist' Nadhatul Ulama stream, to remember someone who's passed away. The event is held on the first until the seventh day of death and then repeated on the 40th and 100th day.
2. David Hanan, *Cultural Specificity in Indonesian Film: Diversity in Unity* (Cham: Palgrave Macmillan Imprint, Springer International Publishing, 2017), p. 218.
3. Ibid., p. 220.
4. Karl G. Heider, *Indonesian Cinema: National Culture on Screen* (Honolulu: University of Hawaii Press, 1991), p. 7.
5. For a detailed discussion on the traditionalist and the modernist Islamic movements in Indonesia, see Suaidi Asyari, *Traditionalist vs. Modernist Islam in Indonesian Politics: Muhammadiyah & Nahdlatul Ulama (NU) in the Contemporary Indonesian Democratic and Political Landscape* (Saarbrücken, Germany: VDM Verlag Dr. Müller, 2010). For an earlier account on Muhammadiyah and Islamic modernism in Indonesia, see Leslie H. Palmier, 'Modern Islam in Indonesia: The Muhammadiyah After Independence,' *Pacific Affairs* 27, no. 3 (September 1954), pp. 255–63.
6. Maria Rzepińska and Krystyna Malcharek, 'Tenebrism in Baroque Painting and Its Ideological Background', *Artibus et Historiae* 7, no. 13 (1986), p. 91.
7. David Bordwell, *Poetics of Cinema* (New York: Routledge, 2008), p. 12.
8. Ibid., p. 3.
9. Ari Purnama, *A Conversation with David Bordwell: Poetics of Cinema, Film Stylistics and Research Valorization*, Vimeo, 23 October 2013, video, 53:28, https://vimeo.com/77626940.
10. Ibid.
11. David Bordwell, *Making Meaning: Inference and Rhetoric in the Interpretation of Cinema* (Cambridge, MA, etc.: Harvard University Press, 1989), p. 269.
12. See Bordwell, *Poetics of Cinema*, Chapter 1: Introduction; David Bordwell, 'Historical Poetics of Cinema,' in *The Cinematic Text: Methods and Approaches*, ed. R. Barton Palmer (New York: AMS Press, 1989), pp. 369–98; David Bordwell and Noël Carroll, eds., *Post-Theory: Reconstructing Film Studies* (Madison, WI: University of Wisconsin Press, 1996); David Bordwell, *Making Meaning: Inference and Rhetoric in the Interpretation of Cinema*, Harvard Film Studies (Cambridge, MA: Harvard University Press, 1989); David Bordwell, *On the History of Film Style* (Cambridge, MA: Harvard University Press, 1997); and David Bordwell, *Figures Traced in Light: On Cinematic Staging* (Berkeley, CA: University of California Press, 2005).
13. Bordwell, *Poetics of Cinema*, p. 12.
14. Richard Rushton and Gary Bettinson, *What Is Film Theory? An Introduction to Contemporary Debates* (Maidenhead: McGraw Hill Open University Press, 2010), p. 132.

15. Bordwell and Carroll, *Post-Theory*, p. 29 (original emphasis).
16. Ibid.
17. Bordwell, *Poetics of Cinema*, 2008, p. 16 (original emphasis).
18. Referential meaning is the most concrete sort of meaning, approximating a straightforward plot summary (e.g., Alfred Hitchcock's *Psycho*: a lady travels from Phoenix to Fairvale and over there she encounters a psychopath). Explicit meaning, on the other hand, is more conceptual; it involves some degree of abstraction (e.g., *Psycho*: madness can overcome sanity). According to Bordwell, referential and explicit meaning constitute what are typically considered 'literal' meanings. See Bordwell, *Making Meaning*, p. 8.
19. Implicit meaning is even more abstract than explicit meaning as it moves beyond the literal and enters the symbolic, covert and thematic realm (e.g., *Psycho*: sanity and madness cannot be easily distinguished). Symptomatic meaning is the sort of meaning that discloses a particular set of societal symptoms, which the film 'divulges "involuntarily"', bearing the traces of political, economic, sexual or ideological mechanisms (e.g., *Psycho*: the male fear of woman's sexuality is symptomatic of modern Western society). See Bordwell, *Making Meaning*, p. 9.
20. Ibid.
21. For a rigorous critique of Bordwell's characterisation of interpretation, see Ira Bhaskar, 'On "Historical Poetics", Narrative and Interpretation,' in *A Companion to Film Theory*, eds Robert Stam and Toby Miller (London: Blackwell, 1999), pp. 387–412.
22. Ibid., p. 392.
23. George Wilson, 'On Film Narrative and Narrative Meaning', in *Film Theory and Philosophy*, eds Richard Allen and Murray Smith (Oxford: Clarendon Press, 1997), 226, cited in Bhaskar, 'On "Historical Poetics", Narrative and Interpretation,' p. 395.
24. Bordwell, *Making Meaning*, p. 21.
25. George Wilson, 'Interpretation,' in *The Routledge Companion to Philosophy and Film*, eds Paisley Livingston and Carl Plantinga (London; New York: Routledge, 2009), p. 164.
26. Bhaskar, 'On "Historical Poetics"', p. 387.
27. My understanding of interpretation as a sense-making activity is informed by Barend van Heusden's theory of semiotic cognition, which refers to the 'double processing of the stream of incoming information' that 'results in a combination of two types of patterns: *stable structures*, on the one hand [...] and a *changing situation*, on the other hand'. According to van Heusden, stable structures are what we recognise as 'schemata', 'scripts', or 'concepts'; meanwhile, a changing situation is what we typically identify as the 'reality', 'object', or the 'thing itself'. Viewed this way, and by way of an analogy, an interpretation is therefore not an instrument like a juice extractor that squeezes out implicit-thematic or symptomatic essences, but 'an activity of relating' (in van Heusden's parlance) the stable patterns (enabled by *memory*) to the more 'floating', changing patterns. Thus, we

can conceive interpretation through this theoretical lens as a doubly occurring process whereby we as human agents rely on stable patterns of structures (cultural, psychological or theoretical schemata) to make sense of the reality ('the here and now'), which in this particular context involves the moving images we see on the screen. As van Heusden aptly puts it: 'The patterns "adjust" as much as possible to what is perceived.' See Barend van Heusden, 'Dealing with Difference: From Cognition to Semiotic Cognition', *Cognitive Semiotics*, no. 4 (Spring 2009), p. 124.
28. Richard Neer, 'Connoisseurship and the Stakes of Style', *Critical Inquiry* 32, no. 1 (Autumn 2005), p. 17 (emphasis added).
29. John Gibbs and Douglas Pye, eds, *Style and Meaning: Studies in the Detailed Analysis of Film* (Manchester: Manchester University Press, 2005), p. 4.
30. Ibid.
31. The idea of symptomatic interpretation or symptomatic reading can be traced to the Structural Marxist philosopher Louis Althusser. Blending Freudian and Marxian theories, Althusser claimed that hidden forces often determine social structures. Consequently, we can understand how societies work by unravelling the *hidden symptoms* that are absent from official conversations ('structuring absences'), but which affect those conversations in much the same way as unconscious wishes affect our conscious thoughts and actions as psychoanalytic theory would describe it.
32. The *long take*, in essence, is a filming technique with which a sequence is captured in a single take, producing one lengthy, unbroken shot.
33. Bordwell, *Figures Traced in Light*, p. 154 (emphasis added).
34. Ibid., p. 157 (emphasis added).
35. I will discuss how cultural schema is helpful to decode facial expression in Indonesian film, which can yield different meaning than the way in which facial expression onscreen is typically 'read' in films from Western cultures in Chapter 3 within the 'On Storytelling and Expressivity' subsection.
36. Gibbs and Pye, *Style and Meaning*, p. 11.
37. Lennard Højbjerg, 'The Circular Camera Movement: Style, Narration, and Embodiment', *Projections* 8, no. 2 (December 1, 2014), p. 86.
38. Ibid., p. 72.
39. See, for instance, the following journalistic pieces: 'Indonesia Ahmadiyah Attack: Outrage over Victim Jailing,' *BBC News*, 15 August 2011, http://www.bbc.com/news/world-asia-pacific-14526299; and Hertanto Soebijoto, 'Lagi, Masjid Ahmadiyah Dirusak Massa,' *Kompas.com*, 3 December 2010, http://megapolitan.kompas.com/read/2010/12/03/15534561/Lagi..Masjid.Ahmadiyah.Dirusak.Massa.
40. Rushton and Bettinson, *What is Film Theory?*, p. 134.
41. Bordwell, *Poetics of Cinema*, pp. 17–18.
42. Jeremy G. Butler, *Television Style* (New York: Routledge, 2010), p. 11.
43. Ibid.
44. Ibid.

45. For an explanation of the circumstances that led to the disappearance of these early films, see Christopher Woodrich, 'Ekranisasi Awal: Bringing Novels to the Silver Screen in the Dutch East Indies' (MA Thesis, University of Gadjah Mada, 2014), pp. 70–2.
46. Hanan, *Cultural Specificity in Indonesian Film*, p. 54.
47. Frans de Waal, *The Ape and the Sushi Master: Cultural Reflections by a Primatologist* (New York: Basic Books, 2001), p. 93 (emphasis added).

CHAPTER 3

What Can Film Style Do in Narrative Cinema?

We've gathered from the last chapter that analytic stylistics uncovers the systematic patterning of a stylistic device in a particular scene of a film or in the entire film, and breaks down the functions and meanings of such a salient stylistic component. Basically, we want to know what visual techniques a film heavily relies on and what aesthetic functions and effects these techniques yield. To do that, we need to know in advance what the explicit and implicit assumptions about the functions of film style are. Put differently, we need a set of theories that explain what film style can do and achieve in narrative cinema. In this chapter, we will look at some theoretical ideas that film theorists and film historians have generated over the last two decades.

In film studies, we can identify at least two types of theories on the functions of film style. The first, I call the *macro functional theory of film style*. This is a set of theories proposed primarily by Noël Carroll and David Bordwell.[1] The second, which I call the *micro functional theory of film style*, has been produced by Patrick Keating, Jakob Isak Nielsen, Jane Barnwell and Charles Tashiro. These film scholars have carried out in-depth research into the workings of specific stylistic devices in the cinematic arts: lighting (Keating), production design (Barnwell; Tashiro) and camera movement (Nielsen).[2] The difference between these two kinds of functional theory lies primarily in their degree of generality. The macro theory proposed by Carroll and Bordwell elucidates the functions of style in narrative film more generally, irrespective of the genre, period or origin of the films. Meanwhile, the micro theory of Keating, Toshiro, Barnwell and Nielsen targets the functions of particular stylistic devices such as lighting, production design and camera movement across a large filmic corpus from a specific period, region or production mode. Let's start with the first type.

THE MACRO FUNCTIONAL THEORY OF FILM STYLE

The macro functional theory of film style explains how film style functions in an individual film, but also across a filmmaker's body of works. Carroll, in 'Film Form: An Argument for a Functional Theory of Style in the Individual

Film', proposes this macro functional theory of style by arguing that when film techniques are organised in a single film, they function primarily to materialise the film's point.[3] Interchangeably applying the terms form and style, Carroll contends:

> According to the functional account of film form, the form [or style] of an individual film is the ensemble of choices intended to realize the point or the purpose of the film. This approach to film form is different from the descriptive account. The descriptive account says that the form of the film is *the sum total of all the relations between the elements of the film*. The functional account says that film form comprises *only the elements and relations intended to serve as the means to the end of the film*.[4]

We should note here that Carroll stresses the difference between descriptive stylistics and analytic stylistics by pointing out that while the former conceptualises style as *the sum of all techniques* chosen in a film, the latter conceives style as a set of film techniques *saliently* applied to realise the point(s) of the film. To make this abstract concept tangible, take, for instance, the heavy reliance on low-key lighting that produces intensified graphic darkness in the film whose visual style I analysed briefly in the previous chapter, *Sang Pencerah* (discussed in more depth in Chapter 5). Low-key lighting in that film is systematically patterned to support the foregrounding of the film's purpose, which is to get across the idea that enlightenment is brought by the modern and forward-thinking Ahmad Dahlan to a 'dark' time of Islam in Java.

Moving from this conception of film style, Carroll further suggests that style fulfils several functions in the process of bringing about a film's point. In some instances, the purpose of style in an individual film is to put forward a viewpoint or a theme.[5] For example, the handheld, free-ranging camerawork with tight framing on the characters' faces and bodies used in Garin Nugroho's *Puisi Tak Terkuburkan* (*A Poet: Unconcealed Poetry*, d.p. Winaldha E. Malatatoa, 1999) evokes the theme of repression through physical confinement and psychological torture in line with the film's subject matter: the imprisonment of alleged communists waiting to be executed. The film is set in a prison cell in the highlands of Aceh during the 1965–6 anti-communist purge, orchestrated by forces associated with the rise of General Suharto's New Order regime.

Carroll maintains that in other cases, film style can 'foreground an expressive property', 'arouse feelings, including feelings of visual pleasure in audiences', or 'communicate ideas about life, society or *even about film*'.[6] How the tracking shot as a mobile camera technique is patterned in the omnibus *Kuldesak* (*Cul-de-*sac, d.p. Yadi Sugandi/Yudi Datau/Roy Lolang/ Nur Hidayat, 1998) illustrates the function of style to communicate ideas about the art of cinema. *Kuldesak* is an independent film put together by *Riri* Riza, Mira Lesmana, Rizal Mantovani and Nan Achnas, who wanted to experiment with cinematic storytelling in ways that people hadn't seen before in Indonesian film. In the segment directed by Riri, an aspiring filmmaker Aksan (Wong Aksan), is seen having a recurring nightmare about being chased and attacked by a 35mm film camera. At one particular point in this dream diegesis, the camera cranes down on him, descending rapidly to assault Aksan ferociously. This sequence is particularly important because soon, we'll discover that these nightmares act as an omen that warns Aksan that if he doesn't start making films, he will die, as captured by his memorable line: 'I must make a film soon! If I don't make one soon, I'll die.'[7] The camera and its tracking movement, along with Aksan's paranoia, suggest the anxiety that Indonesian filmmakers faced in the late 1990s. And the remedy to this anxious state is to make films independently, armed with a do-it-yourself ethos. That's precisely what the makers of *Kuldesak* did in 1998 when they decided to put together resources to get this feature film made even without financial support from the government or a major production company, except the film equipment rental company PT Elang Perkasa.

Finally, Carroll posits that film style can also 'engender a particular experience, such as repose, excitement, suspense, or perceptual delight'.[8] In the short fiction film *Hulahoop Soundings* (Edwin, d.p. Gunnar Nimpono, 2008), the camera repeatedly moves, circling the character Lana (Lidya Cheryl) in a 360-degree fashion whenever she has sex with her lover Nico (Nicholas Saputra). Lana performs a hula hoop dance while having sex, and the rotating camera enlivens the shot by following the circling movement of the hoop around Lana's body. Beyond injecting lively energy into the lovemaking shots, the circular camera movement accentuates the meaning typically associated with it, namely the invigorating and self-interested nature of falling in love or becoming infatuated that Lennard Højbjerg has elucidated in his research article.[9] Meanwhile, in the found footage horror film *Keramat* (*Sacrosanct*, Monty Tiwa, d.p. Ucup Supena, 2009), the handheld camerawork follows the characters tightly from behind, intensifying the suspense of the film's scenes. The film revolves around a crew trying to shoot a dramatic fiction film at a sacred site in Yogyakarta. In the middle of production, the crew members encounter a supernatural being, which causes the mysterious disappearance of their main actress, Migi (Migi Parahita).

We can conclude that through the lens of Carroll's macro functional theory, film style can do many tasks, including those that don't necessarily serve moment-by-moment storytelling objectives such as conveying 'ideas about life, society or even about film' and eliciting 'perceptual delight'.

Thus, film style serves not only narrational and aesthetic functions, but communicative and affective ones, too.

Another contribution to the macro functional theory of film style comes from the theoretical writings of Bordwell. In *Figures Traced in Light: On Cinematic Staging*, Bordwell proposes four broad functions of film style. First, in what he calls the *denotative function*, film style can 'denote a fictional or nonfictional realm of actions, agents, and circumstances'.[10] In this most fundamental function, a stylistic device presents concrete objects, people, settings and so on. This denotative function is activated when film techniques are engineered to display whatever is placed in front of the camera descriptively. For example, in *Laskar Pelangi* (*The Rainbow Troops*, Riri Riza, prod. des. Eros Eflin, 2008), the props arranged in the set of the *toko kelontongan* (neighbourhood convenience store) display the household appliances typical for a mom-and-pop shop in Indonesia. This stylistic device, namely production design, *denotes* figures and settings. In other words, film style here functions to present the diegetic story world of *Laskar Pelangi* at its most elemental level.

Second, the organisation of film techniques also works beyond showing objects and persons descriptively; thus, it 'can display expressive qualities too'.[11] Bordwell calls this the *expressive function*. The arrangement of camera movement, lighting, acting and other stylistic components can imbue the shots or scenes in the film with particular feelings analogous to human emotional states.[12] Bordwell contends, 'In most films expressive qualities can be *carried* by light, color, performances, music; and certain camera movements, such as the blurry swirl that can *express* vertigo.'[13] What Bordwell means by 'expressive' in this context is the ability of film style to represent 'feelingful qualities' ('The shot exudes sadness') rather than 'causing feelings in the perceiver ('The shot makes me sad')'.[14] Bordwell is being careful here not to conflate *representational* expressivity with *cinematic affect* – viewers' emotions and feelings activated by a cinematic experience – which is a whole other area of study within the field of film spectatorship.

A prime example of this expressive function comes from the *Laskar Pelangi* scene cited above. The set design of the *toko*, in addition to denoting the setting, also expresses a feelingful quality in one particular moment in the film. As soon as the main character Ikal (Zulfanny) hears the news that the girl he fancies – the *toko* owner's daughter – has moved to another city, he becomes sad and disappointed. The props (household appliances) that are hung inside the *toko* suddenly begin to fall, one by one; however, this happens without being caused by any diegetic force like strong wind or an earthquake. This particular handling of the props exudes the sorrowful feeling that Ikal is going through at that moment; hence, it works as though these household appliances are *crying with him*. We can infer from this example that set design amplifies the emotive quality of the shot.

Apart from the denotative and expressive functions, film style can also work to connote symbolic meanings; Bordwell calls this the *symbolic function*. For example, shadow and light engendered by low-key lighting in a segment from *Gie* (Riri Riza, d.p. Yudi Datau, 2005) symbolise the iconic Javanese shadow puppet theatre. In this scene, the shadow play represents the anti-communist purge directed by Suharto between 1965–6 that took the lives of hundreds of thousands of Indonesians across the country. The use of installation art as props in Garin Nugroho's *Opera Jawa* (*Requiem from Java*, prod. des. Nanang Rakhmat Hidayat, 2006) symbolises the evil traits of Rahwana – the villain in the Hindu epic *Ramayana*.

Fourth is the *decorative function*; Bordwell claims that in this functional paradigm, film style can operate independently of its purported role in channelling story information.[15] A paradigmatic example of the decorative function of style comes from *Kuldesak*. In one scene directed by Rizal Mantovani, a blue lighting pattern pierces through holes on the office wall of the sexual predator Jacob Gamarhada (Torro Margens) – the villain (see Figure 3.1). But this blue lighting scheme does nothing to advance storytelling as such because there's no diegetic event that caused the holes on the walls like fired gunshots, for instance. Thus, the lighting pattern is put together for a decorative purpose, heightening the shot's visual interest.

The decorative function of film style overlaps with another concept that Bordwell has developed in *Narration in the Fiction Film*, which is the concept of *parametric narration*. Borrowing Noël Burch's use of the term *parameter* to replace *technique*, parametric films are those in which 'the film's stylistic system creates patterns distinct from the demands of the syuzhet system'.[16]

Figure 3.1 *A decorative lighting pattern in* Kuldesak

In a parametric film, 'Film style may be organized and emphasized to a degree that makes it at least equal in importance to the syuzhet patterns.'[17] So in this mode of filmic storytelling, film style is assembled in a way that would call attention to it – foregrounding its artifice rather than simply transmitting story information.

An important premise of Bordwell's theory is that all these functions can emerge simultaneously. So, a particular sequence or a shot can be denotative, expressive, symbolic and decorative at the same time. Now that we've covered the more general theory of the functions of film style from Carroll and Bordwell, let's turn to the more specific ones.

THE MICRO FUNCTIONAL THEORIES OF FILM STYLE

On the Functions of Lighting

In *Hollywood Lighting: From the Silent Era to Film Noir*, Patrick Keating demonstrates that lighting in classical Hollywood cinema is far from invisible or neutral as it had been traditionally understood. Rather than merely illuminating the set or glamorising the look of female movie stars on the screen, lighting can do many more tasks. So, in actuality, classical Hollywood lighting turns out to be multifunctional upon closer examination.[18] Keating proposes that there are at least three major categories of lighting's functions: *storytelling*, *realism* and *pictorialism*.[19] Like Bordwell, Keating also believes that these three functional categories can be fulfilled simultaneously in a shot or a scene.

Keating further theorises that within the category of storytelling function, one important sub-function of lighting is to *express mood*. But Hollywood cinematographers in the classical period invoked 'mood' as an umbrella term to refer to several different things: indicating characters' emotions and personal dispositions; punctuating dramatic points in the film; and, importantly, producing atmosphere.[20] In this case, mood was an all-inclusive concept that Hollywood cinematographers applied in their lighting practices.

Lastly, the handling of light and shadow under specific lighting techniques can also create striking graphic effects. Seen this way, darkness can *enhance* light. When darkness dominates the frame, a small patch of light can make a powerful visual impact. In addition to guiding attention to the important parts of the frame, darkness and light can also re-enact and allude to traditional *chiaroscuro* techniques in the visual arts, such as referencing the look of Baroque paintings from European masters like Rembrandt, Caravaggio and Tintoretto. In this sense, perhaps, light and darkness may invoke cultural gravitas as images on the screen transform into painterly images akin to the masterworks of these celebrated artists.

To illustrate these theoretical points, it is helpful to consider the scene from *Sang Pencerah*, discussed in the previous chapter. The low-key lighting applied in that scene aptly illustrates this multifunctional characteristic of lighting as a stylistic device. As I have explained, low-key lighting produces atmosphere, articulates the film's theme and creates a painterly effect.

Another scene that equally works to illustrate this multifunctionalism of lighting comes from *Hanung* Bramantyo's biopic of Indonesia's president, Sukarno: *Soekarno: Indonesia Merdeka* (d.p. Faozan Rizal, 2013). In this scene, the young Sukarno (Ario Bayu) asks the parents of his then-lover Inggit Ganarsih (Maudi Koesnaedi) for permission to marry their daughter. The scene takes place during the day. The light source in the scene is the sunlight penetrating through a glass window (see Figure 3.2). But the sunlight was de facto artificially constructed from the placement of a strong light fixture outside the window, as an overhead diagram of the shot's camera and lighting setup reveals.[21] In this instance, the cinematographer Faozan Rizal applied a cinematographic convention known as *effect lighting*, in which natural light sources are simulated by artificial lighting, whether in the studio or on location. So, the effect lighting deployed in the scene works to denote the plot time: daytime. But there is another function at play here, which is to give a realistic impression that the scene is shot on location with a natural light source: sunlight. On top of this, the effect lighting also creates a striking graphic effect, which alludes to the paintings of Vermeer. In Vermeer's works, figures are often depicted standing next to windows, and the light source in the scene is typically the sunlight, exemplified by his famous paintings like *The Milkmaid* (1657–61), *The Geographer* (c. 1668–9) and *Lady Writing*

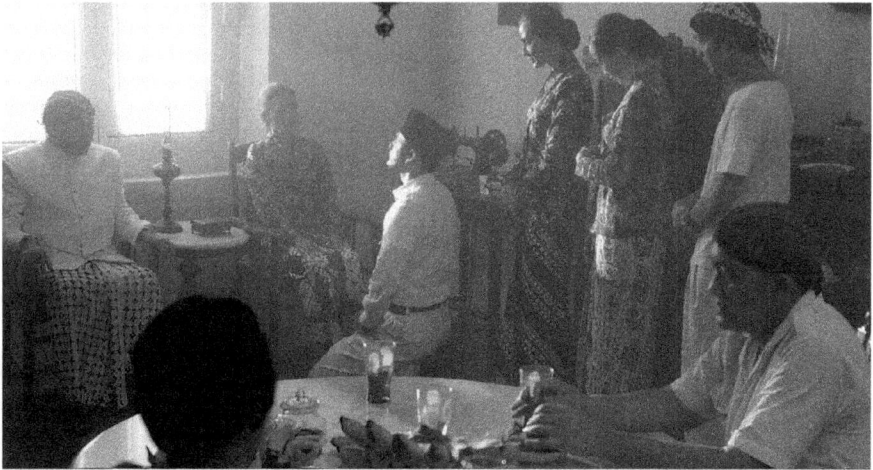

Figure 3.2 *The* effect lighting *convention simulates the sunlight in* Soekarno: Indonesia Merdeka

a Letter with her Maid (c. 1670–1).[22] Thus, lighting here performs a pictorial function. In this one scene alone, according to Keating's concept of multifunctionalism, lighting performs multiple tasks simultaneously: storytelling (indicating the time of day); realism (artificial lighting gives the impression that there is actual sunlight illuminating the space and figures); and pictorial effect (evoking painterly images).

In Chapter 5, I will discuss in more depth how this multifunctionalism of lighting and darkness extends beyond storytelling, realism and pictorial imperatives in post-Suharto-era cinematography.

On the Functions of Production Design

Another contribution to the micro theory of style comes from the scholarship on production design. As a start, Anette Kuhn and Guy Westwell claim that production design has a threefold purpose in narrative film:

> firstly, if a story creates an illusory reality, the verisimilitude of the fictional world must be *consistently convincing*; secondly, production design must *create both an overarching style that gives expression to the film's subject matter or story; and also specific sets, props, and dressings that support that style*; thirdly, production design can *create the fabulous, the spectacular, the extraordinary*.[23]

Echoing Kuhn and Westwell's functions of production design, Vincent LoBrutto asserts:

> The production designer researches the world in which the film takes place to *establish a sense of authenticity*. The production designer must *interpret and transform the story, characters, and narrative themes into images* that encompass architecture, décor, physical space, tonality, and texture. Production designers use sketches, illustrations, photographs, models, and detailed production storyboards to plan every shot from *microscopic to macroscopic detail*.[24]

According to Christopher Frayling, production design can work powerfully as a set of 'visual shortcuts', signifying the characters' social backgrounds and lifestyles, which in a literary work might be described over several pages.[25] For example, in *Kuldesak*, one of the main characters Andre (Rian Hidayat) is introduced to the viewers by way of a single tracking shot scanning his room littered with props related to Kurt Cobain and grunge music, giving us the visual shortcuts to his background: a cosmopolitan middle-class young adult who is well in touch with global pop music and lifestyles. Without relying on any descriptive verbal narration, set design in this establishing shot visually transmits important story information about Andre's identity and cultural milieu.

Filmmakers can use these visual shortcuts as narrative devices to contrast two different worlds in the film. In production design scholarship, scholars refer to this purpose of production design as the *polarisation function*:

> Film narratives often revolve around oppositions that reveal themselves in set design—whether it be the one between a working girl's apartment and a department store magnate's estate in our *Blushing Brides* (1930) or between Kansas and Oz in *The Wizard of Oz* (1939).[26]

We can find an example of the polarising function of production design in contemporary Indonesian cinema, too. The plot of *Republik Twitter* (*The Twitter Republic*, Kuntz Agus, prod. des. Muhammad Ichsan, 2012) – a film about the impact of social media on contemporary Indonesian politics and interpersonal relationships centres on two characters who work for two different organisations. One is an internet wizard who works for a shabby internet company that runs digital campaigns for corrupt politicians, and the other is a journalist who works for a conventional news company. The set design of the first setting (internet company) is frugal and poorly lit, full of worn-out furniture and disorganised workspaces. Meanwhile, the set design of the latter setting is lavish, modern-looking, well-lit and neatly organised. The design for each setting polarises the atmosphere, but also the meaning of office space. In the first one, the office space connotes the idea that they are involved in a sketchy and illegal business, hence the frugal and dark setting. By contrast, in the latter setting, the office space signifies a legitimate, transparent and professional business, hence the extravagant corporate setting.

Another instrumental task of production design is to set the atmosphere of the film or of a particular scene. According to Jane Barnwell, this atmosphere-production function is accomplished 'largely through their evocation of place'.[27] From a practitioner's viewpoint, production designer Léon Barsacq writes the following in his account of film décor:

> As a general rule, airy sets with many windows or other openings give an impression of gaiety, and thick walls, narrow windows and low ceilings create a heavy atmosphere. The designer can play with height and depth, large or small scale, matte surfaces or gleaming floors, gold and mirrors with a range of dull colors or violently contrasting tones. Each combination arouses different feelings that are difficult for the spectator to analyze but of which he is nevertheless aware.[28]

How the apartment building interior in Gareth Evans's *The Raid: Redemption* (prod. des. T. Moty D. Setyanto, 2011) is designed as its main setting sets an entrapping and suffocating atmosphere. The dilapidated courtyard, the dingy rooms, the broken elevator – all of these contribute to the brooding vibe of this home of the criminal mastermind Tama (Ray Sahetapy).

Production design can *enhance* realism, too. Since the advent of neorealism in post-war European cinema, location shooting has become the vogue in many film production contexts around the world.[29] The neorealist mode of production became influential not only for European and American filmmakers, but also for Asian filmmakers, including the Indonesian directors of the 1950s.[30] Important to note here is that, by opting for location shooting, ideas about what constitutes filmic realism shifted from studio-enhanced realism to on-location realism.[31] Garin Nugroho's *Daun Di Atas Bantal* (*Leaf on a Pillow*, prod. des. Roedjito and Tonny Trimarsanto, 1997) exemplifies the realism function of production design. Since the story revolves around the poverty-stricken street children of Yogyakarta, the location chosen for the film comprises low-income neighbourhoods in Yogyakarta itself. Shooting on location in these *kampungs* (urban villages) rather than in a studio in Jakarta enhances the authenticity of the setting where these children roam around.

This specific function of production design vis-à-vis *realism through stylisation* corresponds to a similar function in film lighting, which Keating calls *the realism of detail*.[32] While *realism of detail* in film lighting has to do with the replication of natural lighting phenomena – from the moonlight to the flickering flames of a fireplace –through the application of the effect lighting technique, in production design, realism can manifest in several forms. First, realism can manifest in what Stephen Prince has called 'the illusion of wholeness'.[33] This idea points to the fact that space in narrative films – whether on location or on a studio soundstage – is often partially built and designed; therefore, only the parts that will be shown on screen are constructed and decorated. Thus, they are not as holistic as spaces in our world. To explain this point further, Prince asserts:

> Narrative cinema is an art of the fragment. The viewer's experience of wholeness and contiguity is an illusion constructed by filmmakers, and production design very often is about being co-extensive with a film's story world. In fact, however, the spaces of the story world and production design are fabricated and engineered to sustain the narrative illusions of contiguity and wholeness.[34]

This 'illusion of wholeness' is also achieved by using several different locations to suggest that the events are happening in one place. In *Marlina Si Pembunuh dalam Empat Babak* (*Marlina the Murderer in Four Acts*, Mouly Surya, prod. des. Frans XR Paat, 2017), the setting takes place in a small village located on Sumba Island, eastern Indonesia. Most of its plot takes place inside the house of a widow named Marlina (Marsha Timothy). While the exterior of her house is shot from an actual house located on Sumba, characterised by the island's typical limestone hills, the interior is shot in a studio set designed to match the interior of a local Sumba house.[35] The 'illusion of wholeness' in this sense is achieved by combining on-location shooting (exterior) and studio filming (interior). The result of this combination is that the exterior and the interior of Marlina's house appear unified.

Realism in the context of production design also means that set design, props, CGI-enhanced scenery and other pertinent elements of this craft can heighten the impression of period authenticity. This means that the cinematic images would need to be supplied with large-scale details like location, building, vehicles and so on, and fine-grained details like materials specific to the era (plastic, metal or wood), household appliances, posters, printed advertisements, newspapers and magazines to look authentic. But filling up the images with those details won't be sufficient; these details need to be *congruent* with the spirit of the age depicted in the film as well. As production designer Dean Tavoularis remarks, when making a period film, the filmmaker cannot simply put any kind of soup can on the shelf, 'it has to be the right can of soup'.[36] Of course, we cannot be completely sure if the soup can that appears on the screen is the accurate one for the period. So, authenticity here is only a matter of *mediated congruency*, that is, the soup tin design seems very fitting to that period because of what we know about that era from the mass media and audio-visual arts – photography, painting, newspapers, family album, documentary footage and fiction films from that time. In the scene from *Laskar Pelangi* I cited earlier in this chapter, the set of the *toko* is designed to heighten the period authenticity of the 1970s. The products featured in the film, supplied by the props integrated into the set, are designed to match how the branding of those products looked in that era, such as the Rheumason balm, *kapur* Harimau (blackboard chalk), the ABC AA battery and other products specific to the Indonesian context. These elements of production design enhance the microscopic details of the film, which effectively enhances the realism function.

Finally, visual compositional impact is an equally important function of production design. Art director Sarah Horton remarks that the craft 'establishes a kind of *visual scaffolding*, defined by *color, light, texture,* and *contrast*'.[37] The visual scaffolding that Horton mentions is important to serve not only storytelling and realism goals, but also pictorial goals. What Keating has said about cinematographers as craft practitioners, who see themselves as image-makers as much as they are visual storytellers, can also be said about production designers.[38] Compositional symmetry or asymmetry, geometric patterns, cantering and decentring of objects in the frame, colour juxtapositions and similar aspects of visual composition can all result from the creative choices of the production designer, in consultation with the cinematographer and based on the director's artistic vision. This triangular relationship between the production designer, cinematographer and director is indispensable because the cohesiveness of the film's look is determined by the synchronicity between the visual choices in production design and cinematography. The film frame can be an interesting object visually when it is composed in a certain way; thus, production design serves this objective in tandem with cinematography. For example, translucent curtains, as part of the recurring set design in *Sang Pencerah*, become instrumental tools for visual composition. Figures are usually staged behind and in front of these transparent curtains creating a frame-inside-the-frame motif that gets repeated across the film (see Figure 3.3).

In Chapter 6, I will discuss these functional facets of cinematic production design in more depth, specifically in relation to how the techniques of *location shooting* and *location designing* have impacted the ways in which local-regional cultures of Indonesia are presented and delineated visually in the post-1998 narrative films.

On the Functions of Camera Movement

Jakob Isak Nielsen's research on camera movement in narrative cinema equally furnishes the micro functional theory of film style with indispensable

Figure 3.3 Translucent curtains patterned as a visual motif in Sang Pencerah

insights into the complex functions of camera mobility. Having examined the forms and roles of camera movement in American and European films, spanning from the silent era to the 2000s, Nielsen contends that there are at least six functions of camera movement:

1. *Orientation*: orienting the viewer spatially.
2. *Pacing*: contributing to the cinematic rhythm of the film.
3. *Inflection*: making commentative, suggestive or valuative statements.
4. *Focalisation*: associating the movement of the camera with the viewpoints of characters or entities in the story world.
5. *Abstract*: suggesting abstract ideas and concepts.
6. *Reflexive:* drawing attention to the filmmaker, the craft of filmmaking, the narrative or stylistic patterning at play.[39]

In a recent publication, Nielsen lists only five of these six functions (orientation, pacing, inflection, abstract and reflexive) as 'significant and primary', thus leaving out the focalisation function.[40]

Nielsen contends that, in many cases, camera mobilities work in a combinatory fashion, meaning they do not always fall into one of his functional categories in a neat and clear-cut way. A productive way to analyse the purpose of camera movement, then, is to imagine a 'flow chart of layered functions'.[41] On this idea, he explains:

> At one point a single function or a certain combination of functions will be engaged, sometimes to be replaced by another combination later in the same shot. Thus the taxonomy can be applied to both synchronic and diachronic analyses, i.e. establishing what functions are at play in a particular segment of a shot and establishing how one set of layered functions weaves into another in the course of a shot.[42]

Nielsen invokes literary theorist Roman Jakobson's concept of the *dominant*[43] as a useful framework to make sense of the layered functions of camera movement in a single shot or a single scene: what is the dominant function at play? But Nielsen also believes that there is a set of foundational functions of camera movement that usually work as the springboard for the other functions to emerge, such as the orientation function and the pacing function. This is to say that in any narrative film, these primary roles will always be at play. So, one fruitful way of examining the functions of camera movement, according to Nielsen, is to first ask, 'In what ways does this mobile shot orient the viewer in the diegetic space? And how does it temporally unfold?' before moving on to inspect whether there are other functions at play.[44]

Nielsen particularises the first function, i.e., orientation, into three sub-functions: lending more depth and volume to the image, directing the viewer's attention to salient story information, and articulating the scope of action.[45] A case in point is the crane shot in *Darah Garuda* (*Blood of Eagles*, Yadi Sugandi and Connor Allyn, d.p. Padri Nadeak, 2010). In the opening scene, the camera elevates to reveal an overhead view of a truck driven by a band of pro-independence Indonesian soldiers. As the camera cranes, we see a soldier lying on the top of the truck to hide from the Dutch soldiers who check incoming vehicles. In this instance, camera movement directs viewers to an important piece of story information: the fact that a soldier is hiding atop the truck and that this band of soldiers plans to ambush the Dutch military headquarters.

Camera movement often gives us cues about the characters' psychology, physical and behavioural traits, and their situation at a particular moment. Nielsen categorises these tasks as the *inflection* function of camera movement. Essentially, inflective camera movements are those that express 'feelingful qualities', which is in line with Bordwell's concept of the expressive function of film style. In one video essay, Nielsen altered this inflection function to *expressive function*, aligning it even closer to Bordwell's idea.[46] A good illustration of this expressive function is the slow push-in – a forward motion of the camera to close in on a subject or an object – in *Perempuan Punya Cerita* (*Chants of Lotus*, Upi Avianto/Nia Dinata/Fatimah Rony/Lasja Fauzia Susatyo, d.p. Ical Tanjung and Teoh Gay Hian, 2007). In the first portion of this omnibus directed by Fatimah Rony – *Cerita Pulau* (*Story from an Island*) – a disabled teenage girl, Wulan (Rachel Maryam), has been raped by a group of men. The doctor who has taken care of this girl, Sumantri (Rieke Diah Pitaloka), is deeply dismayed and enraged by this incident. During a scene in which Sumantri is seen helping Wulan to clean herself after the attack, the camera creeps in at a lethargic pace to show Sumantri's face, accentuating her sadness and fury as tears run down her cheeks. In this example, the *push-in* technique plays an expressive function in that it amplifies the heart-wrenching, sad feeling that the main character is harbouring, signalled by her weeping that's becoming louder and more intense as the camera gets closer to her.

Camera movement can also mediate a character's viewpoint. Nielsen calls this purpose of camera movement the *focalising* function. If expressive, or inflective, camera movements remain external to the character's viewpoint, *focalising* camera movements, by contrast, approximate or invoke the viewpoints of a character or an entity in the story world. He distinguishes between several kinds of focalising camera movements, embodied by three types of point-of-view shots: *optical POV*, *affected POV* and *invoked POV*.[47] While the optical and affected POV shots mediate the viewpoint of a character or an entity in a direct way, invoked POV shots only suggest the presence of a character or entity whose identity remains unknown to the spectator. For example, the POV shots in the found-footage mystic film *Keramat* illustrate the optical POV, since they represent the viewpoint of the cameraperson in charge of making a behind-the-scenes documentary film for the production team. Meanwhile, the focalising camera movement in *Pengabdi Setan* (*Satan's Slaves*, Joko Anwar, d.p. Ical Tanjung, 2017) exemplifies the invoked POV type, as it focalises the viewpoint of a supernatural entity, which is disclosed much later in the film to be the haunting spirit of a deceased woman who worshipped Satan.

Camera movement also performs a *reflexive* function. According to Nielsen, 'Reflexive camera movements can be engrossing in their own right; they only by-pass the storytelling resources of the medium in order to *elicit other types of engagement and appreciation*.'[48] He argues that camera movement can be reflexive in several ways: firstly, it can be reflexive because it self-consciously addresses the operation and mechanics of camera mobility. We can locate this type of self-referential shot in films that contain a parody camera movement or in films about filmmaking. This type of reflexive camera movement can be illustrated by the segment from *Kuldesak*, cited earlier in this chapter, in which the aspiring filmmaker Aksan is chased by a camera in his dream. In this segment, camera mobility alludes to the artifice of the medium of film, but additionally, it also touches on the mechanics of camera movement, suggesting the fantastical idea that the film camera has consciousness and agency.

Secondly, it can also be that the choreography of the camera movement demonstrates the virtuosic sensibility of the film director. We can locate some of these virtuosic mobile shots in long take-oriented filmmaking, in which camera movement captures an entire scene or sequence in a single shot. An example of this kind of reflexivity comes from Hanung's *Catatan Akhir Sekolah* (*High School Diary*, d.p. Suadi Utama, 2005). In the opening sequence's one-shot presentation (totalling six minutes and twenty-eight seconds), the handheld camerawork takes us to the different locales in the high school where the story takes place. The virtuosic mobile camera operation by Suadi Utama in this lengthy opening shot – introducing us to the film's main characters and the various pockets of the setting – reminds us of the similar stylistic arrangement in the opening sequence of Robert Altman's *The Player* (d.p. Jean Lepine, 1992).

Thirdly, camera movement can be reflexive when it alludes to a convention of camera mobility associated with a certain genre, filmmaking movement, cinematic tradition or even a well-known film, without necessarily being a parody or a meta film (a film about filmmaking). The hyper-fast zoom-in shots in *Pendekar Tongkat Emas* (*Golden Cane Warrior*, Ifa Isfansyah, d.p. Gunar Nimpono, 2014), for instance, allude to the quick zoom-in technique applied religiously in the Hong Kong *wuxia* cinema of the 1960s and '70s as well as in the Indonesian *silat* genre of the 1970s and '80s.[49]

In sum, reflexive camera moves are those that 'appeal to a specific sort of engagement, divergent from the viewer's involvement with the ongoing story'.[50] Viewed from Nielsen's theoretical lens, these are the mobile shots that offer the viewer another kind of experience based on the appreciation of camera movement in and of itself. The reflexive function of the mobile frame in contemporary Indonesian cinematography will be discussed in more depth in Chapter 7.

CRANING DOWN, ZOOMING IN

Now that we have considered the main assumptions and propositions of these theories, we need to zoom in and assess the overlaps and divergences among these ideas and identify any conceptual wrinkles that need to be ironed out by means of clarification.

On Storytelling and Expressivity

In many ways, the micro functional theories of film style corroborate and particularise Bordwell's four broad functions of style theory. For instance, the micro functional theories of lighting, production design and camera movement share Bordwell's contention that style in narrative film performs a denotative function. But style does not only describe concrete objects and persons, according to the micro functional theories; it also contributes to storytelling processes. Lighting, production design and camera movement, for instance, orient the viewers in the diegetic universe of the film, create the illusion of three-dimensionality (or, *the illusion of roundness* to use Keating's phrase[51]), reveal the scope of action, heighten the volumetric depth of the space and provide visual shortcuts to the character's background in the story.

These micro theorists also share Bordwell's notion of the expressive function of style, but with some reservations. Nielsen, for instance, takes issue with how Bordwell conceptualises this expressive capacity of film style. He asks sceptically, 'What kind of inflection are we dealing with, i.e., what is the nature of the inflection?'[52] Nielsen claims that Bordwell's expressive theory remains fuzzy when it comes to answering this question. And the vagueness is caused – to begin with – by Bordwell's choice of words when defining expressivity, Nielsen argues. To make this clear, it is helpful to cite at length what Bordwell has asserted when articulating this expressive function of style:

> it [style] can *display* expressive qualities too. A great deal of musical style is devoted to *representing* emotional states, such as majesty, sprightliness, or menace. Abstract Expressionist paintings are often taken to *represent*

turbulence or anxiety. In most films expressive qualities can be *carried* by light, color, performances, music; and certain camera movements, such as the blurry swirl that can express vertigo.[53]

Nielsen argues that Bordwell's use of verbs such as *display*, *represent* and *carry* 'does not refer to the function of a stylistic device but to *the outcome as seen* in a shot wherein a stylistic device was used expressively'.[54] Nielsen subsequently asks, under Bordwell's functional paradigm, 'What is the "it" that is being inflected expressively?'[55] The answer to this question would be 'whatever *has been denoted* beforehand', but:

> by using the [sic] phrases such as 'represent' and 'carry' Bordwell actually downplays the constitutive role of style and instead implies that expressive style is a vessel of states or qualities that are somehow already present in the dramatic action.[56]

I share Nielsen's concern with Bordwell's terminology, which can be imprecise, and I also agree with him on the fact that Bordwell could have made his idea on stylistic expressivity more explicit. But I don't believe that Bordwell's approach consistently 'downplays the constitutive role of style', as Nielsen claims. For example, in an account that Nielsen himself cites,[57] Bordwell clarifies that the expressive toggle switch turned on by the arrangement of stylistic techniques in a shot or a scene often interlocks with the denotative role, as he claims:

> the denotative and the expressive, are often closely welded together. So for instance performance is a borderline case. If we count the actor's performance as part of the style of the film—and it seems to me that we should—there are expressive values there from the very beginning because acting or performance is letting us know what feelingful qualities are at stake in the scene.[58]

In this respect, Bordwell's description demonstrates that he does understand style to function in a constitutive manner. The performance of actors, which is also a stylistic device,[59] denotes 'the realms of agents', to use Bordwell's words; but at the same time, the actors' facial expressions, body language, dialogue content, lighting and music, for instance, all imbue the shot or scene with feelingful qualities.

Nielsen more or less agrees with Bordwell on this point, though he still raises questions about how Bordwell addresses the relationship between denotative and expressive functions:

> If emotional states, expressive and feelingful qualities are introduced by performance, then it would make sense to investigate how *the more mechanical of stylistic devices* such as cinematography and lighting can be expressive of the actor's performance. If that is the case it should have been made more

explicit because the expressive function of style could in fact inflect both denoted action and *denoted action already inflected expressively*.[60]

Yet, Nielsen's critique raises further questions; what is meant by 'the more mechanical of stylistic devices' and 'denoted action and denoted action already inflected expressively'? In what ways is Nielsen's understanding of the relationship between the expressive and denotative functions of style fundamentally different from Bordwell's, apart from arguing for a more precise terminology? While Nielsen's proposed inflection concept is valuable for it helps clarify some issues regarding this relationship between the denotative and expressive functions of film style, it doesn't fully resolve the question he has posed regarding Bordwell's concept of expression: what is it exactly that style *inflects*? Furthermore, while both Bordwell and Nielsen have tackled the relationship between denotation and expression, a critical question remains largely unaddressed: if the denotative function is the baseline for every other function that follows, at what point does the expressive function *begin* in an unfolding shot or scene?

My answer to this question is that this is where interpretation comes into play. I contend that we can modestly resolve this issue of the expressiveness of style by welcoming the idea that interpretation facilitates our understanding of the relationship between the use of film techniques and the inflection of feelingful qualities. From my perspective, a degree of interpreting activity is necessary in order for us to identify that an expression or inflection of feeling has taken place and to decipher the ways in which the denotative and expressive functions of style are 'welded together', with the latter building on the former, as Bordwell and Nielsen claim. An actor's performance alone doesn't automatically present to us the emotional states or feelingful qualities that Bordwell and Nielsen claim already exist (in the shot or scene) for the stylistic device to inflect, display, represent, magnify or add to.

If we take Bordwell's example of the technique in which the 'camera tracks in to the face', to help us decode this shot, we need to draw on cultural schemata to understand that the facial expression, the music and the camera tracking into the actor's face exude a sad feeling.

Karl G. Heider, in his study of non-verbal communication in Indonesian cinema, has found that some facial expressions displayed in Indonesian films connote different meanings to Indonesian audiences compared to how these expressions are conventionally 'read' by Western audiences. For instance, analysing the films of the Indonesian comedian and singer Benyamin S, he demonstrates how raising the eyebrows ('brows up' rather than 'brows down'), as performed by Benyamin's characters, conveys a negative emotion: extreme anger. This interpretation of the raising eyebrows is consistent with his findings during his research on emotions in Indonesia, especially in the Minangkabau community of West Sumatra.[61] Heider finds that in Indonesia, there is 'an anger face which is not an anger face'.[62] Although one can also find the more pancultural version of anger face in Indonesian films – characterised by eyebrows down, lips hard-pressed or parted to show clenched teeth[63] – it is the culturally specific version of this facial expression (eyebrows up) that requires one to learn the particular cultural schemata. It is only if one understands the local meaning of this facial expression that one will be able to decode this seemingly non-angry gesture (at least in Western cultures) as an expression of extreme anger in Indonesian cinema.

What this tells us is that the expressive or inflective function of film style is more complex as it is not as straightforward as we might think. Although resolving this theoretical problem is outside the scope of this book, an awareness of the issue does inform my analysis. The expressive dimension of film style needs to be examined very carefully on a case-by-case basis, and interpretation informed by a film's cultural context must come into play in the examination as well.

On Setting the Filmic Atmosphere

Bordwell's idea of the expressive function and Nielsen's of the inflective function only partially tackle the meaning of *artistic expression*. They focus primarily on what scholars and film practitioners often refer to as mood, which is the 'quality of a work of art or literature which evokes or recalls a certain *emotion* or *state of mind*'.[64] In this context, film style is considered to be the facilitator of art mood articulation, to use cognitive film theorist Carl Plantinga's concept.[65] But there is another meaning of artistic mood that film style has a huge role in articulating: 'the pervading atmosphere or tone of a place, event, or period.'[66]

Atmosphere in this context is understood experientially as a *feeling* related to space, which is activated when a subject and object enter the space.[67] We can refer to atmosphere phenomenologically through our lived-body experience as something that is 'in the air'. But this does not mean that this expression is plainly anecdotal. Julian Hanich stresses the importance of atmosphere in eliciting cinematic fears like dread and terror. As he contends:

> In ordinary language, we acknowledge these phenomena by talking about elating, depressing, comfy, inviting, erotic, or dreadful atmospheres. These atmospheres are *gushed out spatially*, but *cannot be pinpointed locally*. They cloak and thus pre-reflectively affect and modify in very specific ways those who enter them.[68]

The implication is that we can't designate where exactly atmosphere comes from in a space with absolute certainty; however, we can feel it as a 'vibe' as soon as we enter the space. The location choice, décor, lighting and darkness matter in 'gushing out' the vibe in which the setting coats us. For instance, the exterior and interior of the two-story house where the characters live in Joko Anwar's *Pengabdi Setan* exude an eerie vibe due to the house's characteristics as an old Dutch-colonial style structure that had been left unoccupied and underkept for decades. Shot on location in Pangalengan, West Java, using an existing house built during the Dutch colonial era, the interior of the house – with its decaying wood and shabby staircase – gushes out the atmosphere of *suasana mencekam* (a sinister vibe).[69]

Due to its immersive qualities, film is one the artforms most well-equipped to produce atmosphere. Filmmakers construct atmosphere through the employment of sound, music, set design, colour, wardrobe and lighting, to name but a few stylistic devices. In horror and thriller genres especially, according to Hanich, 'The threatening aspect of dread scenes is also felt directly because the film draws on atmospheric elements that correspond to and support experiences as typical of the phenomenology of fear: constriction and isolation.'[70] Light and darkness, in this respect, are fundamental devices, alongside location choice and set décor, to bring about such an atmosphere of constriction and isolation. In the example from *Pengabdi Setan* cited earlier, the state of the house (exterior and interior) already radiates an eerie atmosphere, but the deployment of minimal lighting inside the space that creates extreme visual darkness powerfully enhances the unsettling vibe.

Darkness in horror and thriller films emphasises the negative attributes of darkness: the ghost, monster, rapist or murderer lurks in the dark. Hanich stresses that this is the exact reason why many horror and thriller films are set at night: the night's gloom enhances the atmosphere of constriction and isolation. We can note the preference for darkness and nighttime in horror filmmaking by scanning some of the genre's titles: *Wait Until Dark* (1967), *Alone in the Dark* (2005) or *Night of the Living Dead* (1968).[71] In Indonesian horror films, we can find the same phenomenon: *Malam Jum'at Kliwon* (*Night of Jum'at Kliwon*, 1986), *Malam Satu Suro* (*Night of Satu Suro*, 1988), *Malam Suro di Rumah Darmo* (*Night of Suro at Darmo's House*, 2014), and *Malam Jum'at Kliwon* (*Night of Jum'at Kliwon*, 2007).

Léon Barsacq's statement, cited earlier in this chapter, brings us to what philosopher Gernot Böhme claims about the interrelating dynamics between atmosphere and space.[72] Architecture can exude a certain atmosphere depending on the design of the building and the elements that make up the interior. From this combination of the space and interior components, an atmosphere of cosiness, majesty, formality, conviviality, depression and so on can be created and sustained.[73] Horror, crime thriller and action films rely heavily on the atmospheric quality of space – not only of buildings and architecture, but also of outdoor locations like forests, lakes, corn fields and so on.[74] Hanich further suggests that dread scenes in these films usually depend on 'labyrinth-like places with winding corridors or a dizzying arrangement of rooms as in old castles, tunnel systems or cellars'.[75] To use the example of the house in *Pengabdi Setan* again, the area surrounding the house, namely a pine-tree forest situated nearby the tea plantation of Pangalengan, adds an extra layer of eeriness.

Period dramas equally rely on the atmospheric quality of location, both exterior and interior. Production design helps 'the creation of a spirit or atmosphere redolent of the period'.[76] It does so by utilising specific buildings with certain architectural styles common to the period in which it is depicted in the film – whether it is Art Nouveau or Art Deco or earlier styles like the Roman colosseum or the Japanese eighth century pagoda.

But location and architecture are not the only components used to evoke the atmosphere of an era. In addition to wardrobe and hairstyle, everyday objects, from household appliances to personal accessories as well as interior design, accumulatively contribute to pour out the period's atmospheric quality. Furthermore, the material used for designing the set – whether on location or on the studio soundstage – can enhance the look and atmosphere of the period depicted in the film. For example, specific types of fabric, paper or wood, with particular patterns and colours, added to the set can deepen the nuances of a period feel, whether it is the 1970s' flower power palette or the MTV-inspired neon ambience of the 1980s. This aspect of production design in contemporary Indonesian cinema will be discussed at length in Chapter 6.

On Suggesting Events/Actions

Another important function that the macro and micro functional theorists have overlooked is the capacity of film style to subtly present story events in an indirect way to activate viewers' imagination. The handling of light and darkness, camera movement and set design, for instance, can conceal objects, events or actions that are too unbearable to be shown explicitly. Film style, in this case, can contribute to an aesthetic mode in narrative cinema that invites viewers to imagine rather than merely perceive actions or events. Hanich calls this mode of audio-visual presentation *the aesthetic of suggested horror*. This suggested horror 'relies on intimidating imaginations of violence and a monster evoked through verbal descriptions, sound effects or partial, blocked and withheld vision'.[77] Contrary to *the aesthetic of direct horror*, where viewers perceive the horrific elements *directly* – presented in the most visible fashion – the suggested horror aesthetic stirs viewers to mentally visualise the dreadful or terrifying elements by imagining them in ways that are informed by the use of particular stylistic techniques. In this presentational mode, the filmmaker does not spell out the monster, the rape, the murder or any other unpalatable incident or action, but instead *suggests* it.

Hanich identifies three crucial components of the suggested horror aesthetic: moving images, sounds and verbal description. Staging, camera framing, editing, dialogue and off-screen sounds are the pertinent stylistic elements used by the proponents of suggested horror. These elements are the primary cues for the viewer to embark on a mental visualisation. So, what is lacking in this presentational mode is total visibility. By relying on those primary elements, the filmmaker opts for a strategy of omission, enticing the viewer to fill in what has been excluded in the scene.[78] Blocking the viewer's visual access to the monster or rape is a crucial strategy of omission. This strategic omission can be done either by staging the actors in such a way that blocks our vision or framing the actors' faces in very tight close-ups – perhaps even using extreme close-ups. Lighting also plays a crucial role in executing this suggested horror strategy. Extreme darkness produced by minimal lighting can obstruct the viewer's visual access to the horrible incident or monstrous creature, either partially or completely, by throwing it into the dark areas of the image. By covering it with graphic darkness or by pushing it to an unlit space, mental visualisation of the scary being or horrific action can be elicited in place of direct depiction. Hanich claims that it is exactly this imagined dimension that effectively terrifies audiences. These theoretical ideas are important as an analytical microscope through which I will examine the application of intensified graphic darkness in contemporary Indonesian filmic visual style (Chapter 5) to elicit the viewer's imagination of an otherwise graphically unbearable event such as the rape of a teenager and child abuse, a darkness which also works as a deliberate tactic to circumvent censorship.

On Authenticity and the Reality Effect

Although the micro functional theorists have addressed the realism function of film style, the nature of this realism itself is often taken for granted – as if realism is a given condition. Therefore, I argue that we should consider this role of film style under what Roland Barthes has called *the reality effect* (French: *l'effet de réel*).[79] Basically, through Barthes's lens, realism is seen more as an 'effect' than a transmission of objective reality. The reality effect, as proposed by Barthes, is a textual device employed to make artwork appear or feel realistic, but it does not always serve a narrational purpose. Examining nineteenth-century realist literature, Barthes came to the conclusion that there is a paradox at play: even though these literary works are replete with descriptive details, these details are often insignificant to plot progression.[80] So, Barthes asks, 'if there exist insignificant stretches [in the text], what is, so to speak, the ultimate significance of this insignificance?'[81] Barthes concludes that these 'insignificant' details function more as 'reality effects' that negotiate the complicated relationship between meaning (signified by textual devices) and reality.

In film art, details of place, action, individual, object, and period contribute to giving the story world of a film an authentic feel. This reality effect is also linked to the function of film style to produce atmosphere; so, in this sense, it is possible to conceptualise a function whereby cinematic techniques are put together to create a realistic atmosphere. The concept of reality effect is helpful in repudiating some of the assumptions often held by scholars about the relationship between certain film techniques and realism. For instance, in production design and lighting, location shooting is considered more readily capable of attaining verisimilitude. It is often assumed that, as soon as a filmmaker shoots on the streets, in existing apartments, or in nature, with available light, realism is automatically achieved.[82] But in practice, shooting on location poses its own problems and thus *requires creative stylisation* to appear realistic. As Barnwell notes, location shooting is not always ideal, so 'designers prefer to build, because they can control exactly what the setting will include, whereas in existing locations there is often a conflict of imagery that can confuse and detract from the overall design concept'.[83] Moreover, as many practitioners of production design have argued, shooting on location does not mean that there will be no *location designing* involved.[84] Even when an existing location is chosen, most often, it requires some art direction and design work based on the concept envisioned by the production designer. On this issue, Barnwell contends:

> Actually choosing the location is in no way an arbitrary task, as the places chosen will be loaded with meaning. Selecting exactly what to include, taking into account the action, dialogue and the look is the next stage. What to take away or add to this real place can be transformational.[85]

In *Pretty Pictures: Production Design and the History Film*, Charles Tashiro argues:

> Film design works from the difference between the physical world as it exists and the requirements of a particular narrative. This is another way of saying that *the real world is lacking*, is not good enough to provide an idealized, designed image. If the space in which a film is shot does not meet the story's needs, it has to be "designed" to fit the bill, so that, for example, the television antennas in the background of a period shoot have to be moved or avoided, and so on.[86]

What Barnwell and Tashiro are claiming accords with a prominent discourse in the practice of film and television production design, namely that shooting for realism without any creative intervention at all is an illusion.[87] Consequently, we should not assign immediate primacy to location shooting as a guarantor for realism and assume that once the filmmakers decide to shoot in existing locales, they will shoot it *as it is*. Location shooting and location designing supplement each other in constructing and heightening the reality effect. In my analysis of two production design cases in contemporary Indonesian cinema (Chapter 6), I will show how this interlocking principle of location shooting and location designing is at work to achieve the reality effect.

On Reflexivity

Finally, regarding the reflexive function of film style, we need to deepen Nielsen's theoretical assumptions by looking at concepts that pertain to reflexivity in other media. An important concept in media studies that connects with the topic of reflexivity is the *operational aesthetic*. Cultural historian Neil Harris introduced this idea in his book on the American showman P. T. Barnum.[88] According to Harris, Barnum's cunning hoaxes and stunts induced his audiences to engage in an operational aesthetic, whereby the excitement of witnessing the creative mechanics at work to pull off these stunts became the ultimate pleasure in which his audiences revelled.[89] In short, an operational aesthetic solicits a different kind of engagement from the audience in which an awareness of the creative mechanics, or 'the how' aspect of the media, becomes the source of pleasure.

The operational aesthetic as a concept in relation to audience reception has gained currency in the past decade within the scholarship of audio-visual media. Transposing Harris' idea onto the medium of film and television, Tom Gunning and Jason Mittell have found it useful to understand various filmic and televisual works that invite spectators to embrace an operational aesthetic.[90] What this aesthetic induces in the audiences is not the 'what will happen?' reaction, but rather the 'how did the maker(s) do that?' response. Although Gunning and Mittell have applied this concept to analyse their respective objects of study on the level of narrative, I am interested in applying it to analysing Indonesian cinematic visual style, particularly as it is engendered by camera movement. In Chapter 7, I will discuss how this operational aesthetic as a form of viewer engagement is activated by the exploration of reflexive camera movement in post-Suharto cinematography, which demonstrates technical and artistic virtuosity.

Zooming Out, Craning Up

In the preceding pages, we have closely looked at the theoretical assumptions that several film theorists, film historians and film philosophers have put forth regarding the functions of film style in narrative cinema. We've seen that these scholars agree on the fact that film style is *multifunctional*; however, when it comes to specifying what the exact functions of film style are, they have overlapping but also diverging ideas about it.

Curiously enough, the micro theories we have reviewed and assessed overlap more with Bordwell's than with Carroll's macro theory. Carroll's proposition that film style can 'foreground an expressive property'[91] corresponds well with the expressive function of film style that Bordwell and the other theorists have suggested. But none of the theorists (apart from Carroll himself) argue explicitly that film style can 'communicate ideas about life, society or even about film'.[92] Perhaps, this is because the communication model of film as a message-sending medium is no longer tenable in contemporary film theory. But it could also be that this assumption is far too general for it to work as a precise conceptual tool to analyse the function of specific stylistic devices like lighting, production design and camera movement. Nevertheless, this discussion of theories is helpful for us to use as a barometer to read the degree to which film style in Indonesian cinema plays a complex, nuanced set of functions in the post-1998 era.

In the next chapter, as we're tracing the evolution of the Indonesian visual aesthetic, we will see that the salient stylistic devices crucial to the transformation of Indonesian films in the post-1998 era (lighting, production design and camera movement) are much more restricted, both in form and function in the previous eras of Indonesian cinema history. To put it bluntly, before 1998, specific techniques of lighting, production design and camera movement that post-1998 filmmakers have leveraged, had much simpler forms and capabilities.

Notes

1. See, for instance, Noël Carroll, 'Film Form: An Argument for a Functional Theory of Style in the Individual Film', *Style* 32, no. 3 (1998), pp. 385–401; and David Bordwell, *Figures Traced in Light: On Cinematic Staging* (Berkeley, CA: University of California Press, 2005).
2. See, for instance, their following publications: Patrick Keating, *Hollywood Lighting: From the Silent Era to Film Noir* (New York, NY: Columbia University Press, 2010); Jakob Isak Nielsen, 'Five Functions of Camera Movement in Narrative Cinema', in *Transnational Cinematography Studies*, eds Lindsay Coleman, Daisuke Miyao and Roberto Schaefer (Lanham, MD: Lexington Books, 2017), pp. 25–53; Jakob

Isak Nielsen, 'Camera Movement in Narrative Cinema: Towards a Taxonomy of Functions' (PhD Thesis, University of Aarhus, 2007); Jane Barnwell, *Production Design: Architects of the Screen* (London: Wallflower, 2004); and Charles. S. Tashiro, *Pretty Pictures: Production Design and the History Film*, 1st edn (Austin, TX: University of Texas Press, 1998).
3. Carroll, 'Film Form'.
4. Ibid., p. 276 (original emphasis).
5. Ibid.
6. Ibid., p. 275 (emphasis added).
7. Original Indonesian: 'Kayaknya gua harus segera bikin film. Kalo gua gak segera bikin film, gue bisa mati!'
8. Ibid.
9. Lennard Højbjerg, 'The Circular Camera Movement: Style, Narration, and Embodiment', *Projections* 8, no. 2 (December 1, 2014), pp. 71–88.
10. Bordwell, *Figures Traced in Light*, p. 33.
11. Ibid.
12. Ibid.
13. Ibid. (emphasis added).
14. Ibid.
15. Ibid., p. 35.
16. David Bordwell, *Narration in the Fiction Film* (Madison, WI: The University of Wisconsin Press, 1985), p. 275 (original emphasis).
17. Ibid.
18. Keating, *Hollywood Lighting*, p. 6.
19. Ibid., pp. 5–6.
20. Drawing on the conventions of lighting in the theatrical arts, cinematographers, via the role of directors trained in theatre, carried this discourse on mood to motion picture cinematography. See Keating, *Hollywood Lighting*, pp. 56–81.
21. See the shot's overhead diagram of the camera and lighting setup here: bit.ly/Soekarno-effect-lighting.
22. 'Complete Catalogue of the Painting of Johannes Vermeer', accessed 7 November 2018, http://www.essentialvermeer.com/vermeer_painting_part_one.html.
23. Annette Kuhn and Guy Westwell, 'Production Design', *Oxford Dictionary of Film Studies* (Oxford: Oxford University Press, 2012), accessed 7 September 2015, http://www.oxfordreference.com/view/10.1093/acref/9780199587261.001.0001/acref-9780199587261 (emphasis added).
24. Vincent LoBrutto, *The Filmmaker's Guide to Production Design* (New York, NY: Allworth Press, 2002), p. 1 (emphasis added).
25. Christopher Frayling, 'Perspectives on Production Design', a keynote lecture delivered at LICA-Lancaster University, Lancaster, 5 March 2013, accessed 27 October 2015, https://www.youtube.com/watch?v=HFZSuNdT5vo.
26. Lucy Fischer, ed., *Art Direction and Production Design: A Modern History of Filmmaking*, Behind the Silver Screen (London; New York, NY: IB Tauris, 2015),

p. 16. The term *polarisation* in the context of production design/art direction originally comes from Jane Barnwell, *Production Design: Architects of the Screen* (London: Wallflower Press, 2004).
27. Barnwell, *Production Design*.
28. Léon Barsacq, *Caligari's Cabinet and Other Grand Illusions: A History of Film Design*, 1st English language edn (New York, NY: New York Graphic Society, 1976), p. 126.
29. Saverio Giovacchini and Robert Sklar, eds, *Global Neorealism: The Transnational History of a Film Style* (Jackson, MS: University Press of Mississippi, 2013).
30. Ekky Imanjaya, 'Revisiting Italian Neorealism: Its Influence toward Indonesia and Asian Cinema or There's No Such Thing Like Pure Neorealist Films,' *Jurnal Kajian Wilayah Eropa*, IV, no. 3 (2008), pp. 57–66.
31. Merrill Schleier, 'Postwar Hollywood, 1947–1967,' in *Art Direction and Production Design*, ed. Lucy Fischer, Behind the Silver Screen (London; New York: IB Tauris, 2015), pp. 73–96.
32. Keating, *Hollywood Lighting*, p. 5.
33. Stephen Prince, 'Hollywood's Digital Backlot: 2000–Present', in *Art Direction and Production Design*, ed. Lucy Fischer, Behind the Silver Screen (London; New York, NY: IB Tauris, 2015), p. 155.
34. Ibid.
35. This mix method of on-location shooting and studio shooting is corroborated by the behind-the-scene documentary made by the production team. See Sabina Renika, 'Di Balik Layar: Membingkai Marlina', Cinesurya, 17 November 2017, video, 6:15, https://www.youtube.com/watch?v=TPVJH9mDKQE.
36. This quotation can be found in Cathy Whitlock, *Designs on Film: A Century of Hollywood Art Direction* (New York, NY: It Books, 2010), p. 190. The statement originally appeared in Harlan Lebo, *The Godfather Legacy* (New York, NY: Fireside, 1997), p. 68.
37. Sarah Horton, 'The Craft of Art Direction,' *Pushing Pixels*, last modified 16 August 2011, accessed 24 July 2015, http://www.pushing-pixels.org/2011/08/16/the-craft-of-art-direction-conversation-with-sarah-horton.html.
38. Keating, *Hollywood Lighting*, p. 5.
39. Nielsen, 'Camera Movement in Narrative Cinema'.
40. Nielsen, 'Five Functions of Camera Movement in Narrative Cinema', pp. 25–53.
41. Nielsen, 'Camera Movement in Narrative Cinema', p. 261.
42. Ibid., pp. 261–2.
43. Roman Jakobson, 'Closing Statement: Linguistics and Poetics', in *Style in Language*, ed. Thomas A. Sebeok (Cambridge, MA; New York, NY; London: The Technology Press of Massachusetts Institute of Technology and John Wiley & Sons, Inc., 1960), pp. 350–77.
44. Nielsen, 'Camera Movement in Narrative Cinema', p. 262.
45. Ibid.
46. Jakob Isak Nielsen, 'Camera Movement in Narrative Cinema', 16:9 filmtidsskrift (2015), accessed 8 December 2015.

47. Nielsen replaces the term *focalising* with the *point-of-view* function in a video essay published in the Danish film studies journal 16:9. His intention is to make this functional category more accessible to a broader audience (point of view, or POV, is a more readily recognisable term than focalisation, according to Nielsen). See Jakob Isak Nielsen, 'Camera Movement in Narrative Cinema', *16:9*, 2 February 2015, http://www.16-9.dk/2015/02/camera-movement-in-narrative-cinema/ The relationship between camera, narration and point of view is a complex problem in film theory. For an extensive meta-theoretical exposition on this matter, see Edward Branigan, *Projecting a Camera: Language-Games in Film Theory* (New York, NY; Abingdon: Routledge, 2006).
48. Nielsen, 'Camera Movement in Narrative Cinema', p. 248 (emphasis added).
49. For a discussion on the preponderant use of zoom shots in Hong Kong martial arts cinema, see Chapter 8 of David Bordwell, *Planet Hong Kong: Popular Cinema and the Art of Entertainment*, second edn (Madison, WI: Irvington Way Institute Press, 2011).
50. Nielsen, 'Camera Movement in Narrative Cinema'.
51. *The illusion of roundness* refers to the role of lighting to create depth in a two-dimensional image. Keating, *Hollywood Lighting*, p. 5.
52. Nielsen, 'Camera Movement in Narrative Cinema', p. 69.
53. Bordwell, *Figures Traced in Light*, p. 34 (emphasis added).
54. Nielsen, 'Camera Movement in Narrative Cinema', p. 69.
55. Ibid.
56. Ibid., p. 70.
57. This account I am referring to is an interview with Bordwell conducted by Nielsen for 16:9, see Jakob Isak Nielsen, 'Bordwell on Bordwell: Part II – Functions of Film Style,' *16:9*, September 2004, http://www.16-9.dk/2004-09/side11_inenglish.htm.
58. Ibid.
59. See the anthology on cinematic acting edited by Claudia Springer and Julie Levinson to learn more about the role of onscreen performance as a stylistic device in film art and its evolution: Claudia Springer and Julie Levinson, eds, *Acting* (New Brunswick, NJ: Rutgers University Press, 2015).
60. Nielsen, 'Camera Movement in Narrative Cinema', p. 70 (emphasis added).
61. Karl G. Heider, *Landscapes of Emotion: Three Maps of Emotion Terms in Indonesia* (New York, NY: Cambridge University Press, 1991).
62. Karl G. Heider, *Indonesian Cinema National Culture on Screen* (Honolulu: University of Hawaii Press, 1991), p. 65.
63. Paul Ekman and Wallace V. Friesen, *Unmasking the Face* (Englewood Cliffs, NJ: Prentice-Hall, 1975), pp. 78–98.
64. 'Mood', *OED Online* (Oxford University Press), accessed 7 July 2018, http://www.oed.com/view/Entry/121878.
65. Carl Plantinga, 'Art Moods and Human Moods in Narrative Cinema', *New Literary History* 43, no. 3 (2012), pp. 455–75.
66. 'Mood', *OED Online*.

67. Philosopher Gernot Böhme highlights atmosphere as a space of condition(s), independent from both object and subject. According to Böhme, atmospheres are re-positioned as an autonomous entity but have a co-presence within the space of subject and object. See Gernot Böhme, 'Atmosphere as the Fundamental Concept of a New Aesthetics', *Thesis Eleven* 36, no. 1 (1993), pp. 113–26.
68. Julian Hanich, *Cinematic Emotion in Horror Films and Thrillers: The Aesthetic Paradox of Pleasurable Fear* (New York, NY: Routledge, 2010), p. 170. For more detailed discussion on the phenomenological characteristics of atmospheres, see Tonino Griffero, *Atmospheres: Aesthetics of Emotional Spaces*, English Edition (Surrey: Ashgate Publishing Limited, 2014).
69. In Java, local people often believe that abandoned old houses from the Dutch colonial era are haunted. This is one of the reasons why Joko Anwar and his production designer Allan Sebastian chose this particular house as the main setting for the film, and shot the film on location (both for exterior and interior shots), instead of on a soundstage. See the documentary on the making of *Pengabdi Setan*: 'Behind the Scene Film Pengabdi Setan', Rapi Films, 28 September 2017, video, 20:14, https://www.youtube.com/watch?v=C2_D0-GNdYI.
70. Ibid.
71. Hanich, *Cinematic Emotion in Horror Films and Thrillers*, p. 178.
72. Böhme, 'Atmosphere as the Fundamental Concept of a New Aesthetics'.
73. Ibid.
74. For an analysis of outdoor locations in horror and thriller films see Chapter 6 of Hanich's *Cinematic Emotion in Horror Films and Thrillers*, entitled 'Anxious Anticipations: A Phenomenology of Cinematic Dread'.
75. Ibid., p. 167.
76. Barnwell, *Production Design*, p. 80.
77. Hanich, *Cinematic Emotion in Horror Films and Thrillers*, p. 109.
78. For more elaboration on this omission strategy and its filmic examples, see Julian Hanich, 'Omission, Suggestion, Completion: Film and the Imagination of the Spectator', *Screening the Past*, no. 43 (April 2018), accessed 24 September 2018, http://www.screeningthepast.com/2018/02/omission-suggestion-completion-film-and-the-imagination-of-the-spectator/.
79. Roland Barthes, 'The Reality Effect', in *French Literary Theory Today*, trans. Tzvetan Todorov (New York, NY: Cambridge University Press, 1982), pp. 11–17.
80. Ibid.
81. Ibid., p. 12.
82. See the discussions on location shooting and realism in Saverio Giovacchini and Robert Sklar, eds, *Global Neorealism: The Transnational History of a Film Style* (Jackson, MS: University Press of Mississippi, 2013). For the Indonesian context see Imanjaya, 'Revisiting Italian Neorealism'.
83. Barnwell, *Production Design*.
84. See the introductory chapter to Fischer, *Art Direction and Production Design*.
85. Barnwell, *Production Design*.

86. Tashiro, *Pretty Pictures,* pp. 17–18 (original emphasis).
87. This line of thought also reverberates in the writings of and conversations about production design. See for instance: Vincent LoBrutto, *By Design: Interviews with Film Production Designers* (Westport, Connecticut: Praeger, 1992); Christopher Frayling, *Ken Adam and the Art of Production Design* (London: Faber and Faber, 2005); and Peter Ettedgui, *Production Design & Art Direction* (Hove: RotoVision, 1999).
88. Neil Harris, *Humbug: The Art of P. T. Barnum* (Chicago, IL; London: University of Chicago Press, 1981).
89. Ibid.
90. See Tom Gunning, 'Crazy Machines in the Garden of Forking Paths', in *Classical Hollywood Comedy*, eds Kristine Brunovska Karnick and Henry Jenkins (New York: Routledge, 1995), pp. 87–105; and Jason Mittell, 'Narrative Complexity in Contemporary American Television', *The Velvet Light Trap* 58, no. 1 (2006), pp. 29–40.
91. Carroll, 'Film Form', p. 275.
92. Ibid.

Part 2: Rising Action

How Indonesian Cinema Has Evolved Aesthetically

CHAPTER 4

Evolution by Means of Stylistic Suppression

To understand how film style in post-Suharto era Indonesian cinema has changed in terms of its form and function, we need to discern its development over time. In this chapter, we will trace the evolution of film style in the four periods of Indonesian cinema history – from the colonial era to the Suharto era – by focusing on the stylistic devices that have shaped and characterised Indonesian cinematic visual style: lighting, production design and camera movement. More specifically, we will look at the changes and continuities of key techniques and conventions within those three stylistic devices salient to the transformation of Indonesian cinematic visuals, including the low-key technique in lighting, location shooting and location designing in production design and the prowling camerawork in camera movement. It makes sense to focus on those techniques because, as my central argument posits, these techniques leveraged by Indonesian filmmakers in the post-Suharto years to transform Indonesian cinematic visual style didn't emerge abruptly in the 2000s and 2010s. These techniques had appeared in the previous eras of Indonesian film history. But as we will see, they were suppressed, underutilised and restrained until the circumstances changed in the post-Suharto era when filmmakers found themselves working in a much more favourable environment to explore visual stylisation more robustly across genres, production modes and target audiences.

How, then, have the forms and functions of those techniques evolved over time? Let's start with the most fundamental component of cinematography: lighting.

Lighting

Known as *tata cahaya* ('the arrangement of light') in Indonesian filmmaking parlance, lighting has been an indispensable part of Indonesian film artistry. While the popular assumption suggests that low-key lighting as a technique of film lighting emerged only in the 1950s in *Usmar* Ismail's war-themed films, particularly *Lewat Djam Malam* (*After the Curfew*, d.p. Max Tera, 1954), we can detect the application of this technique already in the cinematography of the colonial era.

Low-Key Lighting as Scene Lighting in the Colonial Era Cinematography

The low-key lighting technique was rarely applied in the films of the Netherlands Indies. In fact, of the six colonial-era films I viewed closely, *Tjitra* (*Image*, Usmar Ismail, d.p. A. A. Deninghoff-Stelling, 1949) is the only film that demonstrates the employment of this technique. Furthermore, low-key lighting in this film is deployed exclusively in one particular scene involving a murder. In this scene, Harsono (Rd. Sukarno) has fled to the city after stealing the virginity of a village girl, Suryani (Nila Djuwita), on his family's tea plantation. In the city, Harsono meets Sandra, a flirtatious carefree girl with whom he shortly falls in love. But when she betrays him, Harsono strangles her to death. During this homicidal moment, the lighting is kept minimalistic, with only a harsh key light illuminating one side of Harsono's face – leaving the other side of his face in thick darkness. Later, as Harsono chokes Sandra on her bed, the low-key lighting mode is sustained; but this time, we get an overhead light that shines on her face as she dies while leaving Harsono's face completely engulfed in shadow. As a result, the light-to-dark contrast in the images is high and the room becomes very dark, producing a strong *chiaroscuro* effect (see Figure 4.1).

It is possible that low-key lighting was underutilised in the cinematography of colonial-era films because of the prominence of scenes taking place outdoors, and these scenes mostly being during the day. This idea is not too far-fetched because, as Misbach Yusa Biran has explained, after 1937, following the success of *Terang Boelan* (*Full Moon*, Albert Balink, 1937), most filmmakers modelled their films on *Terang Boelan* by relying on three key ingredients: exotic sceneries, popular songs and romantic plots.[1] Setting most of the film scenes during the daytime rather than nighttime and opting for brightly lit rather than darkly lit images would help these filmmakers accentuate the exotic landscapes featured prominently in their movies.

But any explanation for why low-key lighting was hardly applied in colonial-era filmmaking remains hypothetical since we don't have a sufficiently large filmic corpus at our disposal to fully assess the claim that low-key lighting was in fact underused. One thing that we can establish from the low-key lighting applied in the murder scene in *Tjitra* is that A. A. Denninghoff-Stelling – the cinematographer and camera operator – chose this technique to accompany the emotional content of the scene. In this respect, low-key lighting was employed primarily as *scene lighting*, which is a cinematographic convention for lighting a film based on the presupposed mood of a particular scene.[2]

Evolution by Means of Stylistic Suppression 81

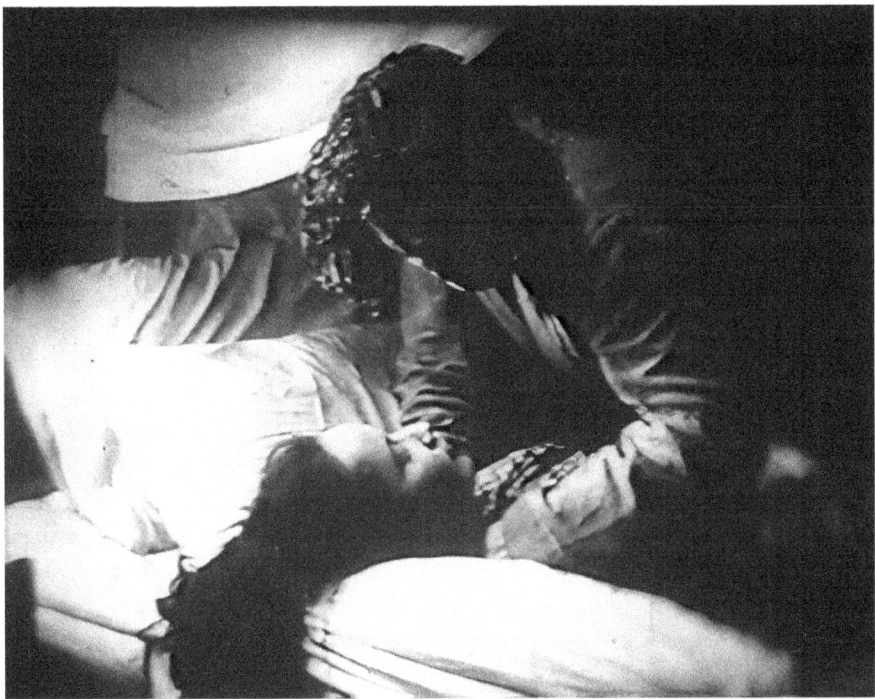

Figure 4.1 *Low-key lighting in* Tjitra

This norm of using low-key lighting primarily as scene lighting, however, changed as the indigenous film industry took off after Indonesia became an officially recognised sovereign republic in 1949 and Sukarno became its first president.

Low-Key Lighting as Genre Lighting in Cinematography of the Sukarno Era

Low-key lighting emerged as an important component of Indonesian cinematography during the Sukarno era. Made in the early 1950s, Usmar's films like *Darah dan Doa* (*The Long March*, d.p. Max Tera, 1950), *Enam Djam di Djogja* (*Six Hours in Djogja*, d.p. Max Tera, 1951) and *Lewat Djam Malam* (*After the Curfew*, d.p. Max Tera, 1954) demonstrate the pervasive application of low-key lighting as *genre lighting*. Slightly different from the scene lighting convention, the genre lighting convention relies more on the mood or feeling that certain genres are presumed to possess. For instance, the mood of horror and crime films is commonly perceived to be dreadful and morose. By contrast, the mood of comedy and musical movies is traditionally taken to be cheerful and gleeful. Based on this assumption of mood, cinematographers would then apply the appropriate lighting style to the film accordingly: dark, contrasty lighting to horror and crime films, but bright flat lighting to comedy and musical movies. Under this genre lighting prescription, low-key lighting became associated with horror and crime films. In the Indonesian context, we can detect low-key lighting in the genre of war films made during the Sukarno years.

Darah dan Doa is a case in point. Low-key lighting pervades many nighttime and daytime interior scenes in the film. In this film, low-key lighting is implemented with the use of a single light source that produces high-contrast images in which dark tonality overrides bright tonality. *Darah dan Doa* centres on the story of Sudarto (Del Juzar), an ex-teacher who joins the Indonesian armed forces in the war against the Dutch occupation forces. The plot chronicles Sudarto's involvement in the infamous long march that the Siliwangi Division of the Indonesian Republican Army undertook from Yogyakarta (Central Java) to Bandung (West Java). The wives of these soldiers accompany them on the journey. In the film, one of them is about to give birth, so they take shelter in a simple bamboo hut along the way. The interior of this hut is lit with a single artificial key source, supposedly simulating the flames of a wooden stove. When a helper enters the hut, she carries an oil lamp, but it isn't strong enough to substantially add any further illumination to the scene. The oil lamp casts a solid shadow on her lower chest, corroborating my contention that an artificial key light source is employed here to imitate the billowing wooden stove flame. This minimalistic lighting scheme is sustained in the exterior scene, too. As the nurse Widya (Farida) meets the protagonist Sudarto for the first time, this initial encounter is lit harshly by a single key light that shines on one side of Farida's face. But no additional fixture is deployed to compensate for the thick shadow that this single light paints on the other side of her face. The exclusion of fill light in this scene leaves a shadowy gap in the right area of the frame, causing Sudarto's presence to be submerged in thick darkness (see Figure 4.2).

These scenes' darkly lit images represent how low-key lighting is applied as genre lighting. The *chiaroscuro* effect resulting from the consistent application of the low-key lighting mode suits the type of story that Usmar tackles in *Darah dan Doa* as well as the other two war films mentioned above. In *Darah dan Doa,* Usmar transforms a solemn subject matter, i.e., the struggle of Indonesian men and women in the Revolution against the Dutch military aggression – a bloody episode in the modern history of the Indonesia-Netherlands relations known as *politionele actie* (on the Dutch side) and *agresi militer* (on the Indonesian side). When Usmar made the film in 1950, this

Evolution by Means of Stylistic Suppression 83

Figure 4.2 *Low-key lighting in* Darah dan Doa

revolutionary war had just ended, so the topic was extremely sensitive for the country that had just gone through the atrocity of fighting back to reclaim its independence declared in 1945.

Using the Siliwangi Division's long march to West Java as the main plot, Usmar wanted to emphasise the dark side of the Revolution. The protagonist Sudarto is depicted more as a common soldier, who is prone to make mistakes, sensitive and at times weak, rather than as an archetypical war hero who is flawless, matter-of-fact and strong-minded. In an essay about the film, Usmar wrote: 'Sudarto's tale is a sad one. Sudarto is not a hero in the traditional sense of the word, but he is an Indonesian man who is dragged into the swell of Revolution before he can judge what is consciously happening around him.'[3] The film's plot also reveals the horizontal conflict between various factions in post-war Indonesia, including one involving the Siliwangi force led by Sudarto, combating, firstly a communist militia, and secondly, the Islamic insurgents Darul Islam. The fact that the story is told from Sudarto's point of view – wherein he is engulfed in tragedy throughout his journey to find security and love – reinforces the film's pathos. Building on this understanding of the story's tenor, the low-key lighting is chiefly employed to serve, on the one hand, the depiction of Sudarto's wretched fate and, on the other, to underline the subject matter's solemnity.

The corollary of this use of low-key lighting as *genre lighting* is that there is little variation in lighting modes applied to different moments in the film's plot. For instance, based on dramatic tone, the above-cited scenes (the birth of a baby and the intimate encounter between Sudarto and Widya) would typically require a high-key lighting technique to evoke an exciting, happy or romantic atmosphere. The birth of a baby is a celebratory event that usually sparks joy. Similarly, an encounter between male and female protagonists usually calls for a diffused and bright lighting style to emit a romantic air – at least if we base this on the conventions of classical Hollywood lighting that Keating has delineated in his book.[4] Additionally, if the female star were very recognisable in the film industry, then a backlight would highlight the glamour of her onscreen persona.[5] But Max *Tera*, the film's director of photography, chose to eschew the bright, high-key lighting style here. Instead, he opted for a darker lighting style by using only one source to light the scenes. As a result, dark tonality reigns. In sum, the low-key lighting approach in *Darah dan Doa* is applied to match the genre and subject matter, even though different moments in the film might usually be deemed to require different lighting techniques. This is genre lighting par excellence.

Sustaining the Low-Key Lighting as Genre and Scene Lighting in Suharto-Era Cinematography

In the Suharto-era cinematography, melodrama and horror films sustained the low-key lighting schema as a genre and scene lighting convention. In melodramatic films of the 1970s, for instance, films that centre on the stories of female prostitutes, low-key lighting accompanies scenes involving sexual violence. *Bernapas dalam Lumpur* (*The Longest Dark*, Turino Djuanedy, d.p. Andy Sadikin, 1970) is a film that initiated the proliferation of prostitute films in Indonesian cinema. The story is about Supinah (Suzanna), who ends up becoming a sex worker in Jakarta after being mistreated and abused by men. While on a search for her husband, who has left the village to find a better job in the capital city, Supinah is raped by multiple men. In the first rape scene, a *becak* (rickshaw) driver pretends to help her settle in. As they are having a casual, friendly conversation, both figures are equally lit with a cross key technique where two key sources are pointed diagonally to get both of their faces in crisp illumination. But as the *becak* driver starts forcing Supinah to undress, the scene's tone shifts radically from congenial to hostile and eventually to life-threatening. With tight close-ups, a single light source shines on Supinah's face very slightly as she struggles to release herself from the rapist. A series of extreme close-ups of body parts partially show Supinah's body as the rapist takes off her clothes. Subsequently, the rapist's male friend takes over to rape her also. In these horrific scenes, low-key lighting accompanies the shift of dramatic mood from friendly (a man helps an innocent young woman from the village) to menacing (men sexually assault her) as Supinah's world collapses (see Figure 4.3).

Although reserved mostly for scenes of sexual violence, low-key lighting in these prostitute films isn't necessarily applied to scenes of pathos. In *Bernapas dalam Lumpur*, when Supinah pours out her wretched feelings to Budiman (Rakhmat Kartolo), sharing with him her life's journey – trapped in the immoral world of prostitution – it's high-key lighting instead of low-key lighting that's applied in this sad scene. Correspondingly, when she dies, high-key lighting is applied consistently throughout the scene (see Figure 4.4). In another prostitute film, *Bumi Makin Panas* (*The Earth Gets Hotter*, Ali Shahab, d.p. Andi Sadikin, 1973), the protagonist Maria (Suzanna) is a victim of domestic violence. She must kill her father due to his abusive behaviour toward her mother. When she is imprisoned, although her look exudes sadness and regret, the lighting does not support this emotional state. The high-key diffused style is employed in full blast; even the shadow of the prison bar is made soft because of this lighting scheme. But there is one scene in *Bumi Makin Panas* in which low-key lighting is employed to enhance a melancholic moment visually. In one scene, Maria's prostitute friend is

Figure 4.3 Low-key lighting *in* Bernapas Dalam Lumpur

about to kill herself. Maria, however, manages to stop her before it's too late. The friend explains that her son in the village is sick, and she doesn't have money to send medication to him, so she feels she has failed. Maria is lit from the side, creating a thick attached shadow on the left side of her face. When we get a reverse shot, her friend is lit in a softer low-key style. Nevertheless, this use of low-key lighting for a scene of pathos, as the last example demonstrates, is more an exception than the norm.

Along with melodrama, the horror genre equally sustained the use of low-key lighting. In one of the early mystic horror films in this period, *Ratu Ular* (*The Snake Queen*, Lilik Sudjio, d.p. Harry Susanto, 1972), low-key lighting is associated with the Snake Queen who transforms into a human being to prey on rich women adorned with jewellery. The setting of the Snake Queen's house is lit very darkly, especially the rooms where she keeps her cousin Siti (Leni Marlina). At nighttime, she performs a ritual to summon the spirit of the Snake King; she makes love to the snake to gain supernatural power. Low-key high-contrast lighting sets a mystical and mysterious atmosphere for the scene. Another use of the low-key mode in the film is to accompany dreadful scenes where the cousin ventures into the dark alone as she investigates if her aunt is in fact the wicked Snake Queen.

Evolution by Means of Stylistic Suppression 87

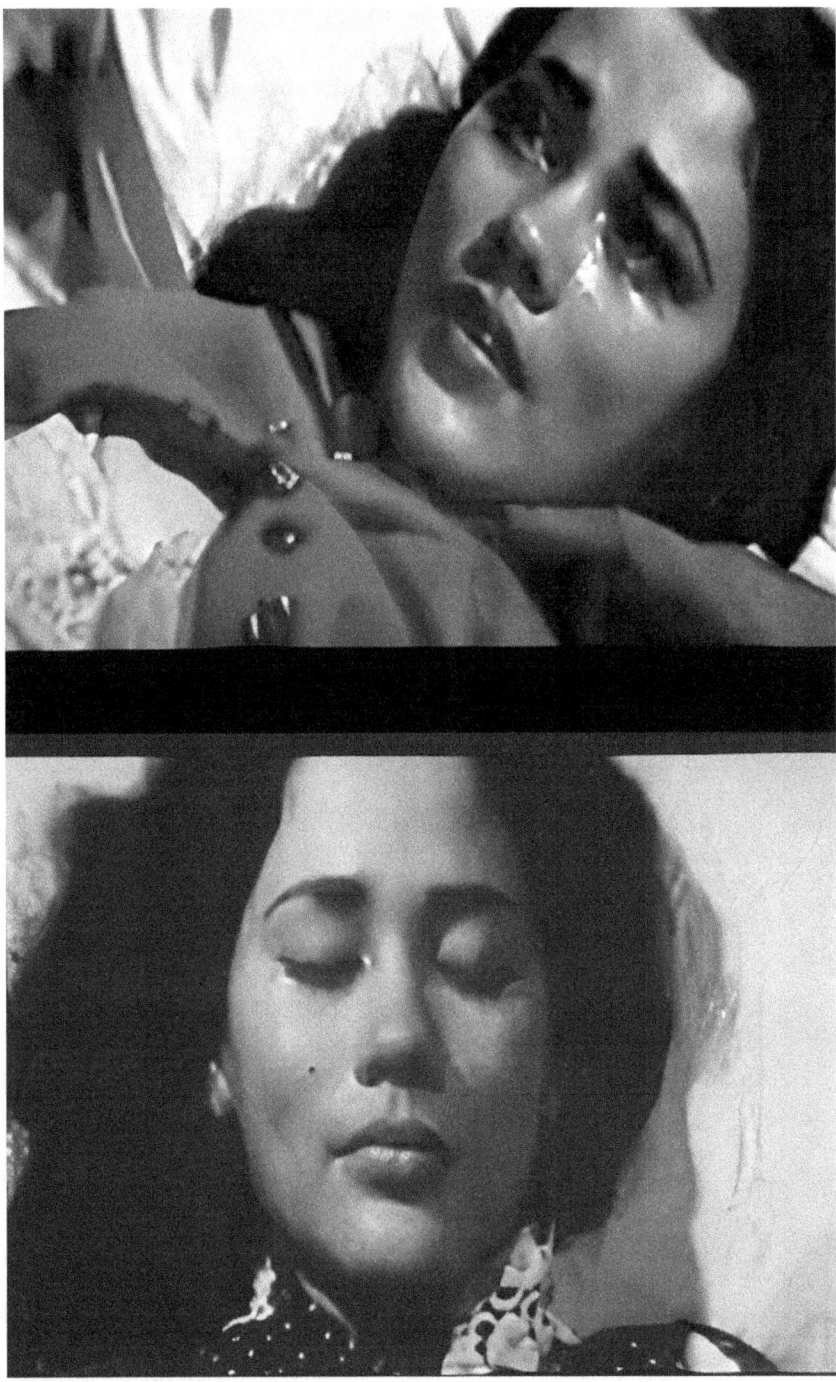

Figure 4.4 *High-key lighting applied to scenes of pathos in* Bernapas Dalam Lumpur

In many horror films of the 1980s, low-key lighting is applied to accompany the appearance of a ghost or monster. But the low-key mode can appear ostentatiously and abruptly without any diegetic justification. In one of the most well-known horror films of the Suharto era, *Sundel Bolong* (Sisworo Gautama Putra, d.p. F.E.S. Tarigan, 1981), when the female ghost appears before her enemy to seek revenge, the lighting in the environment changes from high-key to low-key in a rapid manner (see Figure 4.5). The cinematographer F. E. S. Tarigan simply dims the light as the ghost emerges. But by decreasing the key light's intensity as the scene unfolds, the transition from bright to dark becomes visually conspicuous. Even so, the low-key lighting scheme in this scene doesn't produce striking visual darkness. Nevertheless, it still operates as scene lighting, imbuing the scene with a chilling atmosphere. Here, low-key lighting isn't anchored in the convention of *effect lighting*, that is, the use of artificial lights to simulate a natural light source. Put differently, the transition from bright to dark is not equally motivated by location or time, but solely by atmosphere. In an ideal horror scenario, the haunted house or ghost usually tries to cut off the electricity and kill all the lights, making it impossible for the victim to flee. So, in this sense, the effect lighting convention (the switching off of household lamps) could activate atmospheric lighting. But in *Sundel Bolong*, effect lighting plays no

Figure 4.5 *As the ghost appears to avenge her death, the intensity of the key light gets reduced to create a sinister atmosphere in* Sundel Bolong

role. We can conclude from this *Sundel Bolong* case that there is little interaction between low-key lighting as a genre/scene lighting mode and low-key lighting as an effect lighting mode in the film lighting practices of that period.

Another piece of evidence that substantiates my contention about the loose relationship between effect lighting and genre/scene lighting in Suharto-era cinematography is the use of practical light sources as mere props. The household objects that may appear as light sources, for instance, a table lamp, overhead fluorescent light, or a living room standing lamp, don't provide actual illumination in the shots. For example, in another famous horror film *Malam Jum'at Kliwon* (*Night of Jum'at Kliwon*, Sisworo Gautama Putra, d.p. Thomas Susanto, 1986), the main character Ayu (Suzanna) is a mystery novel writer. She intentionally stays for a month in an old mansion to get writing inspiration but she doesn't know that the mansion was the site of the ruthless murder of a woman: the landlord's wife. One night she hears strange noises from the guestroom upstairs. She decides to go upstairs herself to investigate. She carries a flashlight, but the flashlight is merely a prop because the room is lit so brightly that it hardly requires extra illumination. In another scene, she carries a candelabrum as she seeks out the source of the strange noise (see Figure 4.6). Again, this candelabrum does not add any light to the scene because the whole hallway is lit very brightly without a trace of shadow. In these examples, there is hardly any interlocking mechanism between the effect lighting convention and the genre/scene lighting convention. As a result, the lighting method neither paints a verisimilar situation nor evokes a dreadful atmosphere. In these cases, lighting is purely exploited for *exposure* purposes; that is, lighting is pursued for no other reason than to make the images clear and the characters' actions maximally visible.

A final point that I want to make to support my argument about the use of low-key lighting as genre lighting in Suharto-era cinematography is the sharp division between the lighting styles of the dramatic genres and comedy films. While melodrama and horror employ low-key lighting in moments where needed, comedy films hardly use lighting to differentiate tone. Sombre moments that would typically call for a dimmer and darker lighting mode are handled in full blast brightness. In one of the most popular comedies of the 1970s, *Bing Slamet Koboi Cengeng* (*Bing Slamet the Weeping Cowboy*, Nya Abbas Akup, d.p. F. E. S. Tarigan, 1974), many scenes of terror are presented in a flat and diffused lighting style. Similarly, in a satirical comedy involving well-known stars of the 1980s, *Kipas Kipas Cari Angin* (*Running Free*, Nya Abbas Akup, d.p. F. E. S. Tarigan, 1989), emotionally charged moments are presented in flat high-key visual tone. In this scene, the protagonist Bambang (Mathias Muchus) finds out that his girlfriend (Misye Arsita) is upset because she has finally discovered that he has been manipulating her throughout

Figure 4.6 *A flashlight and a candelabrum acting merely as props than practical light sources in* Malam Jum'at Kliwon

the time they have been in a relationship. She is disappointed and angry, so much so that she wants to end the relationship. The emotional content of the scene is despondency; for that reason, a much darker lighting style might have been more appropriate – if we view this from the rationale of the genre/scene lighting convention. But the cinematographer F. E. S Tarigan instead chose to light the shots in an evenly diffused way – not leaving any portion of the image in darkness. Comedy lighting in Suharto-era filmmaking strictly adheres to the genre association of bright lighting with farce and slapstick. As such, comedy lighting uses the genre's overall perceived tone (i.e., cheerful) as the guiding parameter for lighting, more than a particular scene's dramatic tone. Thus, it doesn't matter if the scene is gloomy, emotional or terrifying – the lighting style will be bright and flat through and through.

All these examples suggest that Suharto-era film lighting adhered only loosely to what Keating has described as *the strategy of differentiation*[6] whereby cinematographers apply different lighting styles to different scenes in the film to match each scene's dramatic or comedic mood. Through this differentiation strategy, each scene will be lit distinctively, depending on the time, place and location as well as the scene's dramatic tone, irrespective of the film's genre identity. In contrast, the strategy of differentiation figures more in the lighting practices of post-Suharto-era cinematography, which we'll discuss in Chapter 5.

PRODUCTION DESIGN

The culture of film production in a specific country impacts how production design as a craft practice is organised and implemented. In the Anglo-American film industry, it is the production designer who is typically responsible for the overall design of the film, collaborating with the director and cinematographer.[7] Meanwhile, the art director works under and reports to the production designer, covering many tasks, from supervising the execution of the design concept to managing the art department's budget and schedule.[8] But in the Indonesian context, the titles production designer and art director are used more loosely. In low-budget and independent productions, these roles may not even be recognised as such. The term *tata artistik* is traditionally used to refer to the craft of design, while the title *penata artistik* is given to the head of the art department. Before the 2000s, it was common to find a myriad of titles signifying the role of art director, such as *penata set*, *dekor*, *artistik* and so on in the films' credits. In the 2000s and 2010s, we can find the title of *desainer produksi* (production designer) more regularly listed in the film credits, even though the titles *tata artistik* or *penata artistik* remain in use. Despite the pervasive usage of the latter titles, in practice, the range of tasks that a *penata artistik* covers tends to include those of a production designer. Indonesian art director Angela Halim explains:

> We can find many art directors working for films, which means they are the designers of the settings and they also work full time in the field, lead the art department from preparation until production days, visualising their designs into real sets. It's like those art directors *do both what a production designer and art director should work on*.⁹

Considering the fluidity of these two terms in Indonesia, I will use *tata artistik* to refer to production design and art direction simultaneously in the following pages as we trace the evolution of the key Indonesian film production design techniques: *location shooting, studio filming* and *location designing*.

Location Shooting and Studio Filming in Colonial-Era Production Design

In the early years of film production in the Netherlands Indies, the norm of *tata artistik* consisted of on-location shooting mixed with set building in film studios. Filmmakers went on location to film exterior scenes; meanwhile, they built sets in the studios to capture interior scenes. In his account of the production of *Loetoeng Kasaroeng* (*The Lost Lutung*, 1926) – the first feature film produced in Java – Misbach Yusa Biran notes that the film director L. Heuveldorp shot the film in Batu Karang, near Padalarang, about 23.5 kilometres from Bandung.[10] Heuveldorp and Raden Wiranatakusumah V (the Regent of Bandung) took this location as the setting for the main character, Sunan Ambu, who is depicted as living in a cave. For the female protagonist's house, 'a majestic bamboo house' was built especially for the film.[11]

In the years after *Loetoeng Kasaroeng* was made, location shooting continued to be one of the primary methods chosen for filming exterior scenes. Outdoor settings such as the *sawah* (rice fields), *kebun teh* (tea plantations), *sungai* (rivers) and *pantai* (beaches) can be seen populating the films of the 1930s and '40s. Albert Balink's film *Pareh* (1936) features the vast cascading rice paddies of West Java quite prominently, delineating the film's title and topic, *pareh* (Sundanese for rice). In *Tjitra* (1949), a tea plantation is chosen as its main exterior setting to connote the characters' socio-economic background as plantation owners. In some instances, filmmakers opted for on-location shooting because they needed a unique type of vegetation or other natural elements that could not be replicated in the studio during that period. For example, in *Srigala Item* (*Black Wolf/De Zwarte Wolf*, 1941) – one of the first action films made on the archipelago – the Zorro-like masked vigilante known as 'The Black Wolf' deceives his enemies by leaping onto a

Evolution by Means of Stylistic Suppression 93

Figure 4.7   *The masked vigilante 'The Black Wolf' leaps onto the sacred* beringin *tree during one of the chase scenes in* Srigala Item

beringin tree during a suspenseful chase scene (see Figure 4.7). The *beringin* tree couldn't have been replicated in a studio due to its scale, as the shots in this scene indicate.[12] Moreover, the environment where this particular scene takes place shows an actual outdoor location, as the background elements in the shots reveal, such as rows of coconut trees and rice paddies.

In the 1930s and 1940s, Chinese and Dutch film production companies owned and operated film studios in the Netherlands Indies. The Teng Chun of Java Industrial Film Company is reported to have turned a housing complex into a film studio equipped with a film development lab and an open-roof set through which the sunlight could enter for lighting purposes.[13] The Wong Brothers owned the film studio Legok Bidara Cina until the Chinese film businessman Tan Khoen Yauw decided to recruit them for his film production venture. Consequently, he rebranded Legok Bidara Cina to Tan's Film Co Studio.[14] Albert Balink built ANIF (Algemeen Nederlandsch Indische Film Syndicaat) thanks to a partnership with the Dutch film company Profilti and the American RKO Radio Pictures.[15] The intertwining of studio filming and location shooting continued into the Sukarno era.

Location Shooting and Studio Filming in Sukarno-Era Production Design

In the Sukarno era, filmmakers made use of location shooting primarily to achieve a greater sense of geographic and regional authenticity. In *Darah dan Doa*, for instance, Usmar and his art director Basoeki *Resobowo*[16] chose to shoot on location at the temple of Borobudur when depicting the start of the Siliwangi Division's long march from Central Java to West Java. To illustrate concretely how arduous the group's journey was, Usmar and Resobowo used an actual location, Subang in West Java, which is replete with natural obstacles. So hazardous was the terrain of this location that one member of the Division was depicted falling down a hill to his death in the film.

Besides Usmar, D. *Djajakusuma* also went on location to shoot his regional films. Under Usmar's film company Perfini, he was able to make *Harimau Tjampa* (*Tiger from Tjampa*, 1953) and *Tjambuk Api* (*The Whip of Fire*, 1958). According to David Hanan, it is appropriate to call these works 'regional films' because they

> initiate a concern with peasant life and particular regions based not only on location shooting in poor rural areas but on the utilisation of regional performance traditions as a key signifier of regional cultures, as though regional culture is performance as well as a tradition.[17]

Set in the 1930s, *Harimau Tjampa* (prod. des. Ali Akbar) tells the story of Lukman (Bambang Hermanto), who is on a mission to avenge his father's death. To do so, he needs to learn the martial art *pencak silat*. The film's plot development mostly revolves around the conflict between him and his *pencak silat* master. The master condemns Lukman's intention to use *pencak silat* as a way to get even, because it is against the principle of self-restraint advocated in Islam.[18] The characters' engagement with *silat* and the Minangkabau's (ethnic group from West Sumatra) traditional dances and performances such as the *randai* (local dance performed by men) and *adat pantun* (folk proverbs) underscore the regional cultural attributes of West Sumatra. Most notably, the film's location shooting emphasises the uniquely shaped Minangkabau's *rumah gadang* or *rumah bagonjong* (traditional spired roof houses) and the traditional costumes typically worn by Minang women. These shots were captured on location in the villages of West Sumatra, thus endowing the film's visual style with an ethnographic documentary feel.[19] Like *Darah dan Doa*, *Harimau Tjampa* features landscape shots, too, which include cascading rice paddies, hills and valleys. The most memorable of all these exterior shots is the climactic *silat* duel between Lukman and the villain Datuk Langit (Raden Ismail), taking place outdoors atop a Minangkabau hill. Whether in rural or urban areas, these filmmakers explored location shooting to imbue their films with a sense of authenticity as regards regional cultural identity and milieu.

Location shooting during this period, however, remained primarily a means to capture exterior shots, while interior shots were still captured mostly in the confines of a studio. In this respect, there is a continuity to this norm of *tata artistik* that was established in the colonial-era production design. For example, in *Darah dan Doa,* although we are presented with highly dramatic exterior scenes depicting the epic battle and harsh journey of the republican army from Central Java to West Java, when we enter the interior spaces, we can detect the studio environment. The painted backdrop providing the view of the rice paddies accentuates the stage-like quality of the set. In one scene, the main character Sudarto (Del Juzar) is romantically involved with a female German expatriate Connie (Johanna). Because of the fervent nationalistic and anti-imperialist temperament of the time, his fellow soldiers discourage him from continuing this romantic affair. In one scene, a colleague confronts Sudarto about this issue, and he is ordered to send the woman away to another city. Similarly, in *Harimau Tjampa*, the majority of its interior scenes take place inside the village mosque. These scenes were captured in the studio (most likely at Perfini), and the mosque itself was a built set as the construction of the *mihrab*[20] inside the mosque displays.[21] Another Djajakusuma's film *Embun* (*Dewdrop*, prod. des. Soemardjono, 1951), also mixes location shooting with studio filming, or *studio opname*, as it was then called in Dutch.[22] Here, the main character Leman (A. N. Alcaff), who has murdered his boss, is lured into conducting illegal business by his village friend Barjo (Raden Ismail). In the long shot, we get a natural location, namely a hut situated atop a hill. When we get a closer shot of the characters inside the hut, however, a white studio backdrop – enhanced by assertive background lighting – becomes more visible. So, in these two shots, we get an on-location shot for the exterior and a studio shot for the interior.

Hanan's writing about these films supports my contention that this dual practice of studio filming and on-location shooting in the Sukarno era was the norm.[23] But Hanan seems to have overlooked the fact that microscopic detailing in the art direction of these studio shots is very minimal. If we look at the settings of the interior scenes of these films, we find only the most basic layer of art direction. That is to say, furniture, household objects, wall decoration and so on are used to establish the locale where the action takes place. But they do not convey information about the characters' cultural background, lifestyle or social position; thus, through the lens of Christopher Frayling's concept

I invoked in Chapter 3, the *tata artistik* of these Sukarno-era films does not function effectively as a 'visual shortcut'.²⁴ For example, in *Embun*, the contrast between the haves and the have-nots is hardly articulated onscreen. Leman's family, which comes from a lower-class background, is seen having dinner in their living room without much decoration, and its walls are made of *bilik* (sheets of woven bamboo). By contrast, the house of the affluent entrepreneur, who later falls victim to Leman and Barjo's crime, is made of bricks, and its interior is furnished with modern-looking appliances – from electric lamps to a bookshelf. Besides these elements, though, there are hardly any props that flesh out microscopically who these characters are. The same goes for *Darah dan Doa*. The German woman Connie, whose story is quite important in the film as Sudarto's potential lover, is depicted living in a modern house in Bandung; Sudarto pays her a visit at one point in the film. The only object in the set that slightly conveys her Western background is an electric lamp located next to the sofa. Other than this, there is not much detailing in the set dressing, thus rendering her house characterless. Put bluntly, it could have been *anyone's* house, not just a German expatriate's house.

These findings shed light on the important position of studio filmmaking as much as location shooting in the first decade of postcolonial Indonesian cinema history. In the literature on Indonesian film, location shooting is considered the most important defining feature of these Sukarno-era films. In fact, one can find many more references to location shooting than to studio filming.²⁵ Usually, this line of thought is supplemented by references to the influence of Italian neorealist films on these filmmakers, specifically on Usmar Ismail.²⁶ Accordingly, location shooting has been heavily emphasised, while studio filming has been downplayed, even though the existence of film studios at that time is well-documented.²⁷ To be sure, I don't want to suggest that location shooting was insignificant; what I want to stress is that this mode of shooting was chosen *partially*, not completely. That is, it was used mostly for obtaining exterior shots, or *opname luar* (exterior filming).²⁸

Still, what's missing in the discussion of these films is how Usmar exploited one of the functions of production design with respect to location shooting, namely to construct what Stephen Prince has called 'the illusion of wholeness', as I have explained in Chapter 3. In the case of *Darah dan Doa*, although the story is set in several places in East and Central Java such as Madiun and Yogyakarta, Usmar shot most of the exterior scenes in Subang and Purwakarta – both located in West Java.²⁹ He claimed in his writing that he wanted the film to look as authentic as possible, as if 'it happened in its original location'.³⁰ In this case, Usmar managed to accomplish this 'as if' effect by shooting the scenes in multiple locations without necessarily being at the actual places where the film's story is set.

Location shooting as a technique to capture exterior scenes carried over to the ensuing period, but with a slight adjustment and bigger role.

Expanding the Role of Location Shooting in Suharto-Era Production Design

In the Suharto era, filmmakers expanded the role of location shooting to be an all-encompassing technique. While during the Sukarno period, filmmakers used location shooting to capture exterior shots only, in the Suharto era, filmmakers used it to capture interior shots as well. Two scenes from a bestselling film of the period, *Si Doel Anak Modern* (*Doel the Modern Kid*, Sjuman Djaya, prod. des. Djufri Tanissan, 1976), can illustrate this shift of convention. Set in Jakarta, the film is about Doel (Benyamin S), an unemployed man from a village who goes to the capital city to find his childhood sweetheart Kristin (Christine Hakim). When he arrives in Jakarta, he joins in an export-import business venture with his best friend Sapii (Farouk Afero). Doel assumes that Sapii can help him find Kristin, and Sapii feels that Doel could be a great asset to his company. When Doel arrives at Sapii's office, a long shot shows both characters entering the space. In the background, we see Jakarta's towering skyscrapers, signifying the unfolding modernisation of this capital city. Inside, we see Doel browsing through popular magazines featuring shots of Kristin, who has apparently become a famous supermodel, while Sapii is shown collecting more magazines with images of Kristin in them for Doel to look at. But Doel then asks Sapii to take him to Kristin's house. Sapii comes closer to Doel and explains to him that he should be more patient. As the camera focuses on Sapii, we pan rightward to follow Sapii approaching Doel. As soon as the shot gets reframed as a two-shot, we see the environment in which this office is situated in the background. Again, we can see the skyscrapers, but now we can also see a row of banana trees in the lower part of the frame, indicating the peripheral location of Sapii's office. Within this one shot, we get an interior shot that simultaneously shows the exterior environment.

Another scene follows a similar pattern. Kristin turns out to be already engaged to a rock star, Achmad (Achmad Albar). Due to Achmad's promiscuous behaviour, however, Kristin often gets into arguments with him. After making up, they share a romantic moment together at Achmad's house. In this scene, set in the daytime, we see them serenading each other while Achmad is mixing some alcoholic concoctions. In a medium long shot, we get a vision of Achmad's living room as the two of them are singing and exchanging affectionate glances. In the far background, as the door stands ajar, we see the street with vehicles passing by, denoting that Achmad's house is situated in one of the busiest parts of Jakarta. Similar to the earlier example, this shot gives an indication that the scene is captured wholly in an existing location instead of partially captured in the studio.[31] These instances may point toward the changing mode of production design in Suharto-era filmmaking, whereby shooting a film at existing places became one of the creative options.

While the use of location shooting was expanded to capture interior shots, location designing, however, still figured very little. In other words, when shooting on location for interior and exterior scenes, the existing location didn't get much additional designing, whether through props furnishing, set decoration, or other tools in the production design and art direction departments. To illustrate this, let's consider one of the bestselling *period films* from the Suharto era: *Sunan Kalijaga* (Sofyan Sharna, prod. des. Ardi Ahmad, 1983). *Sunan Kalijaga* is one of the well-known *legenda* films centring on the life of the 'nine saints' of Islam who spread Islamic teaching in fifteenth and sixteenth-century Java. As the title suggests, this film features the transformation of Raden Mas Said (Deddy Mizwar), the son of a Javanese aristocrat who converted to Islam and earned the title of *sunan* (Islamic apostle) in the latter part of his adult life.

Set in 1477, the film first chronicles the upbringing of Sunan Kalijaga in an aristocratic family: that of the Regent of Tuban in East Java. After the opening credit title, the baby Raden Mas Said is depicted going through the *tedak siten* ceremony.[32] The scene opens with his father coming home from a trip and entering the *kraton* (Javanese palace). The exterior shot reveals the sumptuous design of the palace, supposedly fitting the Majapahit era style of architecture.[33] The most iconic part of this design is the *wrigin lawang*, the tall split gate made of brownish red bricks, typically erected as an entrance to a palace or royal compound. Inside the *kraton*, we see the father, Wira Tama (W. D. Mochtar), seated on the throne, accompanied by his wife (Sunarti Rendra), and together they bless the child before the ceremony commences. While the exterior shot indicates the grandiose Majapahit architecture, the interior shot does not reveal much similar splendour. Medium shots reveal different groups seated on the floor – from female dancers to priests, each distinguished by their distinctive costumes. The social standing of the Regent and his wife is also signified by the golden jewellery decorating their bodies, such as the crown, armband and necklace.

The focal point of the scene (the *tedak siten* ritual), however, is not visualised in great detail. Instead of the parents who guide the child through all the steps required in the ceremony, it is a female subordinate who does it for them. More critically, however, the props utilised in the ceremony, for instance, the *sesajen* (offerings) are not adequately particularised; hence, the whole scene leaves the impression of frugality, even though the context of

Figure 4.8 *The* tedak siten *ceremony in* Sunan Kalijaga

the ceremony is an aristocratic setting. The peak of the scene comes when the baby is placed inside the rooster's cage (see Figure 4.8). A medium shot shows the child picking up an item, but it's not clear exactly what this is until one dancer whispers to her colleague, saying that if the baby picks up the *keris* (sacred Javanese dagger), then he will replace his father's position as the Regent. But a close-up reveals the baby covered in white powder, followed by a shot of two clerics whispering to each other the following words: '*putih, diputihkan*' ('white, being purified'). It isn't clear, however, whether the powder is rice or flour; thus, microscopic detail is less of an aesthetic priority here.[34] Rather, it is the verbalisation of these objects through dialogue that transmits the information about what these objects are and their symbolic significance. In sum, macroscopically, this scene may denote the period setting through its seemingly authentic exterior setting and costuming, but microscopically it doesn't articulate it in great detail.

Although location designing was not a prevalent practice in the production design of Suharto-era films, there were a few filmmakers who explored this technique. But even when this method was pursued, the degree of macroscopic and microscopic detail was imbalanced. For instance, in the period film *R.A. Kartini* (1982), Sjuman Djaya and his art director Djufri Tanissan put a premium on location designing. Like *Sunan Kalijaga*, *R.A. Kartini* also features a scene involving the *tedak siten* ceremony – similarly shown at the film's outset. A biopic of Raden Ajeng Kartini – an emancipationist of women's rights in colonial Indonesia – the film is set in the late 1800s in the coastal town of Jepara, Central Java. The film opens exactly on the evening when Kartini was born on April 21, 1879. Her father, R. M. Aryo

Sosroningrat (Wisnu Wardhana), is the *wedana* (district chief in the colonial era) of Jepara.³⁵ In this scene, we see him anxiously expecting the baby as his *selir* (concubine) Mas Ayu Ngasirah (Nani Wijaya) is giving birth in the main bedroom. As soon as the baby is born, her father holds her in his arms and gives her the name Kartini. We cut to the credit title, and then the ceremony scene follows. The ritual is held on the front porch of the house; family, relatives and guests are seated on the floor. The father and his legitimate wife are seen holding the baby, guiding her through all the necessary steps of the *tedak siten* procession. Herein, the ceremony's stepping-on-the-earth stage is presented in detail as a closer shot of the baby's feet reveals the multi-coloured stones symbolising the different stages of life. When we get to the most important part (i.e., placing the baby inside the rooster's cage), the details of the objects housed within the cage are not concretely specified. Compared with the scene from *Sunan Kalijaga*, this crucial element of the sacred ritual is hardly emphasised. Instead, the father quickly takes the baby out of the cage and puts her on his lap as he utters some words of wisdom, telling her that she will enlighten the 'dark soil of Java' ('*tanah Jowo yang gelap!*') on which she has just stepped. Furthermore, the offerings, which should figure centrally in the syncretic Javanese-Islamic culture, are barely presented in detail (see Figure 4.9).

As we've seen, the visuals of these films put small-scale particularities on display, but only to some degree. Large-scale details, on the other hand, are fully fleshed out. For instance, the interior décor of the *rumah joglo* (Javanese traditional house for the upper class) denotes not only the period setting, but also the social standing of Kartini's *priyayi* (aristocratic) family. A well-sized veranda populated by wooden chairs and a table made from *kayu Jepara* (a type of wood native to the region) and a vintage kerosene-powered hanging lamp – known as *lampu gantung katrol* – supply the image with macroscopic details, epitomising the prototypical Javanese noble class of colonial times (see Figure 4.10).

We can see from these cases that even though these two *period films* are some of the most artistically ambitious films of Suharto-era cinema, they point toward the imbalance between the broad brush and the precise details. Although the two directors have different cultural statuses in Indonesian cinema history, these films share similarities. Both films received awards from Festival Film Indonesia (in 1983 and 1984, respectively)³⁶ but neither of the two won the Best Art Direction category. There is a different degree of detail concerning set decoration and props in the two scenes we examined above. The *R.A. Kartini* scene is slightly more vivid in its visualisation of the ceremony, whereas the *Sunan Kalijaga* scene relies heavily on dialogue to make it understandable. The former also provides us with more visual shortcuts to

Figure 4.9 The tedak siten *ceremony in* R.A. Kartini

the social and economic position of the characters. But neither film brings out the fine-grained details of the essential ritual items onscreen. Thus, we can conclude that in this era, macroscopic details were prioritised over microscopic ones.

This mixed method of production design has sustained into the post-Suharto era; however, as we will see in Chapter 6, it undergoes a striking transformation in the way it levels out the imbalanced proportion between the macroscopic and microscopic visual details, rendering Indonesian films diegetically meticulous.

Figure 4.10 *Macroscopic details in the production design of* R.A. Kartini

CAMERA MOVEMENT

In the Indonesian filmmaking context, camera movement is commonly referred to as *gerak kamera* (camera motion). As in other film-producing countries, *gerak kamera* belongs to the wider craft of cinematography or *tata kamera* in Indonesian. In the following pages, we'll look at the prevailing norms for the use of camera movement during the three periods of Indonesian film history. As in the previous sections, our journey into the historical stylistics here is aimed at comparing and contrasting how filmmakers in these different periods have explored camera movement as part of their cinematographic toolkit. By doing so, we will discern the significant continuities and changes regarding the use of camera movement in Indonesian film and reveal a historical dimension to the innovative camera techniques that have emerged in the post-Suharto era.

Panning and Tilting in the Colonial-Era Cinematography

In colonial-era films, camera movement relies primarily on the combination of two techniques: *panning* and *tilting*. It is common to find a pan deployed to follow a character's movement horizontally across space in the films of this era. For example, in *Gagak Item* (*Black Crow*, Joshua and Othniel Wong, 1939), panning is employed to accompany characters walking or running across the landscape. In one scene, as an attractive village girl (Roekiah) is bathing in the river, a peeping tom secretly observes her from the top of a huge rock.

Figure 4.11 *A pan shot tracks the peeping tom's movement in* Gagak Item

When she notices this, she immediately flees, only to be chased by this perverse man who will play an important role as the antagonist in the story later on. The camera pans leftward, tracking his motion across the river as he tries to catch her (see Figure 4.11). Another conventional way of using the pan technique is to anticipate a character's entrance into the diegetic space, as a fragment from *Singa Laoet* (*The Sea Lion*, Tan Joei Hock, 1941) exemplifies. Since panning was the prevailing norm for camera mobility in this period, one may conclude that not only is the use of camera movement quite straightforward in its structural form but its purpose is also limited to mainly orient the film viewer's gaze. More specifically, it is mostly restricted to following moving characters in the diegetic space.

Despite this restrictive norm, however, there are still examples of creative use of the mobile frame in this era of Indonesian cinema. For example, Usmar's rarely discussed *Harta Karun* (*The Treasure*, d.p. A. A. Deninghoff-Stelling, 1949), demonstrates a rather curious application of the panning technique. Panning in this film is employed to accomplish two objectives: first, to thwart our expectation of a repeated motif; second, to operate as a surrogate for the main character's optical point of view. *Harta Karun* tells the story of an exploitative money lender – known colloquially as a *rentenir* in Indonesian – named Abdul Kadir (Raden Ismail). Abdul is very protective of his wealth, to the point of being suspicious towards his household members. His main source of paranoia comes from the fact that he possesses a cabinet full of jewellery and money in his study room. Even with locked doors, Abdul feels extremely insecure about leaving these valuable possessions in the wooden cabinet, especially since his own *budjang* (male domestic helper) is present everywhere around the house. His suspicion towards the *budjang* grows over time, climaxing at one particular moment when he 'sees' the reflection of his *budjang* in the mirror. While Abdul is shaving, a laughing face appears in the upper right corner of the mirror. Abdul thinks that the *budjang* has suddenly entered the room without knocking, so he turns his head to see if he is at the door. We pan leftward to follow his head turning (see Figure 4.12). But the door is actually shut, and no one is standing there. Is the *budjang* pulling a prank on him? That's highly unlikely, considering how subservient the *budjang* has been to his superior. As Abdul continues to shave, the reflection reappears, making contorted facial expressions as if mocking Abdul's paranoia. Again, Abdul turns his head, then the camera pans to follow this movement, but the door remains shut, and no one stands there.

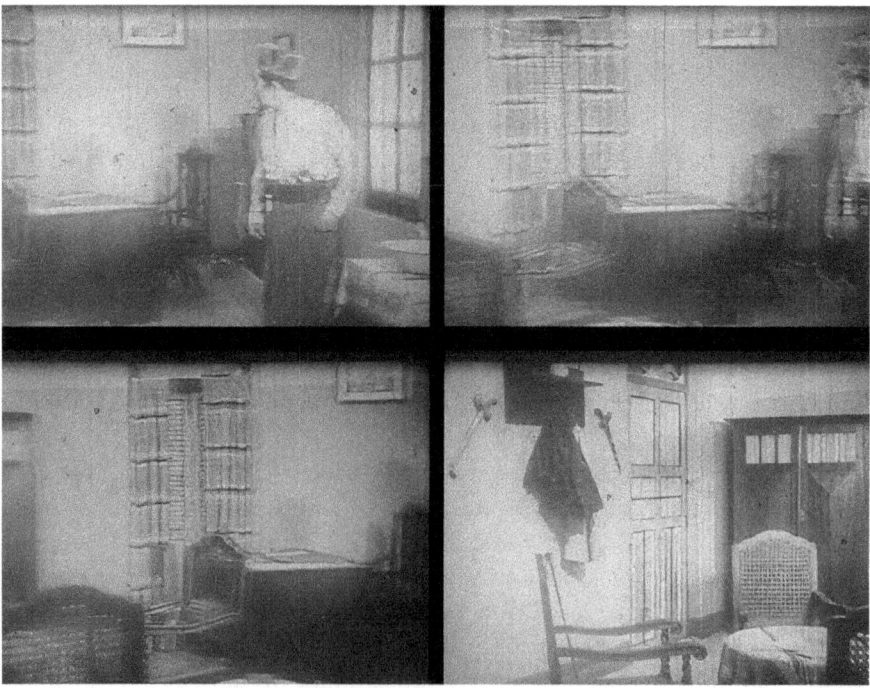

Figure 4.12 *A pan shot elicits a comic effect in* Harta Karun

For the second time, Abdul thinks that he sees the *budjang* peeking at his jewellery and money, waiting to find the right moment to steal them. Enraged, Abdul opens the door and finds the *budjang*, who is apparently preoccupied with the household chores in another section of the house. Abdul confronts him with interrogative questions regarding his ulterior motive for working in the household, that is, to rob Abdul's treasure. The *budjang* denies this allegation. The fear of losing his material possessions gets to Abdul to the point that he starts having bizarre hallucinations.

What appears to be an ordinary panning shot is in fact a clever demonstration of camera movement used for expressive and focalising effects. Before this scene, a leftward pan is applied a few times in the film for its typical purpose, that is, directing the viewer's attention to a character's entrance. But in this particular scene, which by the way, exemplifies Usmar's propensity for humour also, such a pan shot is used to raise the expectation that the *budjang* is about to enter the room – only to emphasise that there's no one there. This example displays the playful application of a simple technique to inflect a character's behaviour and traits, central to the film's theme of materialistic greed and class-based suspicion.

Despite the interesting use of panning in the previously cited scene, the rest of the film is handled stylistically in a parsimonious fashion; tracking shots, for instance, are mostly absent. In fact, tracking movement was extremely rare. Based on my viewing of the other colonial-era films, only one film features a tracking movement on a dolly: *Srigala Item* (Tan Tjoei Hock, 1941). But this example of a dolly shot was an exception to the norm.

In sum, if you were a filmmaker working in the Netherlands Indies, making sound films under the Chinese and Dutch production companies between 1926 and 1949, it is highly likely that you would shoot the film in the following manner: capture the majority of the scenes inside a studio; use trained actors, but with you mainly acting as a dialogue coach;[37] stage the figures quite laterally; frame the actors at a distance (primarily in a medium long shot); and opt for panning as the most readily available resource for camera movement. But the range of options did become slightly broader in the subsequent period as film production companies like Perfini and Persari took the indigenous film industry to a different level in the newly independent Republic of Indonesia.

Widening the Camera Movement Vocabulary in Sukarno-Era Cinematography

Just one year after Usmar made the Dutch-controlled film *Tjitra*, he made *Darah dan Doa* – his 'true' first film, according to his personal notes.[38]

Although the time gap between the making of *Tjitra* and *Darah dan Doa* is not that long, a closer look at the latter's camera movements reveals a very different approach to cinematography. In *Darah dan Doa*, Usmar and his cinematographer Max Tera expanded the camera movement vocabulary of Indonesian cinema by incorporating *tracking shots*, consisting of several techniques, including the *push-in*, *pull-back* and a lateral tracking movement in many of its scenes.

Although the film begins with an exterior scene of the Republican Army exterminating the communist insurgency in Madiun, interior scenes quickly follow. One of the first interior scenes revolves around a discussion about the shooting of the communists by a Republican soldier, Mula (Aedy Moward), and the moral implication of such a questionable action. Sudarto, the captain, raises an objection to the shooting. This issue is central to the film's exploration of the horizontal conflicts that permeated the newly born Republic of Indonesia during the Revolution of 1945–9. In many interior scenes that show the dispute between Sudarto and his fellow soldiers, the pull-back technique is used to open the scene. This method of opening an interior scene is repeated across the film, except in one scene, which involves the Siliwangi Division soldiers collectively singing the Indonesian folk song *Rasa Sayange* ('Loving Feeling'). Imbued with an upbeat mood, the scene is presented with a lateral tracking shot from right to left, enveloping the group as they take turns filling in the verse of this popular song. The film also contains a walk-and-talk shot in one segment, in which Sudarto is escorting the Red Cross nurse Widya (Farida) as the two are becoming closer romantically (see Figure 4.13).

These examples indicate that *Darah dan Doa* puts on display a richer palette of camera mobility compared with the films that Usmar had made one year before at the Dutch-owned South Pacific Film. In a single film, Usmar and Tera were able to utilise several forms of camera movement, three of which are mobile tracking shots enabled by a type of dolly support. Considering this is Usmar's first film project in which he operated independently with a shoestring budget, *Darah dan Doa* accomplished a lot when it came to introducing camera mobility to Indonesian cinematographic evolution.

Besides Usmar, another Perfini filmmaker Djajakusuma, in his regional films like *Harimau Tjampa* (*Tiger from Tjampa*, d.p. Max Tera, 1953) and *Tjambuk Api* (*The Whip of Fire*, d.p. Kasdullah/R. Husein/Kosnen, 1958), puts an interesting twist on the tracking shots that Usmar had introduced in *Darah dan Doa*. An interesting variation of the *push-in* and *pull-back* convention is visible in the ways in which they orchestrated the camera to move past objects diagonally, for instance, in the scene from *Tjambuk Api*. Even more remarkable is how the pull-back technique is implemented to de-dramatise emotionally-charged moments. As an example, in *Harimau Tjampa*, the *silat*

Figure 4.13 *A walk-and-talk shot visualises a pivotal moment between the main characters in* Darah dan Doa

apprentice Lukman (Bambang Hermanto), who is the leading character in the story, has just found out that his proposal to marry a lady from a respected family in the village has been rejected due to their difference in class. Lukman is enraged and devastated to hear this news from the *silat* guru; he resolves to destroy the traditional class structure and whatever obstacles that impede him from marrying his lover. Rather than closing in on his face, we pull back slowly from Lukman and the guru. This is somewhat unconventional because conventionally, a push-in would be employed in an intensely dramatic moment like this – at least in classical Hollywood cinematography. Similarly, in *Tjambuk Api*, when the father reprimands the daughter for preserving the relationship with the village boy who he resents and insists she marry the man he has chosen for her, the camera tracks back as she begins to weep. Through these moments, camera movements in the shape of a tracking shot (diagonal push-in and pull-back) participate in telling the story visually, but this is handled with some degree of reticence rather than direct interference. These Djajakusuma films demonstrate that even within one filmmaking institution (i.e., the Perfini film company), there is variation in how tracking camera movements are implemented.

I should point out, though, that the tracking camera movements in these films are restricted mainly to capturing interior scenes. Pans and tilts are the only camera movements deployed for exterior shots. The only exterior tracking shot that I have found in films made before 1960 is a lateral dolly shot in *Harimau Tjampa,* and even this one was captured in a studio environment that simulated an exterior setting. This curious detail adds further evidence to the argument I presented in the previous section on production design that studio filming was as prevalent (if not even more predominant) as on-location shooting in the first years of the postcolonial film industry.

After 1960, we can find tracking shots in actual exterior scenes shot on location, as in the opening scene of the film *Anak Perawan di Sarang Penyamun (The Virgin and the Bandits,* Usmar Ismail, d.p. Max Tera, Kasdullah and Kosnen, 1962). Based on a story written by the famous Indonesian author Sutan Takdir Alisjahbana, *Anak Perawan di Sarang Penyamun* showcases riveting exterior shots of the forest where the bandits reside. Most of these outdoor scenes are shot on location and accompanied by mobile camera shots that allude to Kazuo Miyagawa's work on Akira Kurosawa's *Rashomon* (1950). The link between these two films is also strengthened by the score composed by Jack Lesmana during the exterior shots in the forest. It is not too far-fetched to claim that this link between *Anak Perawan* and *Rashomon* has reinforced the notion that Usmar and his colleagues at Perfini were highly aware of other developments in world cinema, in addition to Hollywood and Italian neorealism, as often suggested in the scholarly literature.[39]

By the end of the Sukarno period, camera movement in Indonesian fiction films became more diverse. A popular *silat* film like *Matjan Kemayoran (The Tiger of Kemayoran,* Wim Umboh, d.p. Eksin, 1965) contains a wide range of techniques, including those that prefigured the trend of mobile framing in the ensuing period, such as the zoom technique.[40] While the film's visual style sustains the use of pans and tilts in many of its scenes, there are notable techniques that warrant a closer look. First, the tracking shot – whether a pull-back or push-in – is explored more judiciously, reserved for specific moments in the film. While in Usmar and Djajakusuma's films the tendency was to use tracking shots to open scenes with long strokes of movement, in *Matjan Kemayoran* tracking shots tend to be short and concentrated on smaller distances. Moreover, it is largely designed to accompany the walk-and-talk staging of actors. Second, it is in this film that we can detect camera movements that primarily function as *optical* and *affected POV* shots, according to Jakob Isak Nielsen's functional theory delineated in Chapter 3.

An example of this specific form of camera movement comes when Rausin (W. D. Mochtar) has been fighting off paid bandits in the village. During a fight scene, he attacks the bandit in the neck and locks him into a kneeling position. The thug finally collapses to the ground. As he struggles to get up, he looks up to the sky, and a point-of-view shot takes over. The camera rotates to mimic his dizziness. Next to this, a whip pan is also utilised as a visual effect to inject energy into the fighting sequences as well as to simulate the enormous impact of Rausin's first strike of the enemy. Finally, in this film, we are also able to witness the early use of the zoom technique. Halfway into the film, there is a zoom-in on the character Toha (Ratno Timoer), who is depicted just returning from incarceration. The zoom technique here picks him out of the frame filled with foliage, indicating the idea that he has been observing from afar the intrigues and petty bickering among the villagers. This scene of quiet observation is important because Toha is plotting revenge against the bandits who have set him up, getting him incarcerated without a trial. But in other moments, the zoom-out technique is used to replace the pull-back tracking shot that would normally open a scene, as the films of Usmar and Djajakusuma have demonstrated. When the children of the Dutch officer (Hamid Arief) are playing nearby a well, a close-up of a well opens the scene, and then the camera slowly zooms out to a wider view of the yard where the well is located. In a typical film made fifteen years earlier, this particular moment would have been handled with the pull-back technique, but the zoom became a handy substitute for this kind of scene opening. Combined, these mobile frame devices render *Matjan Kemayoran* a visually energetic and kinetic film, which suits its identity as a *silat* film – a genre that became prominent as the film industry became much more commercialised in the subsequent era.

The Predominance of Zoom in Suharto-Era Cinematography

In the Suharto era, not only did the number of films produced increase but the diversity of film types intensified as well. With this diversification came a broadening of the camera movement repertoire. Camera movement techniques that were already in place during the Sukarno period carried over to Suharto-era filmmaking. But there were equally important changes to the vocabulary of camerawork during this period. Among the significant developments, the zoom technique figured prominently.

While Wim Umboh and his cinematographer Eksin had experimented with the zoom technique in *Matjan Kemayoran* in 1965, this technique was only applied very selectively in the film. But from 1969 onward, one can notice how pervasive the zoom technique had become. A good indication of this stylistic development can be gleaned from looking at the films financed and supervised by the Dewan Produksi Film Nasional (National Film Production Council) – a formal body created to produce *film percontohan* (a prototype for 'quality' films) conceived by the New Order government. In *Apa Yang Kau*

Tjari, Palupi? (*What Are You Looking For, Palupi?*, Asrul Sani, d.p. Wagumin Tjokrowardojo, 1969) the zoom takes us from a master shot to a closer shot of actors, providing an alternative option to the push-in and to analytical editing altogether. Similarly, in *Nji Ronggeng* (*The Ronggeng Dancer*, Alam Surawijaja, d.p. Sjamsudin Jusuf, 1969) – another *film percontohan* produced by the Council – a fast zoom-in from a wide exterior shot to a medium close up of the action supplies us with a closer view of the characters interacting in the *sawah* (rice field). In this example, a speedy zoom-in becomes an alternative to the dolly tracks typically applied for exterior shots, which at this point in Indonesian film history had become quite common, as the aforementioned examples from *Anak Perawan di Sarang Penyamun* and *Matjan Kemayoran* testify.

While these instances of zoom shots are rather straightforward and applied singlehandedly, in *Apa Yang Kau Tjari, Palupi?* it is also evident that the zoom and tracking shots are used in combination. For example, the scene that depicts the encounter between the leading female character Palupi (Farida Sjuman) and her unrequited love Chalil (Pietrajaya Burnama) is handled by a mixture of lateral tracking shot and zoom-in. The shot begins with the long shot of Palupi walking along the Bina Ria Beach in North Jakarta. As she approaches Chalil, who is already seated on a plastic chair, we zoom in to get her in a medium close-up, but at the same time, the camera tracks horizontally to follow her motion. The shot is then held for a couple of seconds until Chalil moves to the left of the frame to talk to the *saté* (satay) seller. What we obtain from this orchestration of tracking shot and zoom is an interesting decentring of characters in the visual field. The purpose of camera movement in this scene oscillates from being a reframing device – adjusting the frame when the character moves and settles into a new position – to a compositional device, supplying one of the most intriguingly ornamental shots in the visual fabric of Suharto-era cinema.

In the popular genre films that characterise a large portion of Suharto-era cinema history, the rigorous reliance on the zoom technique is highly noticeable. In the comedies of Benyamin S, for instance, the fast zoom is typically employed as an expressive tool to enhance a character's sudden surprise and realisation. The way in which this zoom is implemented can be conspicuously exaggerated. For example, in *Samson Betawi* (*The Strong Man*, Nawi Ismail, d.p. Cucu Sutedja, 1975), which is an adaptation of the biblical story of Samson and Delilah, the mother (Wolly Sutinah) in her late-50s is pregnant with the baby Samson. Because of this odd occurrence, she is soliciting advice from an *orang bisa* (clairvoyant), played by Edi Gombloh, who can supply her with a prognosis about this unlikely pregnancy. According to his insight and calculation, albeit remaining very dubious, the mother will be pregnant for sixteen months, which prompts her shocked response. The absurdity of the forecast, which is already preceded by the fact that the mother is considered too old to have a baby, is amped up by the aggressive zoom-in on her face when she hears this estimate, while non-diegetic sounds from a beaming synthesiser add comic effect to this outlandish scenario. Fast forward to a couple of scenes later, when Samson is now a five-year-old boy, he is shown singlehandedly devouring all the meals on the dining table, leaving nothing but a few grains of rice and *tempe* (fermented bean, or tempeh as it is known in English). Seeing this, his parents are terribly shocked by the animalistic appetite of their seemingly 'normal' child. Nevertheless, after gorging on the food, Samson demonstrates his strength as he clenches his fist and pushes his chest forward. As the visual effect denotes his power, another sound effect is added to convey this. Witnessing this magical moment, Samson's parents' stunned reaction is again enhanced by assertive zoom-ins (see Figure 4.14). By this time, they know that their son is extremely 'special'.

The zooms in Benyamin S films like *Samson Betawi, Buaye Gile* (*Crazy Playboy*, d.p. Adrian Susanto, 1974), *Musuh Bebuyutan* (*Arch Enemy*, d.p. Adrian Susanto, 1974), *Benyamin Raja Lenong* (*Benyamin the Lenong King*, d.p. Endus, 1975) and *Benyamin Koboi Ngungsi* (*Benyamin the Refugee Cowboy*, d.p. H. M. Taba, 1975) can be very obtrusive. Nevertheless, they powerfully

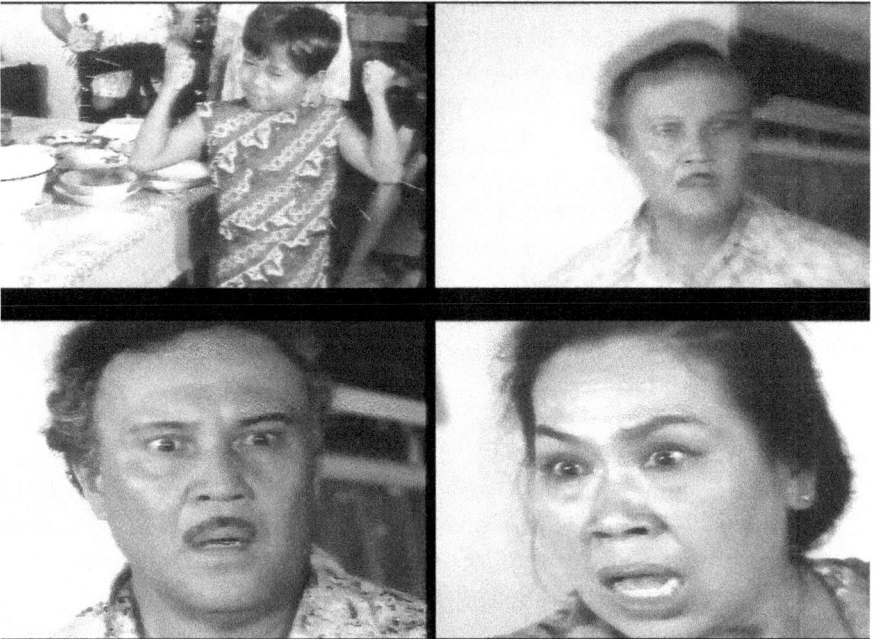

Figure 4.14 *An aggressive zoom-in technique inflects the parents' surprised reaction at their son's superpower in* Samson Betawi

demonstrate the expressive possibility of the mobile frame to a maximum level. With its conscious exploration of the zoom shots, Benyamin's filmic visual style exploits the medium's own technique to externalise a character's emotional state and thereby achieve his comic objective rather than relying solely on physical slapstick and verbal enunciation.

One of the major directors of the New Order era, *Teguh* Karya, incorporated zooms into the visual fabric of his early films. His debut feature *Wajah Seorang Laki-Laki* (*The Ballad of a Man*, d.p. Tantra Surjadi, 1970), displays some interesting uses of the zoom technique. The film is set in the 1800s, and it is told mainly in a flashback mode – analysing an incident that involves the shooting of a thief who turns out to be the son of the shooter. Apparently, the relationship between father and son is a strenuous one, replete with mutual resentment. In one crucial scene, the son (Slamet Rahardjo) confesses why he's so angry at his father (W. D. Mochtar) to a dear female friend (Rima Melati) who has a deep affection for him. This scene is handled as a flashback-within-flashback. It is preceded by a slow zoom-in on his face before the frame settles on his hands; then, the shot becomes blurred as we enter an episode from his childhood. Next, a zoom-out opens the scene as we are presented with a view of children gathering; one of these children is the son when he is a ten-year-old. His mother is dying. Instead of taking care of her, however, his father has sex with another woman in the stable located next to the house, resuming his philandering behaviour. Then, the son observes this erotic encounter through a gap in the door. In this shot, we can only see his eyes through the gap as the zoom closes in on him. His father discovers this and, without any hesitation, beats him severely. But they then discover that the mother has passed away, and the young son blames his father for her death. At the end of this flashback-within-flashback segment, we zoom in on the son's hands as he punches his father in the chest, calling him a murderer; subsequently, the shot is blurred and we get a close-up of the adult son's hands punching at a tree that he leans on while we are slowly zooming out to get a wider view. We are now back in the main flashback.

I need to note that the zoom shots in this film are used prominently to transition from a wider view to a closer shot of the son's face. By doing so, his face becomes an important motif whose salience in the story has a deeper thematic resonance. In other words, the zoom shots do not mainly work to orient the viewer's attention, but to facilitate meaning-making; if we translate the title of the film literally into English as 'The Face of a Man', instead of referring to its official international title *The Ballad of a Man*, then the close-ups foregrounding his face become chief interpretive cues. Therefore, although the film has the time of the resistance against the colonial powers as a historical backdrop, it is ostensibly a character study rather than a prototypical *film sejarah* (historical film set in the colonial period). The film is innovative in the ways in which it relies on the zoom technique and the use of telephoto lenses to magnify details of facial expressions. Despite the fact that closer views of actors had already been part of the visual vocabulary of Indonesian films from the colonial and Sukarno eras, close-ups proper were very rare. Therefore, it is interesting to see that Teguh has made the close-ups of Slamet Rahardjo a predominant graphic motif in the film, contributing to the expression of the pathos of this abandoned man. With zoom shots and close-ups, we are able to study the face of a man who the director has foregrounded as a meaningful object of scrutiny.

Zoom was also widely used in many *silat* films, which was another popular genre during the Suharto period. In these action-oriented films, the zoom shot is mainly used as a device to enliven fight scenes. *Si Bongkok* (*The Hunchback*, Lilik Sudjijo, d.p. Sjamsuddin Jusuf, 1972), a bestselling *silat* movie from the early 1970s, exhibits the use of a fast zoom shot during a critical moment in the film's fighting scene. As a group of outlaws disturb the peace of a family living atop a mountain, the father is ambushed and outnumbered. While he is doing his best to fight off these men with his *pencak silat* skills, one of the men throws his son over the cliff. As he is plummeting down the cliff, a speedy zoom-in follows his movement, just as a bearded old man proves to be fast enough to catch him. We find out that the man is a lone warrior, who later becomes the *silat* guru for this young boy who will eventually become Si Bongkok, the crime-fighting *silat* warrior. In a lesser-known example, *Tengkorak Hitam* (*Black Skull*, Wijsnu Mouradhy, d.p. Harry Susanto, 1978), the zoom visibly enlivens the fight scene as fighters leap into the air to attack and land on their feet again. Toshiro (Bobby Kim) is a Korean who sympathises with the locals as they fight off Japanese forces. A group of local soldiers, however, has a suspicion that he is actually Japanese and that he keeps a pot of gold stolen from a Chinese family during the war. When they are trying to get rid of him, Toshiro combats these men with ferocious energy and spirit. He leaps into the air and attacks one of the leaders with a forceful kick. As he lands, the camera zooms out to reveal the precise location of his landing move. It is also common to find the zoom technique working together with whip pans and fast tilts to follow the quick action of the fighters. Besides revealing scope, the zoom in this film injects kinetic energy into the action scenes. This example shows that the cinematographic convention of East Asian action cinema, mainly developed by Hong Kong martial arts filmmakers, has seeped into the stylistic fabric of Indonesian *silat* films of the New Order era.[41]

Use of zoom as a dominant mobile frame technique endured throughout the Suharto era. In the early 1990s, as the industry entered a period of decline, the zoom technique was still chosen as one of the main methods of visual narration. In Slamet Rahardjo's *Langitku Rumahku* (*My Sky, My Home*, d.p. Soetomo Gandasoebrata, 1990), many of the exterior scenes depicting the slums of Jakarta as the home of one of the protagonists are handled by the zoom device. These instances exhibit the persistence of the zoom as a dominant mode of camera movement. Curiously enough, in the post-Suharto years, the zoom receded into the background as other types of camera movement entered the visual stylistic vocabulary of Indonesian cinema. One striking feature of camera movement in the post-Suharto years, which I will discuss more in Chapter 7, comes in the form of prowling camerawork that contributes to making Indonesian cinema a stylistically complex cinema in the twenty-first century.

Now that we've traced the evolution of visual style in Indonesian cinema through the lens of lighting, production design and camera movement, we are ready to enter the third act of this book in which we'll examine and unravel how exactly these salient stylistic devices contribute to the stylistic complexity of post-Suharto Indonesian cinema.

Notes

1. Misbach Yusa Biran, *Sejarah Film 1900–1950: Bikin Film Di Jawa* (Jakarta: Komunitas Bambu dan Dewan Kesenian Jakarta, 2009), p. 25.
2. Patrick Keating, *Hollywood Lighting from the Silent Era to Film Noir* (New York, NY: Columbia University Press, 2010), pp. 140–51.
3. Original Indonesian: 'Kisah Sudarto adalah kisah sedih. Sudarto bukanlah pahlawan dalam arti yang biasa, tetapi adalah seorang manusia Indonesia yang terlibat dan diseret oleh arus revolusi itu, sebelum dia sempat menilai segala kejadian disekelilingnya dengan sadar.' Usmar Ismail, *Usmar Ismail Mengupas Film* (Jakarta: Penerbit Sinar Harapan, 1983), p. 169.
4. Keating, *Hollywood Lighting*, pp. 140–51.
5. Ibid.
6. Ibid., p. 132.
7. Peter Ettedgui, *Production Design & Art Direction* (Hove: RotoVision, 1999), p. 8.
8. Ibid.
9. Angela Halim, e-mail interview, 21 July 2015 (emphasis added).
10. Biran, *Sejarah Film*, p. 61.
11. Biran also notes that the cave had to be carved out using explosives. See Biran, *Sejarah Film*, p. 66.
12. The *beringin* (*ficus benjamina*), also known as a *banyan*, is a gigantic tree usually planted in the centre of a city or in front of palaces, considered sacred and believed to house ancestral spirits in Java and Bali.
13. Biran, *Sejarah Film*, p. 151.

14. Ibid., p. 174.
15. Ibid., p. 167.
16. Basoeki Resobowo (1916–99) was a painter and a cultural activist before becoming an art director and screenwriter for Usmar Ismail's Perfini in 1950 where he contributed to the film company's seven films. For more insights into his artistic influences on Perfini's filmic mise en scène, see Umi Lestari, 'Basuki Resobowo as a Jack of All Trades: The Intersectionality of Arts and Film in Perfini Films and Resobowo's Legacy in Indonesian Cinema', *Southeast of Now: Directions in Contemporary and Modern Art in Asia* 4, no. 2 (2020), pp. 313–45, https://doi.org/10.1353/sen.2020.0014.
17. David Hanan, 'Moments of Renewal–Alternative Ways of Viewing Indonesian Cinema', *Jurnal Skrin Malaysia* 5, no. 2 (2008), p. 125.
18. Ibid., p. 124.
19. David Hanan, *Cultural Specificity in Indonesian Film – Two Films from West Sumatra*, Lecture at Monash University, Melbourne, 2014, accessed 28 October 2015, https://vimeo.com/89458347.
20. A *mihrab* is a curved niche in the wall of a mosque that indicates the Kiblat (*qibla* in Arabic), which is the direction of the Kaaba in Mecca, Saudi Arabia, towards which Muslims should face when praying.
21. David Hanan's account of the film corroborates this finding as he asserts: 'Extensive outdoor scenes for *Harimau Tjampa* were filmed on location in West Sumatra, the interiors being filmed in a Jakarta studio, using Minangkabau people resident in Jakarta as extras.' David Hanan, *Cultural Specificity in Indonesian Film: Diversity in Unity* (Cham: Palgrave Macmillan Imprint, Springer International Publishing, 2017), p. 98.
22. *Opname* is Dutch for a recording/shooting. See Usmar Ismail, *Usmar Ismail Mengupas Film* (Jakarta: Penerbit Sinar Harapan, 1983), p. 159.
23. Hanan, *Cultural Specificity in Indonesian Film*, p. 98.
24. Christopher Frayling, 'Perspectives on Production Design', LICA-Lancaster University, 12 June 2013, video, 1:24:39, https://www.youtube.com/watch?v=HFZSuNdT5vo.
25. See, for example, Salim Said, *Shadows on the Silver Screen: A Social History of Indonesian Film* (Jakarta: Lontar Foundation, 1991), pp. 49–58; and Krishna Sen, *Indonesian Cinema: Framing the New Order* (London; Atlantic Highlands, NJ: Zed Books, 1994), pp. 13–26.
26. See, for instance, Said, *Shadows on the Silver Screen*; and David Hanan, 'Innovation and Tradition in Indonesian Cinema', *Third Text* 24, no. 1 (2010), pp. 107–21.
27. See Hanan, 'Moments of Renewal'; and Hanan, *Cultural Specificity in Indonesian Film*, pp. 53–90.
28. Ismail, *Usmar Ismail Mengupas Film*, p. 159.
29. The exception to this will be the shot of Borobudur temple in Magelang, Central Java. Usmar narrates the experience of making *Darah dan Doa* in '*Film Saja Jang Pertama*' in *Intisari*, 17 August 1963, reprinted in *Usmar Ismail Mengupas Film*, pp. 164–71.

30. Ibid.
31. For an illuminating discussion about the relationship between the depiction of Jakarta in Benyamin S's films of the 1970s and the social changes caused by the modernisation of Jakarta, see David Hanan, 'Songs and Films of the Betawi Comedian, Benyamin S, in the 1970s: A Popular Culture of the Poor', in *Moments in Indonesian Film History: Film and Popular Culture in a Developing Society 1950–2020*, by David Hanan (Cham: Springer International Publishing, 2021), pp. 165–216, https://doi.org/10.1007/978-3-030-72613-3_5.
32. *Tedak siten* is a Javanese ritual during which a child is given a blessing. One of the significant elements of this ceremony involves the child stepping foot on the ground for the first time. The ceremony is performed when the child is 245 days old. Another important component of this ritual is the *sesajen* (offerings) and delicacies wrapped flamboyantly inside banana leaves. The ceremony consists of seven stages. The most symbolic part of these steps is the fourth one: the child is guided by his mother or father to enter a delicately ornamented rooster's cage. Inside this cage, there will be everyday objects scattered around the floor that include jewellery, books, rice, fabric and so on. Through this ritual, Javanese people believe that whichever item the child picks, it'll be a sign for his or her future profession: if the child picks up the book, then she will become a scholar, but if she picks up a piece of jewellery, she will be proficient in the business world. The cage itself symbolises guardianship, meaning that when entering the real world, the child should be guided by tradition and religion.
33. The Majapahit Empire was a powerful empire based in Java that ruled the archipelago from the late thirteenth to the sixteenth century.
34. Production design/art direction might not be the only factor that created this lack of clarity in the image. Cinematographic processes could also be the cause, for instance, when the film was being developed during postproduction or during the colour correction phase. In addition, the video compact disc (VCD) version of the film – upon which I rely for the analysis – may not give the most optimal rendition of the images because of its low resolution, which is much lower than VHS quality.
35. *Wedana* was also called *districthoofd* or *bestuursambtenaar* during colonial times.
36. See 'Penghargaan Bagi R.A. Kartini (1982)', *Film Indonesia*, accessed 29 October 2015, http://filmindonesia.or.id/movie/title/lf-r011-82-655427_ra-kartini/award#.VjKNKqLATBM; and 'Penghargaan Bagi SunanKalijaga (1983)', *Film Indonesia*, accessed 29 October 2015, http://filmindonesia.or.id/movie/title/lf-s013-83-072357_sunan-kalijaga/award#.VjKNQ6LATBM.
37. Misbach Yusa Biran in his book explains that film directors' primary task during the colonial era was mainly to coach actors to do the dialogue, while decisions regarding visual techniques were taken by the producers in charge at the film production company. Usmar Ismail described this division of duties to Biran in a personal conversation at Perfini Studio in 1956. See Biran, *Sejarah Film*, p. 365 and p. 376.
38. Ismail, *Usmar Ismail Mengupas Film*, p. 164.

39. See, for instance, Thomas Barker, 'A Cultural Economy of the Contemporary Indonesian Film Industry' (PhD Thesis, National University of Singapore, 2011); David Hanan, 'Innovation and Tradition in Indonesian Cinema', *Third Text* 24, no. 1 (2010), pp. 107–21; Ekky Imanjaya, 'Revisiting Italian Neorealism: Its Influence toward Indonesia and Asian Cinema or There's No Such Thing Like Pure Neorealist Films', *Journal of European Studies University of Indonesia* IV, no. 3 (2008), pp. 57–66; and Said, *Shadows on the Silver Screen*.
40. *Matjan Kemayoran* is Wim Umboh's directorial debut. The film features actors who would later become some of Indonesia's major movie stars, including W. D. Mochtar, Dicky Zulkarnaen, Rahmat Kartolo, Ratno Timoer and Rita Zahara. The cast, however, also consists of older actors of the previous generation such as Raden Ismail, Menzano and Hamid Arief who were regularly cast by Usmar Ismail and Nja Abbas Akup at Perfini.
41. For a discussion about the global influence of Hong Kong action film style, see David Bordwell, *Planet Hong Kong: Popular Cinema and the Art of Entertainment*, second edition (Madison, WI: Irvington Way Institute Press, 2011).

Part 3: Climax

The Analyses, or: How Lighting, Production Design and Camera Movement Have Transformed Indonesian Cinema into a Stylistically Complex Cinema

CHAPTER 5

Lighting and Visual Opacity

In this chapter, we'll examine the role of lighting as one of the three chief visual techniques instrumental to the transformation of Indonesian cinema into a stylistically complex cinema in the post-1998 period. As we've seen in Chapter 4, the low-key lighting technique was a suppressed and underutilised tool in the cinematographic toolbox of pre-1998 filmmaking. In the 2000s and 2010s, not only have filmmakers explored low-key lighting more intensively, they have simultaneously augmented the form and function of this lighting technique as a genre/scene lighting convention. I argue that they have done this by transforming two variants of the low-key lighting technique that valorise intensified visual darkness into a multifunctional creative strategy: 1) *single-source lighting*, which is a lighting technique in which the illumination on the subject appears to come from one lamp, with one visible shadow,[1] and 2) *available light shooting*, which is a lighting method in which the source of illumination comes exclusively from the light present in a location without the addition of extra lighting fixtures.[2]

To illustrate this development in post-1998 Indonesian film lighting, let's consider these scenes from two feature-length films of two different genres, a war film and a woman-centred drama:

- **Scene 1**: A Dutch colonial military officer interrogates a wounded Balinese soldier. The soldier is a member of the guerrilla army fighting against the Dutch re-occupation of Indonesia, which has just been recently declared independent. The officer threatens the captured soldier that if he does not disclose the whereabouts of his comrades, he will have to get his right-hand man to come and 'make' him speak. The soldier doesn't give in; instead, he tells the Dutch major that he's been reborn many times, so he fears no death. The major becomes so frustrated that he orders his subordinate to carry on with the full-blown physical torture. He pulls out the Balinese soldier's teeth one by one with a pair of rusty pliers. In this extremely atrocious moment, the lighting comes only from above, shining on the soldier's bare shoulder. The rest of the frame,

Figure 5.1 *Intensified visual darkness in* Darah Garuda

however, is left unlit, producing a thick black visual cloak that envelops the heightening infliction of pain (see Figure 5.1).

- **Scene 2**: A regional police force raids a karaoke club in the coastal town of Parangtritis, near Yogyakarta. The club is suspected of serving alcohol without a permit and of running a prostitution business. One karaoke girl, who has been entertaining some male patrons, attempts to flee from the scene. A policeman notices her walking away, so he shouts, 'Hey, stop! Where do you think you're going?' He follows her into the dark hallway and finally manages to grab her arm. She struggles, releases herself, and replies, 'I need to pee!' She steps into the toilet and closes the door. Because the only illumination in the space comes from the toilet's overhead light bulb, when she closes the door solid, black darkness fills up the entire frame. This total darkness is sustained for fourteen seconds. Our film viewing experience leads us to expect that this is a fade-to-black transition – a device traditionally used to mark the end of a scene or a film. But instead, this complete blackness is part of the unfolding scene. In this wholly blackened moment, we can only hear the sound of the girl urinating. Then, the policeman pounds the toilet door

Lighting and Visual Opacity 123

Figure 5.2 *Intensified visual darkness in* Siti

and shouts, 'Make it quick!' She opens the door. The extremely minimal illumination from the toilet can barely show their mutual aggravated reactions. Then he grabs her arm by force. Dragging her outside, he dumps her in line with the rest of the karaoke bar employees for interrogation. Before answering a question, she collapses abruptly. Handled in one unbroken shot, this scene introduces us to the film's protagonist, Siti (see Figure 5.2).

These scenes from *Darah Garuda* (*Blood of Eagles*, Yadi Sugandi and Connor Allyn, d.p. Padri Nadeak, 2010) and *Siti* (Eddie Cahyono, d.p. Ujel Bausad, 2014) exemplify a particular lighting tendency in post-Suharto Indonesian filmmaking that I call *the intensified visual darkness strategy*. This lighting approach can be characterised as a maximal heightening of the contrast between the illuminated and darkened areas of a shot. In many cases, the dark parts dominate the frame to the extent that they swallow the illuminated sections of the image. In its extreme form, the dominating darkness annexes the illuminated areas, generating a flat plane of blackness. And more strikingly, the darkness obscures details of characters' facial and bodily expressions, which are usually the significant conduits for conveying emotional states pertinent to filmic storytelling.[3]

So, intensified visual darkness is defined here as a condition of tonal value in the image. This means that the tonal quality of shadow and void (unlit area in the shot) resides in the blackest zones (zones 0, I, and II) of the black-to-white spectrum known as the Zone System in photography.[4] In these zones, shadow and void are black instead of grey. As a result, details in the dark area of the image are nearly or completely lost.

Contemporary Indonesian cinematographers implement this intensified visual darkness strategy by leveraging the low-key lighting convention. Within this convention, single-source lighting and available light shooting techniques stand out. As described above, the single source lighting technique is where one light is used as the key illumination source without the addition of a *fill light*[5] or *backlight*.[6] This key light source typically comes from an artificial light fixture, although cinematographers often combine it with natural sources available on location such as sunlight. The available light shooting technique, by contrast, makes use of the light available on location exclusively. This technique is made possible by the development of faster film stocks, faster lenses and digital cinema cameras equipped with more light-sensitive sensors enabling cinematographers to shoot in extreme low-light situations such as the Arri Alexa. At times, cinematographers utilise *practical light sources* – from household light bulbs to oil lamps – to help increase the light level when using the available light shooting technique. Because they are able to view the images on the digital video production monitor, they can control the brightness and darkness levels more readily than was possible before the advent of the digital cinema camera. It is important to note that cinematographers often mix these two lighting techniques (exploiting artificial and available illumination) during filming to attain the intensified graphic darkness as in the examples above.

I began noticing this propensity for intensified darkness when viewing the biographical films that proliferated in the 2000s: *Gie* (Riri Riza, d.p. Yudi Datau, 2005), *Soegija* (Garin Nugroho, d.p. Teoh Gay Hian, 2010), *Sang Pencerah* (Hanung Bramantyo, d.p. Faozan Rizal, 2010) and *Habibie and Ainun* (Faozan Rizal, d.p. Ipung Rachmat Syaiful, 2012). As my research advanced, I have found that films in other genres also explore this dark tendency:

- melodrama (*Cerita Cibinong* [*Story from a Village*, Nia Dinata, d.p. Ical Tanjung, 2009], *Siti* [2014] and *Berbagi Suami* [*Love for Share*, Nia Dinata, d.p. Ipung Rachmat Syaiful, 2006]);
- war film (*Merah Putih* [*Red and White*, Yadi Sugandi, d.p. Padri Nadeak, 2009], *Darah Garuda* [2010] and *Hati Merdeka* [*Hearts of Freedom*, Yadi Sugandi and Connor Allyn, d.p. Padri Nadeak, 2011]);

- action (*9 Naga* [*9 Dragons*, Rudi Soedjarwo, d.p. Edi Michael Santoso, 2006] and *Serbuan Maut* [*The Raid: Redemption*, Gareth Evans, d.p. Matt Flannery, 2011]); and
- road movie (*3 Hari Untuk Selamanya* [*Three Days to Forever*, Riri Riza, d.p. Yadi Sugandi, 2007]).

I discovered that two comedies (*Maskot* [2006] and *Quickie Express* [2007]) and one musical (*Petualangan Sherina* [*Sherina's Adventure*, Riri Riza, d.p. Yadi Sugandi, 2000]) showcase this heightened visual darkness as well. Meanwhile, horror films and thrillers, which have always embraced low-key lighting, have pushed their darkness levels even further in the years after 2000, as the following titles demonstrate:

- *Jelangkung* (Rizal Mantovani and Jose Poernomo, d.p. Jose Poernomo, 2001);
- *Lentera Merah* (*Red Lantern*, Hanung Bramantyo, d.p. Roby Herby, 2006);
- *Legenda Sundel Bolong* (*The Legend of Sundel Bolong*, Hanung Bramantyo, d.p. Faozan Rizal, 2009);
- *Keramat* (*Sacrosanct*, Monty Tiwa, d.p. Ucup Supena, 2009);
- *Modus Anomali* (*The Ritual*, Joko Anwar, d.p. Gunnar Nimpuno, 2013);
- *Pintu Terlarang* (*The Forbidden Door*, Joko Anwar, d.p. Ipung Rachmat Syaiful, 2009); and
- *Pengabdi Setan* (*Satan's Slaves*, Joko Anwar, d.p. Ical Tanjung, 2017).

Intensified Visual Darkness at Work

But even within the horror genre, we can see this intensified visual darkness at work in the post-1998 horror films made by *Joko* Anwar, for instance. To get a better picture of this, let's compare Joko's 2017 remake of a 1980 Indonesian horror film, *Pengabdi Setan* (*Satan's Slave*, Sisworo Gautama Putra, d.p. F.E.S. Tarigan, 1980). The scenes we'll be comparing and contrasting are critical in these films as they involve the apparition of the evil spirit as the proxy for Satan. In the original film, the apparition comes at the end of the first act. A middle-class Indonesian family has recently lost its mother due to mysterious circumstances. Since then, the remaining family members have encountered a series of unsettling occurrences, starting with a Satan-worshipping clairvoyant who shows up at their door unannounced at nighttime, disguised as a housekeeper (Ruth Pelupessy). The housekeeper turns out to be the representative of Satan, sent with a task to turn them into his slaves. She shows up when the family is having dinner (see Figure 5.3). Tomi (Fachrul Rozi), the son, opens the door and finds this lady carrying nothing but a white envelope in her hand. In this instance, the apparition is handled

Figure 5.3 *High-key lighting applied to a scene of apparition in the 1980* Pengabdi Setan

with a high-key lighting technique with a touch of a *beauty lighting* effect. We can see that the housekeeper is lit flatteringly with the symmetrical arrangement of the three-point lighting system wherein the key light is accompanied by a fill light and a backlight. The high-key lighting mode applied to this apparition scene sculps the actor's onscreen appearance, making her face look three-dimensional and glamorous at the same time. This visual outcome reminds us of the beauty lighting effect applied to classical Hollywood actors such as Marlene Dietrich, Joan Crawford, Ingrid Bergman and Barbara Stanwyck in the 1930s and '40s. So, instead of a menacing and terrifying atmosphere, visually speaking, this scene exudes a rather cordial mood. The threatening element in this scene, however, is engendered by sound design, which involves the orchestration of a non-diegetic ominous sonic effect coming from a synthesiser. But lighting, I contend, does nothing to contribute to creating a sinister and scary atmosphere, which is the point of this apparition scene.

In the 2017 remake of the film, the apparition scene similarly comes at the end of the first act. But in this version, the scene is handled differently as far as its cinematographic presentation is concerned. The scene takes place in Toni's (Endi Arfian) bedroom. While he is listening to a radio play at night, he hears the voice of a lady who's calling his name, accompanied by the sound of a ringing bell – like the bell that his deceased mother used when she was bedridden before she eventually died. He tries to ignore it, but the voice gets louder and louder until a ghost appears next to his bed. In this version, the ghost is hardly visible at all due to the intense visual darkness that accompanies her apparition. Rather than lit by a high-key lighting technique, the ghost here is enshrouded by graphic darkness with minimum illumination – just enough to orient us in the space. Like in the 1980 version, the sound design adds a terrifying component to the sound by means of a vocal distortion effect, enhancing the ghost-like presence of this haunting spirit. But lighting (or lack thereof) plays a significant role here in evoking the threatening and unsettling atmosphere. If we take this visual aspect out of the equation, the scene would have been less effective in getting viewers to jump out of their seats.[7]

In sum, lighting in the 1980 version of *Pengabdi Setan* is organised to achieve an *aesthetic of visual clarity* in which the ghost is directly presented and, at the same time, the famous actor is glamorously depicted onscreen. Contrastingly, lighting in the 2017 version is geared towards achieving an *aesthetic of visual opacity*, enhancing an atmospheric expressivity aimed at startling and terrifying the viewers, not by directly presenting the ghost in full visibility but by eliciting the viewers' imagination of it as her presence is cloaked in extreme visual darkness.

So, when we have this number of films across several genres that pursue visual darkness to an intense degree, we can't assume that this is merely a coincidence. Thus, it warrants a closer inspection. We need to ask: what functional possibilities emerge when graphic darkness is pushed to this staggering level? In addition to *denoting* the time of day and location, I contend that the use of intensified darkness as a stylistic strategy has other functional capabilities: to produce atmosphere; externalise a character's emotional states; create pictorial/graphic effects; suggest events or objects and elicit imagination; and direct the viewer's attention to auditory information. But not every function is activated simultaneously. According to my concept of *bounded multifunctionalism*, the context of story development, genre and the filmmaker's artistic motivation promote certain functions, but at the same time restrain the emergence of other possible functions. Nevertheless, there are two salient functions that are worth noting: the creation of pictorial or graphic effects and the externalisation of characters' emotional states.

To support my claims, I will analyse two scenes from *Sang Pencerah* and *Cerita Cibinong*. I am not suggesting that these two films represent all of the lighting developments in contemporary Indonesian cinema, but they are both examples of the intensified visual darkness that demands a critical inspection for reasons that I will highlight shortly. Before we launch into that analysis, though, it is helpful for us to first get a broad-stroke impression of how the low-key lighting convention has changed in the post-Suharto era more generally.

Low-Key Lighting in Post-Suharto-Era Cinematography

The use of low-key lighting as a genre or scene convention applied in the pre-1998 cinematography continued into the post-1998 cinematography as well. But significant changes in how low-key lighting is pursued have taken place in a way that is unprecedented in this period of transformation.

To begin with, as I have alluded to in Chapter 4, *the strategy of differentiation* has become a fundamental principle in the lighting practices of post-Suharto films. For example, *Petualangan Sherina* (*Sherina's Adventure*, Riri Riza, d.p. Yadi Sugandi, 2000) – a children's musical that reignited the film industry in the early 2000s – is generally a high-key lit film. But when a blackmailing gang kidnaps the protagonist's children, the scene's lighting turns to an extremely dark, low-key style. High contrast directional lighting is employed to denote the gang's secret headquarters. But when the criminal mastermind Pak Raden (Butet Kertarajasa) shows up, a solid black shadow falls on his face, signifying a mysterious and volatile persona. Conversely, in a biopic about the first indigenous archbishop during colonial times, *Soegija* (Garin Nugroho, d.p. Teoh Gay Hian, 2012), the majority of the scenes are rendered in low-key lighting. The plot is mostly confined to the interior space of prison camps, a hospital, a restaurant and a monastery. When the female protagonist, whose husband is killed by the Japanese imperial army, engages in a romantic affair with a Dutch journalist, we move outside and the lighting shifts to a high-key mode. In this scene, we see them on a motorbike journey across the plains and beaches, singing a nostalgic Indonesian song while the afternoon sunlight shines from behind them, creating a mild silhouette. This shift contrasts with the way she is lit in an earlier scene, depicting the moments before her husband is shot by the Japanese soldier. Attuning to different purposes – whether realism of time, place, location or the externalisation of a character's emotion – cinematographers of the post-Suharto era flexibly oscillate between the different modes of lighting.

Low-key lighting is transformed into a device that can serve wider purposes in post-Suharto-era cinematography. The functions of this lighting technique are not simply restricted to mood lighting or mystery lighting, depicting graphically taboo scenes (such as rape) or supernatural presence (such as the appearance of ghosts). What's crucial here is that intensified visual darkness has become a creative option, pursued as a distinct variant of the low-key lighting approach. To better understand the aesthetic and artistic possibilities of this variant, let's examine two cases in detail from the films *Sang Pencerah* and *Cerita Cibinong*.

Examining Extreme Darkness: Case Studies

Sang Pencerah (*The Enlightener*, Hanung Bramantyo, d.p. Faozan Rizal, 2010)

In *Sang Pencerah,* the intensified visual darkness strategy is implemented throughout the film – mostly accompanying scenes that involve conflict resolution. This pattern culminates in the climactic scene. The protagonist Ahmad Dahlan (Lukman Sardi), whose story is chronicled in the film as a reformer of Islam in late-nineteenth century Java, is reconciling with his fiercest opponent Muhammad Noor (Agus Kuncoro), who happens to be his own brother-in-law. The ideological clash between Dahlan and Noor has turned into an open physical conflict carried out by their respective followers. The confrontation has escalated and many casualties have been suffered by both sides. It is at this point that the brothers-in-law decide to reconcile.

The sequence opens with a medium long shot of Dahlan and his pupils sitting around the table in a circular fashion. The oil lamp lights the figures in the middle, but an additional light is thrown in the background (see Figure 5.4). Morale is at its lowest point in this scene because Noor's followers have physically harassed and verbally bullied Dahlan's pupils as a result of the rising tension between the two factions. Suddenly, Noor appears at the door, greeting them with '*Assalamualaikum*' ('May peace be upon you.'). He asks to talk with Dahlan privately. But instead of asking the pupils to leave the room so that they can talk in private – which is more customary in

Figure 5.4 *A medium long shot opens the climactic scene in* Sang Pencerah

Javanese culture given the hierarchy between teacher and pupil is still strongly maintained – Dahlan and Noor are the ones who leave privately. The next shot reveals that they are conversing outside, in the courtyard of the *langgar*.

The conversation between Dahlan and Noor lasts for two minutes and fifty-eight seconds and is presented in twelve shots. Across these twelve shots, lighting is extremely minimal; illumination comes mainly from *lampu minyak* (traditional oil lamps) and a few additional light fixtures that work mainly as background light. In the long shots, most of the details of space and figures are crushed into the blacks – making it very difficult to perceive. But even in closer shots, the details of these two central characters in the film are obliterated, submerged in a pool of darkness. When the most important lines, expressing the resolution to the film's dramatic clash and clang, are being articulated by the two characters, intensified darkness prevails.

To analyse the scene in more detail: in the first shot (a two-shot of these two characters), the camera tracks in slowly to approach the two figures as Noor opens the conversation: 'We are family, we should not hate each other just because we want to maintain our different ideals.' *Lampu minyak* from different areas of the courtyard provide very minimal illumination. The two figures are submerged in darkness, making their facial expressions barely discernible (see Figure 5.5). Then we cut to a long shot from a different angle, circling the two leaders from afar. Darkness is sustained throughout the camera movement so that we can only see the oil lamps, while both characters are rendered as sharply delineated silhouettes.

Figure 5.5 *Intensified visual darkness obscures the facial expressions of two major characters in the climatic scene of* Sang Pencerah

Then, the drama heightens, but without the histrionic outburst of a melodramatic film. Subsequently, Noor stresses that each Muslim has a responsibility to carry out the *jihad*,[8] but he asks Dahlan: 'Do we need to sacrifice the unity of our own family for it?' We then cut back to the two-shot featured earlier. Dahlan replies: 'I have no intention to sacrifice anybody.' Their faces are still obscured despite this highly important expression of moralistic principle. Dahlan continues: 'I actually always respect those who have different ideals from mine.' The next shot gives us a moment of reconciliation between the two figures. We cut back to the long shot, oil lamps scattered around the frame, supplying small spots of illumination. But the two characters are still bathed in deep shadows (see Figure 5.6). Noor says, 'This mosque is a witness to the lowest crime that humans have ever committed, to destruct and ruin, whatever the reasons are.' Then we get a close-up of Dahlan – again, lit with the single source lighting technique. He points out, 'Everywhere man can destroy, not only here. But they don't want to be blamed.' Noor sighs and moves away before he says the last words: 'Don't you ever think that I hate you. You are my little brother, my family.' In this two-shot that features the two central opposing figures finally reconciling their differences, darkness is pushed to the limits. The two-shot barely makes their faces visible (see Figure 5.7). The most significant close-up of Dahlan closes the scene, and as Noor declares, 'You are my little brother, my family,' Dahlan is lit extremely minimally. A small illumination casts highlights on his shoulder. The rest of

Figure 5.6 *Intensified visual darkness blankets a crucial shot even though narratively pivotal lines are being uttered by the two main characters in* Sang Pencerah

Figure 5.7 *As the two opposing figures finally reconciling their differences, visual darkness is pushed to the limits in the climax of* Sang Pencerah

his face and body is bathed in blackness. We can barely see how he reacts – facially or bodily – to Noor's final statement.

What functions can we discern from the employment of the intensified visual darkness strategy here? If we use Keating's multifunctional theory of film lighting, which I have outlined in Chapter 3, the extreme graphic darkness generated by this variant of low-key lighting activates storytelling, realism and pictorial functions.

When it comes to storytelling, visual darkness denotes time and space. It is obvious that this highly pivotal scene takes place late at night and in the courtyard of Dahlan's *langgar*, which is lit much more minimally compared with the interior shots presented earlier in this scene (see Figure 5.4). On top of this, it furnishes the scene with realistic detail, imbuing it with an authentic visual representation of the period's atmosphere. In this regard, just like production design and art direction, the darkness helps in portraying the past: pre-electrified Java in the late 1800s and early 1900s. At the same time, by pursuing realism, this intensified darkness strategy is applied to attain expressive purposes in the sense that it is geared toward producing the atmosphere of the period when electricity was unavailable, and the oil lamp was the only means of illumination for household settings. It is interesting to note that, as historian Merle Ricklefs has pointed out, petroleum extraction in the late colonial period in the Netherlands Indies was driven primarily by the need to supply oil lamps.[9] It wasn't until the 1920s that oil became a valuable commodity for fuelling motor cars in the Indies as the automobile industry took off. So, it is not a stretch to contend that the foregrounding of *lampu minyak* as a prominent light source in the scene and throughout the film is compatible with the goal of setting an authentic period atmosphere. Faozan Rizal, the film's cinematographer, further explains the importance of period authenticity as a goal he aimed for through the exploration of intensified graphic darkness:

> For *Sang Pencerah* I didn't want to use any diffusion or muslin cloth because, based on my research, the film is set in early 1900. I wanted to create hard shadows and because, I did not want to use salon lighting; I wanted to be ... if it's dark, it's going to be really dark.[10]

So far, we've moved from a denotative function (indicating time and place) to a realism (displaying period authenticity) and expressive (producing atmosphere) function for the application of intensified visual darkness. But, on top of these functional layers, there is a pictorial goal at play. As I have explained in Chapter 2, by pushing the darkness level, light can be accentuated, and the interplay between the light that comes from natural sources like bamboo oil lamps and the enshrouding darkness creates painterly images, intertextually referencing the artistic tradition of European Baroque paintings of the *tenebrism* vein represented by the masterworks of Tintoretto or Caravaggio. Faozan consciously explores and emulates the *chiaroscuro* effect stemming from the tenebrism style in the film's visual design. In an interview, he confirms this proposition:

> I am more strongly influenced by tenebrism, because since the beginning I always see [sic] tenebrism as having a powerful force that is emphasised in its lighting, whether in Joseph Wright of Derby's or George de la Tour's or Gerrit van Honthorst's paintings, even in Rembrandt's. Single-source lighting in their works contributes to a more powerful and dramatic way of [visual] storytelling.[11]

Furthermore, Faozan stresses that the use of the oil lamp as the primary source of illumination ultimately contributes to the sequence's painterly allusion. He explains:

> In that scene, the influence of tenebrism is more palpable. The light beaming from the *lampu minyak* from afar is the main source of illumination. As a consequence, even though it falls on the actor's figure, it will be so minimal to become the backlight.[12]

Thus, incorporating a particular stylistic tradition from an artform that possesses a high cultural cachet enhances the prestige of a period film based on the biography of a historical figure. Faozan's ability to compose the images by structuring light and shadow to allude to the visual motif of tenebrism showcases his priority of foregrounding pictorial impact. At this point, we have denotative, expressive, realism and pictorial functions all activated alongside one another.

But there's an additional function that Keating's functional categories do not cover. I am referring to the function of lighting – in this case, intensified visual darkness – in facilitating implicit and thematic meaning-making. As I have indicated, the representation of Ahmad Dahlan as the enlightener is crucial to the film's identity as a biopic. The status quo in the film, represented by his brother-in-law Muhammad Noor and the chief of the Great Mosque Kamaludiningrat (Slamet Rahardjo), allegorically represents the unenlightened majority in the Muslim communities of Indonesia. Eric Sasono argues that as an Islamic revivalist film *Sang Pencerah* aims to portray Islam as a progressive religion.[13] An important element of this progressiveness is the desire to accept different interpretations of Islam. Dahlan, as a reformer, carries another interpretation of Islam that he acquired during his time in Mecca. When he wants to apply the teachings and practices of this modernised view of Islam in Java, the forces of the status quo reject and marginalise him. The film points to the intolerance of the Muslim majority in Indonesia, a troubling phenomenon that continues into the present, as with the destruction of mosques belonging to the Ahmadiyah sect in the country in the 2000s, which is allegorically embodied in the film by the destruction of Dahlan's mosque.[14]

But the film also represents Dahlan as a person prone to making mistakes. Instead of glorifying his stature as a historical figure in Indonesian collective memory, the film portrays his image as a non-self-serving individual. In this mode of representation, the sustained extreme darkness that obscures Dahlan's face has a particular significance. Particularly in the last scene, Dahlan and Noor come to terms with their conflict in sheer darkness. Arguably, the intensified graphic darkness hiding their faces de-emphasises the veneration of these figures, particularly Dahlan. Yet, it also gestures to ways of portraying the Prophet Muhammad (through absence/concealment) and thus could be seen as a contradictory technique which attempts to avoid the over-veneration of human figures while simultaneously exalting them as being akin to the Prophet. Of course, the special treatment of the Prophet when it comes to depiction itself comes close to the very deification that the taboo was ostensibly aimed at avoiding.

Apart from that, the extreme graphic darkness here directs our attention to salient auditory information: the words they are saying to each other. Faozan maintains that he also wants to direct the audience to focus on the interpretative potentials of the scene rather than on the stars' faces by employing this intensified visual darkness strategy. He remarks:

> To me, when I read that scene, what comes to my mind is honesty. So, when they reconcile, they become honest with each other, open with each other. In this case, the faces of the figures are not of paramount importance. I want to erase the images of the famous actors Lukman Sardi and Agus Kuncoro on the screen because I want the audience to remember their words, their conversation – not their faces.[15]

This shift of emphasis from 'what's being visualised' to 'what's being said' echoes Michel Chion's point in *Film, a Sound Art* in which he makes a case about the gravity of words in the cinematic arts:

> It has long been evident for the sound film that … with noniconogenic narration, something important is at stake. It gives a particular density and gravity to what is spoken; it creates a specific real time, that of the storytelling accompanied *only by our own individual mental imagery* … In each case *the absence of visualization of what the character recounts focuses our attention* as if to say, 'Get serious, listen up, you have to remember this'; it's as though the cinema were laying itself bare and saying, 'it is all you get, words with the image of the person saying them, believe them or not.'[16]

Interestingly, from a local cultural viewpoint, the way in which intensified visual darkness functions in this scene also parallels how shadow is perceived aesthetically in the art of *wayang kulit* (Javanese shadow puppetry). As Jan Mrázek has indicated in *Phenomenology of a Puppet Theatre: Contemplations on the Art of Javanese Wayang Kulit*, shadow and darkness in *wayang kulit* do not only work to support storytelling, but they can also function as a *visual silence* that activates other senses, other than sight, as well.[17] In this respect, intensified graphic darkness helps us to orient our attention to auditory information more so than to visual information.

Cerita Cibinong (*Story from a Village*, Nia Dinata, d.p. Ical Tanjung, 2007)

But there are other functions of intensified visual darkness that do not come into play in the scene from *Sang Pencerah*. For instance, the use of extreme darkness to imply horrific, deplorable actions or events. In the opening scene of *Cerita Cibinong*, Esih (Shanty) comes home rather early from work. When she enters her *rumah kontrakan* (a humble rented house), she notices something odd happening in the bedroom. She walks toward it and discovers that her male partner Narto is forcing her teenage daughter Maesaroh to give him fellatio. Shocked and furious, Esih immediately reacts by threatening to kill him there and then. But he reacts more aggressively than her; he drags her out of the bedroom to the living room, launches a fist at her, and strangles her mercilessly. Seeing her mother in danger, Maesaroh picks up a wooden chair and hits him in the head with it from the back. He falls instantly. Eshi and Maesaroh leave the house at once without even packing their belongings. This highly intense moment, which sets the tone for the film's subject matter, namely the trafficking of women and sexual abuse, is presented visually in preponderant darkness.

Intensified darkness in *Cerita Cibinong* is created by applying the available light shooting technique. The main illumination comes from two sources: a household tungsten light bulb in the bedroom and an exterior lamp outside the house. The first shot (medium shot), which is the longest shot in the sequence, demonstrates the extreme visual darkness immediately. In conjunction with staging, the director activates the dark-to-light and light-to-dark strategy. Esih opens the door and places her jacket behind it. The only lighting available comes in from the opened window, leaving Esih in a pool of blackness (see Figure 5.8). When she hears the voice of Narto instructing Maesaroh 'Just do the usual stuff; don't you get it by now?', the camera pans right to reframe her as she tiptoes into the bedroom. Opening the bedroom curtain, she shrieks 'Narto, what are you doing to my child?' A small light bulb provides the illumination, which takes the form of compositional lighting in a two-part hierarchy (see Figure 5.9). The foreground is rendered in blackness while the background – as Narto and Esih are staged in depth – is

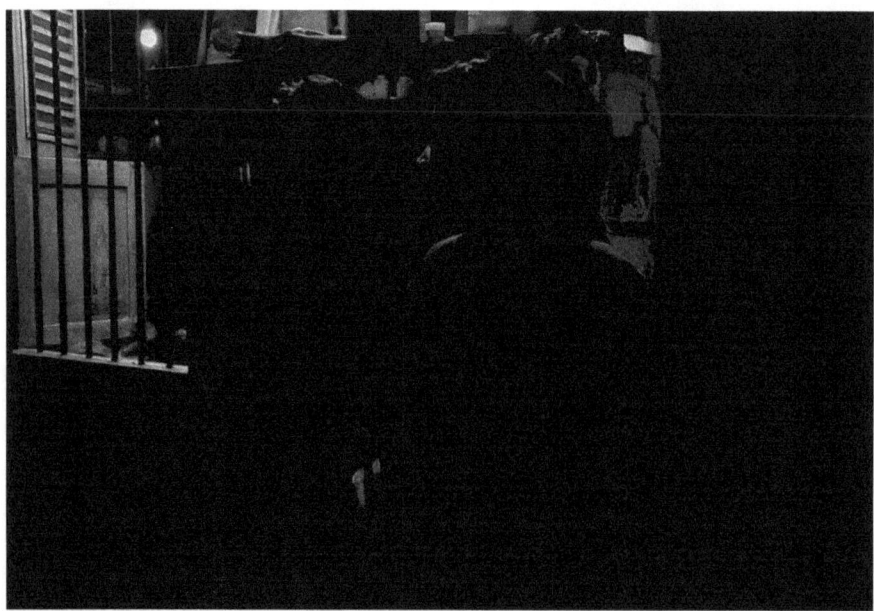

Figure 5.8 *Intensified visual darkness permeates the opening shot of a critical scene in* Cerita Cibinong

Figure 5.9 *A single source lighting technique helps intensifying visual darkness in the most violent scene in* Cerita Cibining

lit to direct our attention to the action. But later on, Esih closes the curtain. As a result, we can only see their shadows wrestling with each other as Esih yells hysterically, 'I will kill you, Narto!' After sustaining this framing for a considerable length of time, Narto comes to the foreground as he drags Esih out of the bedroom; then, the camera pans left.

Now, we have the light coming in from the exterior of the house shining on Esih, but very minimally. This exterior lighting barely shows Esih struggling to escape from being strangled by Narto. As the scene intensifies, Narto threatens to kill Esih if she doesn't shut her mouth. Both figures are presented in a medium shot lit by the single source lighting that creates a stark silhouette effect (see Figure 5.10). By the time Narto severely chokes her, Maesaroh puts an end to this life-threatening situation. In the medium shot showing Maesaroh, the key light from the window and the small light in the bedroom orient our attention to her. When the mother and daughter escape, they search for protection. Overall, in this twelve-shot scene, we see a dynamic interplay between several stylistic features to render this highly intense segment: intensified visual darkness, the intricate staging of actors, framing and sound.

On its basic level, the extreme visual darkness pursued in the scene produces a verisimilar depiction of the story space. Additionally, it denotes the time of day, which is late at night. But space overrides time in this particular case. The extremely low-light condition denotes the setting where the

Figure 5.10 *A striking silhouette effect created by the single source lighting technique as the violent scene reaches its crescendo in* Cerita Cibinong

characters live. Earlier in the film, when Esih comes home from work in the morning, the room is just as dark as when she comes home early. So, to some extent, the intensified darkness applied here tells us something about their socio-economic milieu: a lower-income household. Accordingly, darkness connotes their poor urban background. In conjunction with this purpose, darkness helps produce a gloomy atmosphere stemming from the economic and social situations of the family. Nia *Dinata*, the film's director, has stated many times that she wanted to present the story as it is happening in the poor urban community of Cibinong, not in the glamorous parts of Jakarta. Therefore, shooting darkly in the low-light condition was imperative to her storytelling goal. She remarks:

> It is intentional that the film is made so dark [*gelap*] because [we] want to present the real situation, as it is. The atmosphere over there [Cibinong] is indeed gloomy. The streets of Cibinong have no bright illumination, so when we get to see the exterior scenes, on the streets at night, the actual street lamps are just like that, all gloomy.[18]

Again, this idea of shooting in low-light situations indicates a strong desire to deliver the story with an unpolished, true-to-life feel. This realistic tone goes hand in hand with Dinata's explicit political mission for the film. Intensified visual darkness here functionally works to paint a realistic veneer to the story of the repressed female underclass in urban Indonesia. The thematic weight of the film projects Dinata's political mission to raise awareness about child abuse and child trafficking in post-Suharto Indonesia. This realism of social condition, for this reason, becomes an important goal to which the valorisation of intensified darkness contributes.

Another functional layer follows this atmospheric function: the suggestion of violence and the elicitation of imagination. By presenting the scene in extreme visual darkness, auditory information becomes an important guide for the viewer in experiencing this unbearable scene. When Esih enters and walks slowly in the dark inside the house, off-screen sound (i.e., the dialogue between Narto and Maesaroh) draws our attention to what's currently happening in the bedroom:

> Narto: Just do the usual stuff; don't you get it by now?
> Maesaroh: But I am sleepy, *kang*! (Sundanese for 'older brother')
> Narto: Come on, just for a little while![19]

This auditory information signals to us that Narto is demanding that Maesaroh serves him sexually. Dialogue unfolding off the screen on the right side of the frame pulls us to the bedroom, which is cued by the sound coming from the right speaker. But once Esih is inside the bedroom, she closes the curtain, and the camera doesn't track in to give us full access to the confrontation. Rather, it stays outside in the dark while the interplay of shadows and light, plus the sound, offer us cues that Esih and Narto are engaging in a fist fight.

At this point, the suggestive function of intensified visual darkness takes effect. The scene's distant framing, static camera position, staging in depth, the characters' action with regard to the curtain and the sound of Esih's hysterical shouting – all these contribute to the activation of what Julian Hanich calls the aesthetic of suggested horror, outlined in Chapter 1.[20] Although this scene doesn't involve a masked serial killer or a predatory alien entity that we typically find in slasher or thriller films, in many ways, this scene embodies the horrific element of violently immoral action. This event would repulse the viewer had it been presented in a fully direct and visible manner. Of course, it would still repulse the viewer even if the viewer only needs to imagine it; however, the degree of impact vis-à-vis repulsion is presumably more attenuated than having it shown directly. Receiving fellatio from a thirteen-year-old girl is immoral and illegal. Dinata and Ical Tanjung, the film's director of photography, were faced with a creative problem: how to present this repulsive scene without directly showing it. This strategy of intensified visual darkness was arguably chosen so that they could suggest that fellatio was being performed by Maesaroh without having to show it directly. This stylistic decision also worked as a pre-emptive tactic to avoid censorship from the Indonesian Censorship Board (LSF). If the scene were presented openly and directly through a track-in camera movement, close-ups and bright lighting technique, it might have never passed the Indonesian censorship board without being cut severely. Apart from this, the stylistic handling powerfully leaves dignity to the female character as well.

Finally, intensified visual darkness also offers us a range of interpretive cues such that a larger thematic meaning can be attained. The realism of the film's representational mode, enhanced by the darkly lit images, provides a crucial ingredient for foregrounding the film's theme: the helplessness of women in the male-dominated society of post-Suharto Indonesia. To address the wider social context, the film's use of darkness may invoke the idea that despite the promises of reform after the fall of Suharto in 1998, Indonesian women and girls continue to be subjected to exploitation and abuse. In particular, women from the lower classes who do not receive proper education are subjected to trickery and manipulation. Abuse can also come from people who are close to their victims. Moreover, it happens at home – in the dark – when no one is watching. Metaphorically speaking, stories of child sex abuse and trafficking are systemically kept in extreme darkness. Because sexuality is a taboo subject even in post-Suharto Indonesian society, sex abuse that involves underage girls is even more repressed in the public debate.

Intan Paramaditha argues that the film shows the filmmaker's ambivalent imagination vis-à-vis female sexuality in post-Suharto Indonesia.[21] On the one hand, she contends that Dinata and her creative collaborators imagine Indonesia as a nation free from paternalism; on the other hand, she imagines it as a quite unenlightened nation.[22] It is possible that the extreme visual darkness applied in this scene supports Dinata's ambivalent imagination of Indonesia as channelled through the film's handling of the subject matter. This stylistic strategy is in line with Dinata's mission articulated earlier. She hopes that after watching the film, the audience will be inspired to try to make a change, however small, for the betterment of Indonesian women.[23]

But the functional capabilities of this extreme visual darkness are not limitless. For instance, this stylistic strategy is much less aimed at producing pictorial effects here. Because atmospheric social realism is very important to the film's mission, that is, to present the story as authentically as possible, providing a graphic spectacle would be intrusive to that objective. Indeed, unlike the sequence from *Sang Pencerah*, intensified visual darkness in *Cerita Cibinong* works to suggest a realistic presentation of story events and, in particular, to suggest sexual violence. In the former, intensified visual darkness enhances the atmosphere of conviviality, but at the same time aims to foreground a spectacular graphic effect, which is concomitant to the film's overt visual stylisation. While some other functions for this lighting technique do emerge in *Cerita Cibinong*, its use for spectacular pictorial effect is largely suppressed to enable its primary, realist function to be foregrounded, which is concomitant to the film's subtle visual stylisation.

WHY NO FEAR OF THE DARK?

How come all these developments in Indonesian film lighting have been able to flourish only in the post-1998 era and not earlier? Firstly, the media landscape in Indonesia since the fall of Suharto has changed the ways in which the film industry is run. During the New Order era, the commercial film sector was mostly run by private enterprises that produced films in a very cheap and quick way in order to secure profits. In the early 1990s, the film industry experienced a period of *mati suri* (coma), as I have discussed in Chapter 1, forcing these companies to cross over to television. Since 1998, a new generation of filmmakers has been able to enter the film industry with greater ease than in the previous era. As I have explained, the film industry in the times of Suharto's New Order regime was governed by the professional association KFT (Ikatan Karyawan Film dan Televisi Indonesia/Indonesian Film and Television Workers League), which was an arm of the government and which acted to impede the younger generation from entering the industry. When the regime changed, these stringent rules were eradicated – except for the censorship law.

These new filmmakers established creative companies to produce television advertisements but also expanded into making movies. They brought new approaches to film production, including fresh approaches to cinematography. Believing that these novel approaches have been very successful in bringing Indonesian film audiences to Indonesian movies, the old major production companies are now accommodating the new generation's filmmaking styles. They do this by financing their films. Yet creative control mostly still resides with the new generation's companies.[24] For that reason, there is more openness to stylistic exploration and experimentation in the film industry today.

Secondly, technological changes have also provided Indonesian filmmakers with wider avenues for creative exploration. Working across a spectrum of budgets, Indonesian filmmakers, in general, may not have the same level of logistical resources as their Hollywood counterparts. But for those working on projects financed by major production companies, a sumptuous budget can give access to international standard film and digital cameras and lighting equipment. Riri Riza, as a representative of the younger generation of Indonesian filmmakers, notes that since the 1990s, Indonesian filmmaking has been catching up with the latest developments in technology. Especially with the availability of digital data cameras, he argues, shooting with minimal lighting has become a more viable option, and Indonesian cinematographers have been grabbing this opportunity.[25] As I have indicated in the introduction of this chapter, shooting in low-light situations has been enabled by technological development in various areas of filmmaking – from highly sensitive digital camera sensors to on-set monitoring devices.

Thirdly, it is likely that contemporary trends in transnational cinematography have influenced the ways in which post-Suharto-era cinematographers approach lighting and embrace intensified graphic darkness. According to a study by James Cutting and his colleagues examining the evolution of Hollywood films, the degree of luminance has decreased significantly over the years.[26] In other words, contemporary Hollywood films are much darker than their predecessors. Cutting et al. have discovered that this tendency toward darkness cuts across many genres, including fantasy.[27] Cutting's account may be limited because they looked at the total luminance (overall level of brightness) in the examined films but failed to specify whether this decrease in brightness has to do with the increase of low-key lighting applications. Having said this, this trend toward overall darkness is detectable in contemporary film and television cinematography. Dramatic and even comedic American serialised programmes produced and streamed by content providers like Cinemax, HBO, AMC, USA Network and Netflix have become visually darker over the years.[28] Shows like *The Knick* (Cinemax, 2014–15), *Game of Thrones* (HBO, 2011–19), *Better Call Saul* (AMC, 2015–22), *Mr. Robot* (2015–19) and *Ozark* (Netflix, 2017–22), for example, exemplify this trend toward extreme graphic darkness. On Australian television, even the second-longest running soap opera *Home and Away* (Seven Network, 1988–) has embraced a darker lighting style in recent years.[29] Apart from the advent of digital camera and digital monitoring technology during production and colour grading software during post-production that permit low-light shooting and the rendering of intensified dark images, the switch to HDTV or even 4K UHD TV technology from analogue television broadcast enables cinematographers to keep the high contrast dark looks of their shows intact.[30]

To add to that point, Indonesian filmmakers of the post-Suharto era are also close observers of transnational film and television works, especially Hollywood films. Faozan Rizal, for instance, has noted that American cinematographers like Conrad Hall and his high-contrast dark lighting style in *Road to Perdition* (Sam Mendes, 2002) have been an inspiration, along with European baroque paintings.[31] Ical Tanjung has also expressed how vital the cinematography of neo-noir films like David Fincher's *Se7en* (d.p. Darius Kondji, 1995) is to his artistic sensibility as a cinematographer who embraces visual darkness rather than avoiding it.[32] Though the extent of influence of Hollywood cinematography on Indonesian lighting practices needs to be further investigated, it is possible that trends in global filmmaking have inspired post-1998 filmmakers as well.

These factors clearly cannot capture the intricate complexity of factors that have facilitated the changes to post-New Order cinematography, which includes this characteristic use and valorisation of intensified graphic darkness. However, it is worth noting that this stylistic development, especially in regard to the pursuit of intensified graphic darkness, is distinctive to the post-Suharto era. It was nearly impossible for the cinematographers during the Suharto regime to pursue this technique because of the industrial and political structures that hampered their use of such innovative stylistic gestures.[33] So, the post-Suharto era has been an exciting period precisely because of the qualitative increase in low-key lighting application and, with that, the complexified functions of this mode of lighting thanks to the circumstances under which Indonesian cinematographers currently work, which allow them to pursue more creative possibilities.

VALORISING A MULTIVALENT UNDERSTANDING OF DARKNESS

As a final point, I want to reflect on the implication of the multiple functions of the intensified visual darkness strategy for the cultural meaning of darkness. In some ways, the pursuit of intensified graphic darkness in contemporary Indonesian film lighting practices and the multiple effects it yields also underscore the *positive attributes of darkness*, which often get obscured due to the prevalent negative associations of darkness.

Since medieval times in the West, darkness has been culturally constructed as a metaphor for 'pagan obscurantism—deviancy, monstrosity, diabolism'[34] as well as for witchcraft, devilry, heresy, sin and death.[35] But this negative construction of darkness can be found in Southeast Asia, too. In Indonesia specifically, the negative construction of darkness has been perpetuated by stories of horrifying creatures that lurk at night. Mothers warn their children about the *kuntilanak* – a vengeful female monster with a hole on her back who appears at night to kidnap little children who behave badly. Whether in rural areas or big cities, doors are closed and curtains are drawn as soon as night falls to prevent evil spirits or monstrous creatures like *kalong wewe* and *memedi* from kidnapping family members.³⁶ Darkness is therefore linked with this myth of abduction. Cultural anthropologist Hildred Geertz argues that this kidnapping story is reproduced as part of family education to stay at home during the night.³⁷ Accordingly, these narratives may suggest that fear of the dark persists transculturally.

But recent studies by cultural historians and cultural geographers have shown that there is another side to darkness that is often forgotten. Cultural historian Craig Koslofsky, for instance, has shown that night in early modern Europe is 'diabolical' where one can find, on the one hand, 'nocturnal devotion, honest labor, drunken excess and indiscipline' and, on the other hand, 'conviviality, intimacy, experimentation, excitement and spectacle'.³⁸ Medieval Christian ascetics have explored more positive qualities of darkness as well. Darkness was a valuable avenue for contemplation. In other societies, darkness has also been explored as a positive dimension for retreat and sociality. The Japanese novelist Junichiro Tanizaki in his book *In Praise of Shadow* describes how darkness and shadow are essential to the creation of tranquillity. This book delineates his counter-aesthetic to the over-illumination phenomenon in Japan brought by modern lighting technologies in the first half of the twentieth century. In Indonesia, the Hindu Balinese practise *Nyepi*, which means *total silence*. In this ritual, devotees cut off all lights and avoid using electrical illumination and technology for a day to contemplate and meditate at home. Cultural geographer Tim Edensor has also demonstrated that certain lighting practices in our contemporary urban society have emphasised the positive attributes of darkness. Having studied cultural events and modes of urban illumination that emphasise darkness, such as the Fête des Lumières in Lyon and the Lighting Master plan in Eindhoven, he suggests:

> Dark space also offers possibilities for developing more *intimate, convivial* and *focused forms of communication, unhindered* by multiple visual distractions that sidetrack conversation and storytelling.³⁹

These examples suggest that these positive meanings of darkness can also be found transculturally.

The ways in which low-key lighting is transformed into a multifunctional device, especially through the valorisation of the intensified visual darkness strategy, have activated a multivalent understanding of darkness, as described by the cultural geographers mentioned above. This multivalent understanding entails both positive and negative meanings, which the cases of *Sang Pencerah* and *Cerita Cibinong* analysed above have also demonstrated.

By leveraging intensified visual darkness, Indonesian filmmakers are widening the capacity of this form of low-key lighting beyond merely evoking mystery or 'weird or intense moods' as it is traditionally conceived in the rhetoric of lighting and cinematographic manuals.[40] As such, they have innovated the cinematography of Indonesian films by exploring low-key lighting techniques that, for a long time, had been considered 'taboo' or 'risky' and applying those techniques in a wider set of genres and scenes to achieve a variety of aesthetic functions. By doing so, they have tapped into the creative possibilities of what Conrad Hall calls 'the art of underexposure' – the practice whereby correct or proper exposure is sacrificed to allow more expressive, pictorial, suggestive and thematic forces to 'come to light'.[41]

Notes

1. Patrick Keating, ed., *Cinematography* (New Brunswick, NJ: Rutgers University Press, 2014), p. 190.
2. Ibid., p. 185.
3. From the perspective of cognitive film theory, Carl Plantinga argues further that facial expressions onscreen not only communicate emotion, but also activate and strengthen affective responses of the viewers such as empathetic responses. He makes a strong case that emotional contagion and affective mimicry are the bases that make empathetic responses possible when viewers watch the human face in film, specifically in moments that he describes as the 'scene of empathy'. Carl Plantinga, 'The Scene of Empathy and the Human Face on Film', in *Passionate Views: Film, Cognition, and Emotion*, eds Carl Plantinga and Greg M. Smith (Baltimore: Johns Hopkins University Press, 1999), pp. 239–55.
4. For a pictorial explanation of the Zone System, see the following webpage: https://fstoppers.com/education/how-use-ansel-adams-zone-system-digital-world-417047.
5. *Fill light* is a light source that brightens the shadows created by the key light without being so bright as to eliminate those shadows. See Keating, ed., *Cinematography*, p. 188.
6. *Backlight* is a light positioned behind the subject, pointing toward the camera. It typically produces a rim of light around the subject, separating the foreground from the background. See Keating, ed., *Cinematography*, p. 186.
7. Rapi Films – the production company/studio behind *Pengabdi Setan* – screened the film to a selected audience before they officially released it. As part of their marketing and promotional campaign, Rapi Films decided to film the audiences' reactions when they were watching this scene, among others, and uploaded it to YouTube to generate more buzz around the film's scariness level. This audience's reaction footage has been viewed 1.7 million times on YouTube as of 15 August 2022. The video is available via the following URL: https://www.youtube.com/watch?v=4PRKAdLFu4k.

8. *Jihad* is understood in Islam as the efforts or struggles on behalf of Allah.
9. Merle Calvin Ricklefs, *A History of Modern Indonesia Since C. 1200* (Redwood City, CA: Stanford University Press, 2001), pp. 194–5.
10. Faozan Rizal, e-mail interview, 31 December 2014.
11. Ibid.
12. Ibid.
13. Eric Sasono, 'Islamic Revivalism and Religious Piety in Indonesian Cinema', in *Performance, Popular Culture, and Piety in Muslim Southeast Asia*, ed. Timothy P. Daniels (New York, NY: Palgrave Macmillan, 2013), pp. 45–75.
14. 'Islamic Sect Ahmadiyah Faces Ban in Indonesia', *BBC News*, 21 April 2011, http://www.bbc.com/news/world-asia-pacific-13155924.
15. Faozan Rizal, e-mail interview, 31 December 2014.
16. Michel Chion, *Film, a Sound Art* (New York, NY: Columbia University Press, 2009), pp. 401, (emphasis added). Noniconogenic voice or narration refers to a film sequence in which a character is telling a story. But we are shown only the storyteller and his or her audience; thus, no other supplementary images are provided to us to illustrate or follow up on the narration. This type of narration relies on language alone, and it often occurs during a pivotal moment of the character's journey in the story.
17. Jan Mrázek, *Phenomenology of a Puppet Theatre: Contemplations on the Art of Javanese Wayang Kulit* (Leiden: KITLV Press, 2005), p. 345.
18. *Perempuan Punya Cerita/Chants of Lotus*, DVD Commentary by director Nia Dinata and writer/producer Vivian Idris (Jakarta: Kalyana Shira Films, 2007).
19. Original Indonesian:
    Narto: *Mainin yang biasanya aja … Masak gak ngerti juga sih!*
    Saroh: *Saroh ngantuk, kang!*
    Narto: *Ah, sebentar aja, Roh!*
20. Julian Hanich, *Cinematic Emotion in Horror Films and Thrillers: The Aesthetic Paradox of Pleasurable Fear* (New York, NY: Routledge, 2010), p. 109.
21. Intan Paramaditha, 'Cinema, Sexuality and Censorship in Post-Soeharto Indonesia', in *Southeast Asian Independent Cinema: Essays, Documents, Interviews*, ed. Tilman Baumgärtel (Singapore: NUS Press, 2012), pp. 69–88.
22. Ibid., pp. 85–6.
23. DVD commentary by director Nia Dinata and writer/producer Vivian Idris. *Perempuan Punya Cerita (Chants of Lotus)*, directed by Nia Dinata (Jakarta: Kalyana Shira Films, 2007). DVD.
24. See Krishna Sen and David Hill, *Politics and the Media in 21st Century Indonesia: Decade of Democracy* (London: Routledge, 2011); Thomas Barker, 'A Cultural Economy of the Contemporary Indonesian Film Industry' (PhD Thesis, National University of Singapore, 2011).
25. Riri Riza, 'Diskusi: Sejumlah Masalah Sinema Digital Indonesia', Salihara Arts Center, 25 April 2013, video, 2:17:48, https://www.youtube.com/watch?v=r23P9r-Ey-0.

26. James E. Cutting et al., 'Quicker, Faster, Darker: Changes in Hollywood Film over 75 Years', *I-Perception* 2, no. 6 (2011), pp. 569–76, https://doi.org/10.1068/i0441aap.
27. In fact, from the sample of films Cutting et al. analysed (160 films, made between 1935 and 2010), *Harry Potter and the Deathly Hallows: Part 1* (David Yates, 2010) proves to be the darkest. Ibid., p. 574.
28. Kathryn VanArendonk, 'TV Dramas Are (Literally) Too Dark', *Vulture*, 31 August 2016, https://www.vulture.com/2016/08/tv-dramas-are-literally-too-dark.html.
29. Michael Lallo, 'Will Someone Please Turn on the Lights: Why Have TV Dramas Literally Become so Dark?' *The Sydney Morning Herald*, last modified 9 September 2016, https://www.smh.com.au/entertainment/tv-and-radio/will-someone-please-turn-on-the-lights-why-have-tv-dramas-literally-become-so-dark-20160909-grchcu.html.
30. On this technological aspect of the darker lighting style for television content in the 2010s, see, for example, Matthew Dessem, 'Why TV Shows Are (Literally) Darker Than They've Ever Been', *Slate Magazine*, 29 June 2016, https://slate.com/culture/2016/06/cinematographers-from-game-of-thrones-jessica-jones-and-better-call-saul-on-why-tv-shows-are-darker-than-theyve-ever-been.html; and Rachael Bosley, 'Better Call Saul: Darkness Gains Dimension', *American Cinematographer*, 26 June 2017, https://ascmag.com/articles/better-call-saul-darkness-gains-dimension.
31. Faozan Rizal, e-mail interview, 1 January 2015.
32. Tanjung, 'Belajar Jadi Penata Kamera Ulung Seperti Ical Tanjung'.
33. For a detailed discussion about this topic, see Krishna Sen and David T. Hill, *Media, Culture and Politics in Indonesia* (Melbourne; Oxford: Oxford University Press, 2000); David Hanan, 'Innovation and Tradition in Indonesian Cinema', *Third Text* 24, no. 1 (2010), pp. 107–21; Katinka van Heeren, *Contemporary Indonesian Film: Spirits of Reform and Ghosts from the Past* (Leiden: KITLV Press, 2012); and Thomas Barker, *Indonesian Cinema After the New Order: Going Mainstream* (Hong Kong: Hong Kong University Press, 2019).
34. Galinier J. et al., 'Anthropology of the Night: Cross-Disciplinary Investigations', *Current Anthropology* 51, no. 6 (2010), p. 820.
35. Craig Koslofsky, *Evening's Empire: A History of the Night in Early Modern Europe* (Cambridge: Cambridge University Press, 2011).
36. Clifford Geertz, *The Religion of Java* (Glencoe, IL.: Free Press, 1960).
37. Hildred Geertz, *The Javanese Family a Study of Kinship and Socialization* (Prospect Heights, IL: Waveland Press, 1989).
38. Koslofsky, *Evening's Empire*, p. 5.
39. Tim Edensor, 'Reconnecting with Darkness: Gloomy Landscapes, Lightless Places', *Social & Cultural Geography* 14, no. 4 (June 2013), p. 463.
40. In the discourse on motion picture lighting, John Alton, who's considered to be one of the most influential noir cinematographers in Hollywood, has famously stated: 'Where there is no light, one cannot see; and when one

cannot see, his imagination starts to run wild. He begins to suspect that something is about to happen. *In the dark there is mystery.*' John Alton, *Painting with Light*, With a New Foreword by John Bailey (Berkeley and Los Angeles, CA: University of California Press, 2013), p. 44 (emphasis added). In cinematographic and film/television production handbooks, the connection between low-key lighting and mysterious/sinister mood has been articulated in the following publications: Blain Brown, *Cinematography: Theory and Practice* (Oxford: Focal Press/Elsevier, 2012), p. 69; Bruce Mamer, *Film Production Technique: Creating the Accomplished Image*, sixth edn (Boston, MA: Cengage Learning, 2014), p. 294; and Nikos Metallinos, *Television Aesthetics: Perceptual, Cognitive, and Compositional Bases* (Mahwah, NJ: Lawrence Erlbaum Associates, Inc., 2009), p. 242.
41. *Visions of Light: The Art of Cinematography*, directed by Todd McCarthy, Stuart Samuels and Arnold Glassman (Kino International, 1992).

CHAPTER 6

Production Design and Diegetic Detail

In this chapter, we'll shift our attention to the role of production design in revamping the visual style of Indonesian cinema. I contend that in the post-Suharto era, filmmakers have leveraged production design to refurbish the look of Indonesian films by further exploring two techniques of production design for interior and exterior shots: *location shooting* and *location designing*. Location shooting is the practice of shooting the film at an existing location rather than in the studio on a soundstage or backlot. Location designing is the practice whereby an existing location is modified to meet the demand of the story whether through analogue means such as set decoration and set dressing or through computer-generated imaging methods. Combining these two techniques, contemporary Indonesian filmmakers not only go to existing locations and make use of these real places, but they also *design* these locations by decorating and dressing them or even building entirely new sets on site. This dual pursuit of location shooting and location designing has impacted the level of visual details that post-1998 Indonesian films put on display.

As we've seen in Chapter 4, this current practice of production design is different from that of the Sukarno and Suharto eras. In the production design of the Sukarno period, location shooting was mainly exploited for capturing exterior scenes, while studio filming was the primary method for capturing interior scenes. Although the practice shifted gradually in the Suharto period – that is, towards location shooting for capturing both exterior and interior scenes – there was a discrepancy in how details were prioritised in the production design of that era: while macroscopic details were attained, microscopic details were not extensively elaborated. In post-Suharto films, by contrast, there is as much attention to the microscopic details as to the macroscopic ones. Just to be clear about my terminologies, macroscopic details refer to the 'big picture' elements of production design and art direction such as natural landscape, architecture, automobiles and so on; microscopic details refer to the minuscule components that include props, fabric, furniture, technological gadgets, paper, typeface and so forth.

I further argue that the accumulation of these microscopic details in post-Suharto production design serves multiple aesthetic functions. But the highly foregrounded aesthetic functions are mainly aimed at achieving a more intense 'reality effect',[1] in Roland Barthes's terms, or at achieving specific pictorial goals such as emphasising visual composition (e.g., colour and geometric patterns) or accentuating specific traits of local-regional cultures of Indonesia.

To explore these arguments, I am going to analyse the production design of two films from the post-1998 era, namely *Laskar Pelangi* (*The Rainbow Troops*, Riri Riza, prod. des. Eros Eflin, 2008) and *Sang Pencerah* (*The Enlightener*, Hanung Bramantyo, prod. des. Allan Sebastian, 2010). These films have been chosen for several reasons. Firstly, they both represent the efforts by a new generation of filmmakers to revamp the period drama genre. *Riri* Riza and *Hanung* Bramantyo are two of the most prolific filmmakers of period films in the post-Suharto era whether as directors or producers.[2] Secondly, although the production design and art direction of these films exemplify the norm of mixed mode location shooting and location designing in post-New Order filmmaking, each filmmaker approaches it differently. So, it will be illuminating to see the consequences of these different approaches for the accumulation of macroscopic and microscopic details in the films. Thirdly, these films have been selected because, even though they both are categorised as period dramas that showcase a visual ambition, the visual details yield different emphases of aesthetic functions. By comparing and contrasting the production design of these two films, we will see that some aesthetic functions are prioritised while others are curbed, thus supporting my argument for the bounded multifunctionalism of visual style in contemporary Indonesian cinema.

Like in the previous chapter on lighting, it will be helpful for us to get a sense of the major shift in production design practices in the post-Suharto era before we delve into our case studies.

Interlocking Location Shooting and Location Designing in the Post-Suharto Era

Production design has been strengthened in post-Suharto Indonesian cinema through a closer interlocking of the modes of location shooting and location designing. This strategy to bring the techniques of location filming and location designing closer together can be demonstrated by the period films made in the 2000s and 2010s.[3] Curiously, many of these films are set in various locations across the Indonesian archipelago and overseas. Examples here include, but are not limited to:

- *Marsinah: Cry Justice* (Slamet Rahardjo, prod. des. Berthy I. Lindia, 2000);
- *Pasir Berbisik* (*Whispering Sands*, Nan Achnas, prod. des. Frans XR Paat, 2000);
- *Ca Bau Kan* (*The Courtesan*, Nia Dinata, prod. des. Iri Supit, 2002);
- *Gie* (Riri Riza, prod. des. Iri Supit, 2005);
- *Kala* (*Dead Time*, Joko Anwar, prod. des. Wencislaus, 2007);
- *May* (Viva Westi, prod. des. Eros Eflin, 2008);
- *Sang Pemimpi* (*The Dreamer*, Riri Riza, prod. des. Eros Eflin, 2009);
- *Merah Putih* (*Red and White*, Yadi Sugandi, prod. des. Iris Supit, 2009);
- *King* (Ari Sihasale, prod. des. Budi Riyanto, 2009);
- *Perempuan Berkalung Sorban* (*Woman with a Turban*, Hanung Bramantyo, prod. des. Oscart Firdaus, 2009);
- *Darah Garuda: Merah Putih II* (*Blood of Eagles*, Yadi Sugandi and Connor Allyn, prod. des. Iri Supit, 2010);
- *Habibie dan Ainun* (*Habibie and Ainun*, Faozan Rizal, prod. des. Fauzi, 2012);
- *Atambua 39 Derajat Celcius* (*Atambua 39° Celcius*, Riri Riza, prod. des. Eros Eflin, 2012);
- *Soegija* (Garin Nugroho, prod. des. Ong Hari Wahyu, 2012);
- *Soekarno: Indonesia Merdeka* (*Soekarno*, Hanung Bramantyo, prod. des. Allan Sebastian, 2013);
- *3 Nafas Likas* (*Likas' Three Breaths*, Rako Prijanto, prod. des. Frans XR Paat, 2014);
- *Sang Kiai* (*The Clerics*, Rako Prijanto, prod. des. Frans XR Paat, 2013);
- *Gending Sriwijaya* (*The Robbers*, Hanung Bramantyo, prod. des. Budi Riyanto, 2013);
- *Pendekar Tongkat Emas* (*Golden Cane Warrior*, Ifa Isfansyah, prod. des. Eros Eflin, 2014);
- *Cahaya Dari Timur: Beta Maluku* (*We Are Moluccans*, Angga Dwimas Sasongko, prod. des. Yusuf Kaisuku, 2014);
- *Guru Bangsa Tjokroaminoto* (*Tjokroaminoto: Teacher of the Nation*, Garin Nugroho, prod. des. Ong Hari Wahyu, 2015);
- *Pengabdi Setan* (*Satan's Slaves*, Joko Anwar, prod. des. Allan Sebastian, 2017) and
- *Kartini* (*Kartini: Princess of Java*, Hanung Bramantyo, prod. des. Allan Sebastian, 2017).

In order to show how this interlocking principle between location shooting and location designing works, and the functions activated by this strategy, let's examine the production design of two of the popular films from the post-Suharto era: *Laskar Pelangi* and *Sang Pencerah*.

Examining Detailed Diegesis: Case Studies

Laskar Pelangi (*The Rainbow Troops*, Riri Riza, prod. des. Eros Eflin, 2008)

If there's one film that truly represents the reawakening of Indonesian film in the 2000s, it must be *Laskar Pelangi*. Attracting 4.6 million viewers upon its release in 2008, the film has become one of Indonesian filmmaking's success stories in the post-Suharto era.[4] *Laskar Pelangi*'s widespread popularity sparked optimism among Indonesian filmmakers that local films were capable of attracting a substantial local audience, despite the year-in-year-out domination of Hollywood products.[5] An adaptation of Andrea *Hirata*'s bestselling novel of the same title, the film was directed by Riri Riza based on a script written by Salman Aristo, supervised by Riri and producer *Mira* Lesmana.[6] As a box office hit, *Laskar Pelangi* cemented the reputation of Riri and Mira as filmmakers who strive to 'bridge idealism and commercialism' in feature film production, as Ekky Imanjaya has noted.[7] Since the pair's first collaboration on the film *Kuldesak* (1998), their production company Miles Films has risen to become one of the most respected film companies working in Indonesia today. I contend that this success has to do with their meticulous approach to film production – avoiding the habit and pitfalls of Suharto-era commercial filmmaking rationale: *filem asal jadi* (half-baked films). They invest a great deal of time, money and energy in every step of the production process, particularly during the preproduction phase. In addition to developing their script slowly and carefully, they also take research into the story's background and the characters' identities very seriously.

Building on this scrupulous work ethic, the production design for the film was conceptualised and developed rigorously. Location scouting is usually carried out before the completion of the final shooting script, and the tone of the film is discussed throughout the preproduction phase. Instead of using a location near the headquarters of Miles Films in Jakarta, which theoretically could stand in for Belitong – a small island on the coast of South Sumatra where the story is set – they shot the film entirely in Belitong. The novel *Laskar Pelangi* is partly a biographical account of Andrea Hirata's recollections of growing up in Belitong in the late 1970s. At the time, the island was mainly exploited for its tin. The mining company PN Timah – a nationalised company that was originally owned by the Dutch colonials – provided the main livelihood for the island's population. Hirata grew up in a small village named Gentong, so Riri and Mira didn't only use Belitong as its main location, but they also insisted on shooting the film in Gentong itself and several other areas nearby. Indeed, among the various factors that made *Laskar*

Pelangi appeal to contemporary Indonesian audiences – besides its status as an adaptation of a successful novel, strong ensemble casting and catchy original soundtrack by the popular rock band Nidji – is the fact that the film features Belitong as its main setting.

Before *Laskar Pelangi*, Belitung – as it was called then – was mainly known as a tin-producing island, and indeed this was the only fact that many Indonesians would have known about the island. Now, a simple Google search for Belitong uncovers a multitude of personal accounts – whether text-based, photographic or videographic – that document visits to the locations featured in the film.[8] Travel agencies have also exploited this aftereffect of the film by selling packaged tours to Belitong – usually advertised as *paket tour Laskar Pelangi* (*Laskar Pelangi* tour package).[9] The success of *Laskar Pelangi* and its impact on Belitong's tourism has also triggered the Indonesian government, especially the Ministry of Tourism and Creative Economy, to realise the 'the power and the economical [sic] potential of film tourism'.[10]

The film's achievement can be attributed to the ways in which production design is executed to fill the film with a high degree of accumulated details. How is this level of detail attained in the film? The first degree of detail is attained by shooting on location, but this is not all there is to it. Shooting the film in the exact location where the story is set does not automatically make the film so saturated in detail. Rather, it is the further augmentation and modification of that location that provides such detail. Thus, the location needs more designing to bring out the details for exterior and interior shots.

Based on my classification of details, we can consider this location choice a component of macroscopic detailing. There are three locations that are central to the film's plot: the Muhammadiyah school, the granite rock formation on the beach at Batu Berlayar and the neighbourhood convenience store *toko* Sinar Harapan. The town itself, although present in the film, is kept in the background. All of these central settings are shot on location in Belitong. For instance, the Muhammadiyah School, where the children of Rainbow Troops receive their education in the film, is located in Gentong. The granite rock formation is shot on the shore of Batu Berlayar; as a note, this location is quite central in the film because the name 'Rainbow Troops' is derived from the fact that these children visit this place after school, bonding together to look up at the sky and the rainbow that appears prominently. The *toko* Sinar Harapan is located in the town where the kids get their school supplies. It is also the place where one of the characters falls in love with the *toko* owner's daughter. So, all of these places permeate the film's texture with visual detail, which in this case takes the form of an isolated island far away from the hustle and bustle of the capital city, Jakarta.

But even though they shot these scenes in these existing locations, they also exploited the mode of location designing to the fullest extent. Set building, set decorating and set dressing figured prominently. Let's take the *toko* Sinar Harapan setting as a case in point. The physical *toko* itself was an existing structure, but Eflin and his art crew further designed this existing *toko* to achieve the look of a typical *toko kelontongan* (mom and pop store) in the 1970s.[11] The exterior shot displays the *toko* situated in a central location in Gentong; the *toko* is sandwiched in between other establishments in an existing strip of shops. The artistic team placed the signage Toko Sinar Harapan to add a visual identity to it. From the outside, we can already get the impression that it is a humble 'mom and pop' store of the sort that was so common in Indonesia before modern mini-market chains became ubiquitous in the 2000s.

When we enter the *toko*, other layers of details start to emerge. The shop is stocked with items that one could only find in an Indonesian *toko kelontongan*, selling anything from household appliances to sweets. Typical Indonesian household appliances are the *sapu lidi* (broomstick), *sapu rayung* (grass broom), wooden brush, kitchen utensils made of aluminium and rattan, *tikar* (rug) and other daily tools (see Figure 6.1). Although these props provide the basic signifiers of a *toko kelontongan*, they don't necessarily indicate the specific time period in which the film's main plot is set. It's the smaller objects that

Figure 6.1 *Typical Indonesian household appliances denote the interior of a* toko kelontongan *in* Laskar Pelangi

project a more detailed period visualisation. Among these objects, the most significant of all is the Rheumason package seen in the lower left of the shot (see Figure 6.2).[12] This tired-looking box is among many of the original versions of the objects used for the film that production designer *Eros* Eflin and his art department searched for, and he refused to simply use the contemporary version for the sake of convenience.[13] Inserting this Rheumason box into the shot is one of the important elements to particularise the period design of the film. It aptly demonstrates Dean Tavoularis's maxim, which I have cited in Chapter 3, about the significance of the specificity of props to intensify microscopic details in a period film. In this regard, Eros has not put just any kind of Rheumason box, but a particular Rheumason box graphically designed to match the brand's product identity as marketed in the 1970s. Another example of the microscopic detail in the film is the placing of a warning sign at the tin mining facility written in Dutch '*Verboden Toegang Voor Onbevoegden*' ('Prohibited Access for Unauthorised Persons') – connoting the vestiges of colonial administration in Belitong. All of these details are accrued, stacked on top of each other – as it were – throughout the film.

Another important setting that attests to the intensified exploration of location designing to complement location shooting is the school, Sekolah Muhammadiyah. In the novel, this autonomous Islamic primary school is located on the outskirts of Gentong. The school is extremely central to

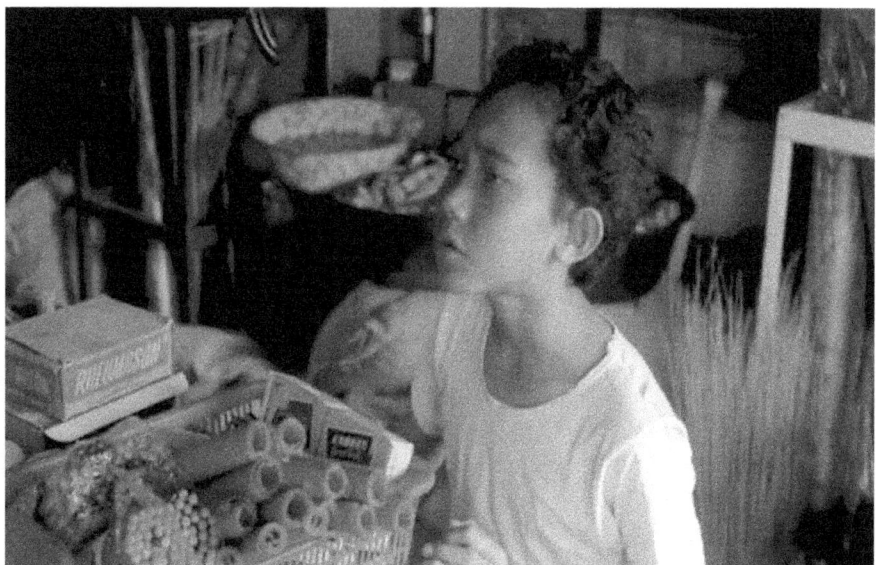

Figure 6.2 Smaller objects specify the time period of Laskar Pelangi, *most notably the 1970s Rheumason box*

the film, appearing prominently in many scenes. It is also shot on location in Gentong. But many buildings described in the novel have been renovated, redeveloped or demolished altogether, including the original Sekolah Muhammadiyah. The school has been transformed into a *madrasah* (Islamic school) with a permanent construction made of concrete. To get the setting back into its original state, Riri and Eros decided to build it completely anew on location.[14] But this presented the additional challenge of making this completely newly built school look as if it was a poorly made and dilapidated structure as the school looked in the late 1970s, based on Hirata's description in the novel. One of the ways in which Eros and his team accomplished this '*kesan tua dan kusam*' (old and worn out) look was to get second-hand material for building the school. Because they couldn't purchase used material anywhere in the area, they made a deal with the locals to trade their used wood for some new material – purchased by the art team from hardware stores in Belitong.[15] Even so, the worn-out look was not achieved effectively because they also needed to use new material for some parts of the school. Ultimately, they had to add an 'ageing effect' by adding *lumut* (green moss) on the walls, especially on a well in front of the school.[16] Additionally, the biggest marker that conveys the school's precarious condition is the gigantic piece of wood installed on the right side of the building to support the whole structure. Another 'effect' that the artistic team added was the repainting of the school's walls with earthy colours so that it looked as if it had aged naturally. This decision was also triggered by a discussion between Eros and cinematographer Yadi Sugandi who urged the production designer to choose those colours so that when sunlight hit the building, some details could be preserved in the image.[17]

This replica of Sekolah Muhammadiyah was built with care for over two weeks. It consists of two classrooms and a small teachers' office attached to it (see Figure 6.3). By going the extra mile to build the school from scratch, instead of using the existing renovated building, they utilised the mixed method of location shooting, set building and set decorating to bring the *suasana* (atmosphere) of the late 1970s Sekolah Muhammadiyah onto the screen.[18]

Microscopic details are further amplified in the interior design of the replicated school building. Set decoration and set dressing work together to bring out the texture of an unkempt school. The roof, made from rusty zinc instead of *genteng* (terracotta tile), is seen leaking tremendously during a torrential downpour. Chairs, desks and blackboards are all made from used wood, boosting the *kesan tua dan kusam* look. More evocative are the props arranged in the classrooms, which include a poster of 1970s *dangdut* star Rhoma Irama on the classroom wall. Moreover, in the teacher's office, 1970s-style folders

Figure 6.3 *A replica of the Sekolah Muhammadiyah, a central setting for* Laskar Pelangi, *built and designed on location in Gentong, Belitong*

and worn-out books clutter the space. These props significantly add more small-scale layers of detail to the film's period setting (see Figure 6.4).

What aesthetic functions do these details perform? Firstly, they are aimed at achieving a strong 'reality effect'[19] for the film. On this level, the selection of location and the manipulation of that location through set construction, decoration and dressing are primarily geared toward capturing a realism of environment and period. Shooting in Gentong gives a very authentic impression because the exteriors are so unique to that place. For instance, its white sandy beaches with rock granite formations are native to the island, and the film capitalises on these notable features extensively.[20]

Figure 6.4 *A poster of 1970s* dangdut *star Rhoma Irama (top) and 1970s-style paper folders (bottom)* add micro details *to Laskar Pelangi's* visual style

But it is also the authenticity of the period that is crucial to the film's aesthetic. Belitong of the late 1970s is depicted here with saturated details through, for instance, using Japanese automobiles from the period, *oma fiets* (Dutch-style bicycles) and signage that shows the vibrancy of the region due to the tin mining company PN Timah. More important is the Sekolah Muhammadiyah's very run down and underfinanced appearance. So, authenticity here is one of the prioritised goals, but to achieve this, Eros had to *rely on artifice*. By shooting the scene in a real location and further designing the location to look authentic with added effects such as green moss and certain colours of paint, Eros simulated the look of the original Sekolah Muhammadiyah. This artistic strategy is, in some ways, equivalent to the use of *effect lighting* in cinematography, in which artificial lighting fixtures are used to simulate naturalistic lighting. In this instance, location shooting combined with location designing worked to create an illusion of naturalism – as if the film had been shot at the original Sekolah Muhammadiyah in 1979.

Authenticity, however, isn't the only function that these details serve; they also play a vital role in transmitting crucial narrative information. In this sense, the Sekolah Muhammadiyah set and its hyper-elaborated interior details are designed to accentuate the abandonment of these enthusiastic and passionate children from low-income families in this part of Belitong. The details in Sekolah Muhammadiyah are often contrasted with those in the more upscale school financed by PN Timah. For instance, the minimalistic and unkempt look of the Sekolah Muhammadiyah is juxtaposed with the modern and pristine look of the Sekolah Dasar (elementary school) PN Timah. The interior of the latter is also filled with newer furniture, glass windows and clean sheets on the teachers' desks. Another important layer of detail when it comes to the contrast between the two schools is the utilisation of interior accessories. Where the Sekolah Muhammadiyah has a Rhoma Irama poster in its classroom (see Figure 6.4), the SD PN Timah has photographs of New Order-era President Suharto and Vice President Adam Malik (see Figure 6.5). This is congruent with the ways in which public schools were supposed to venerate the president and vice president in the classroom – a practice that persists until today. Between the two photographs, the national Garuda Pancasila emblem is framed centrally. These details certainly articulate the contrast between the two settings very sharply; one is a *kampung* school, neglected and

Figure 6.5 *Photos of New Order-era President Suharto and Vice President Adam Malik authenticate Laskar Pelangi's period specificity*

taken for granted, while the other is an upscale school, well-financed, well-furnished and taken much more seriously.

Another interesting detail that complements this contrast is the way in which the props are used by the characters. At the SD PN Timah, the teacher (Tora Sudiro) gives away electronic calculators to the students to be used during mathematics lessons. The next shot reveals the children of Sekolah Muhammadiyah using wooden sticks bundled together by an elastic band for solving math problems (see Figure 6.6). Last but not least, Sekolah Muhammadiyah's signage is hand-painted with the logo of the Islamic organisation Muhammadiyah whereas SD PN Timah's is made of steel. This pattern of comparison and contrast through elements of production design is developed throughout the

Figure 6.6 *Electronic calculators (top) and bundled wooden sticks (bottom) visualise a socio-economic contrast between two elementary schools in* Laskar Pelangi

film, providing cues to the economic gap in the provision of education. The set dressing of these two scenes activates what Jane Barnwell has called the polarisation function of production design – as discussed in Chapter 1 – whereby the opposition between the two worlds in the film's story is accentuated by interior design, accessories, utilities and so on.[21]

Another important function at play is the production of atmosphere. While underdressed and dilapidated, Sekolah Muhammadiyah's details seem to set a rather humble yet warm atmosphere, while the overdressed setting of SD PN Timah's classroom invokes a stuffy and cold atmosphere. The contrasting atmospheres of these two places also affect the activation of another equally important function of production design, namely to 'create an overarching style that gives expression to [a] film's subject matter and story'.[22] Therefore, sets, props and location are manipulated to give the film an appropriate tone congruent with its central theme: the basic right to education. The overarching style of the film may be discerned as a social realist approach. Nevertheless, this realism doesn't mean that it avoids all stylisation in regard to colour scheme and texture. Here, brown and pale blue colours are used throughout the film as a visual blanket that ties together the film's various settings. When bright colours such as red and white are presented in a scene, they usually connote contrast, as in the case of the setting of the SD PN Timah school against the muted colours (dark brown and grey) of the Muhammadiyah school. This is all put together to delineate one of the central issues that the film explores, namely the lack of access to education for the underclass and underprivileged children in Indonesia, expressed more explicitly in the closing title card citing an item in the Indonesian 1945 constitution: 'Article 31 Verse 1: Every citizen has the right to education.' By doing so, the filmmaker's political mission cannot be more apparent – a mission which is also represented visually through the filmmakers' commitment to a subtle, subdued stylisation of the film's look as opposed to an overt stylisation.

Despite the multifunctional possibilities activated by the accumulation of detail, not every possible function is activated in *Laskar Pelangi*'s production design. To single out one of these, the potential function of foregrounding pictorial composition is much less apparent. Even though shots of exteriors on location depict Belitong's real natural beauty, these shots only function denotatively to provide the background to the story and to give it a feel of location authenticity – the reality effect par excellence. Moreover, although the setting of Sekolah Muhammadiyah is multilayered with macroscopic and microscopic details to achieve an authentic impression, produce a low-key yet congenial atmosphere and materialise the film's thematic concerns, my assessment is that compositional considerations are less of a priority in *Laskar*

Pelangi. This is in contrast to the ways in which production design is explored in another period film that we will now turn our attention to: *Sang Pencerah*.

Sang Pencerah (*The Enlightener*, Hanung Bramantyo, prod. des. Allan Sebastian, 2010)

As I have outlined in the previous chapters, *Sang Pencerah* chronicles the life of Kiyai Haji Ahmad Dahlan (1868–1923), the founder of Muhammadiyah, Indonesia's second-largest Islamic organisation. *Sang Pencerah* begins with Ahmad Dahlan's birth (August 1, 1868) and ends on the day he establishes the organisation (12 November 1912). The film's plot revolves around Ahmad Dahlan's process of reforming Islam in Kauman, Yogyakarta. Made with a budget of Rp. 12 billion (US$ 1.3 million) – just slightly above *Laskar Pelangi*'s budget – the film was greeted with a mixed reception. Despite the fact that it managed to attract 1.2 million viewers after premiering on the Idul Fitri (Eid) holiday, 10 September 2010,[23] and managed to attract segments of society that rarely go to the cinema,[24] *Sang Pencerah*'s reception was rife with controversy. After initially being listed for several nominations at the annual Film Festival Indonesia, the initial selection committee was disbanded; as soon as the new committee was formed, it disqualified *Sang Pencerah* from the competition.[25] This controversy has effectively obscured the film's artistic ambition, which deserves critical inspection as much as its dramatic depiction of Ahmad Dahlan. One way the film achieves this artistic ambition is by exploring the creative potentials of production design and art direction.

Like *Laskar Pelangi*, macroscopic details through production design techniques also permeate *Sang Pencerah*'s visual style. However, how the macroscopic details are achieved in *Sang Pencerah* reveals a different approach from that of *Laskar Pelangi*. Shooting the film primarily on location in Yogyakarta is a choice that Hanung and his producer Zaskia Adya Mecca had already thought about before production commenced.[26] Their biggest challenge, however, was to transform contemporary Yogyakarta to appear as it would have in the late 1800s. To meet this challenge, production designer *Allan* Sebastian had to incorporate various art direction elements that aimed to portray this, even when he had to use other locations outside of Yogyakarta.

One of the most apparent results of this detail-oriented production design is the re-creation of Tugu Station. In this shot, we see native Javanese in their *batik sarung* and headscarves selling goods, trading farm animals, and disembarking from the train; meanwhile, the Europeans in their Victorian dress and safari jackets stride along the platform. Moreover, Dutch male business owners are conversing in a coffee shop at the station – designated for white Europeans only. From the costume and casting alone, these images denote the colonial-era Tugu Station. To enhance the atmosphere of the period, however, Sebastian incorporated other essential elements into the scene, including the use of the steam engine train, items that people carry at the station such as bamboo-woven baskets, *sepeda kumbang* (Dutch-style bicycles also known as *omafiets*) and other related items congruent to this 'late colonial' era of Java.[27]

Besides this, an important setting which was transformed to evoke 'the spirit redolent of the period',[28] – citing Barnwell's period design concept – is the central part of Yogyakarta itself. Today, Malioboro Street, which has become one of the busiest streets in contemporary Yogyakarta, is cluttered with shopping stalls and department stores. So, they had to find a solution to accomplish the evocation of the past. As a result, they used parts of the Botanical Garden in West Java to stand in as late-nineteenth century Malioboro Street. Last but not least, the *alun-alun* (city square) of Yogyakarta, which is the heart of the city where the sultan's palace is also located, is depicted in the shot as an open space with the original palace in the background. To construct this nineteenth-century *alun-alun*, they used the green screen technique, taking advantage of computer-generated imaging technology. What these settings project is Yogyakarta's past. Whether or not it is entirely accurate, on the surface, it gives the impression that we are in another era, which is different from the 2010s, or the Yogyakarta that we currently know. Important to note here is that, instead of using one location and designing this single location to enhance period realism as in the case of *Laskar Pelangi*, Hanung and Allan opted to use a number of different locations to construct what Stephen Prince has called 'the illusion of wholeness', which we have touched on in Chapter 3. Put differently, these various locations, supplemented by visual effects (CGI), are employed to represent one supposedly holistic setting, Yogyakarta, in the colonial era.

The most significant setting in the film is Ahmad Dahlan's *langgar* (mini mosque). This set was built and shot on location in Yogyakarta.[29] However, there is additional design work involved here. The *langgar* is decorated in an extremely minimalistic fashion. Apart from the signage that announces '*Langgar Kidoel KH Ahmad Dahlan*', there is nothing that signifies Islamic architecture. Adjacent to this *langgar* is Dahlan's residence, a humble *rumah joglo* (Javanese style house with a veranda), mainly used as a place for the students to gather to recite the Holy Qur'an. At nighttime, the *langgar* is mostly lit with *lampu sentir* (bamboo-based oil lamps), making the interior as well as the exterior staggeringly dark. This set dressing is very important for cinematographic considerations, supporting the valorisation of the intensified visual darkness strategy I described in the previous chapter.

How are the microscopic details foregrounded in the film? Set dressing plays a prominent role in bringing minute details into legible visibility.

Similar to the period films in the Suharto era discussed in Chapter 4, namely *R.A. Kartini* and *Sunan Kalijaga*, *Sang Pencerah* also opens with the *tedak siten* ceremony. This ritual of blessing the newborn baby – in this case Ahmad Dahlan – is held on the veranda. One of the first shots reveals the camera roaming around the space occupied by essential components of the ceremony. In this context, the *sesajen* (offering) becomes one of the highlighted objects of interest. Unlike in *R.A. Kartini* and *Sunan Kalijaga*, in which these offerings are scantily visualised, in this scene from *Sang Pencerah* they are specified in great detail (see Figure 6.7). In the upper left of the frame, we see the elaborated *nasi tumpeng* (pyramid-shaped rice) circled by seven hard-boiled eggs placed atop the vegetable *urab* (grated coconut salad). *Nasi tumpeng* is an irreplaceable item in *selametan* (Javanese rituals of celebration); it is the centrepiece of celebrations, including birthdays, personal achievements and business openings. Next to it, in the right hand section of the frame, we have an assortment of snacks, including *serabi* (Javanese pancake), *ketan* (sticky rice), *singkong* (cassava roots) and *kembang* (flowers). Finally, we also have an assortment of fruits, most notably bananas, which are an essential part of the offering package. In the next shot, we get a close-up of the baby's feet stepping on different plates of food, guided by his mother, symbolising the different stages of life. The rooster's cage is decorated with quintessentially Javanese ornaments such as the *rantaian sedap malam* (strings of tuberoses) (see Figure 6.8). This microscopic detailing of a cultural event is echoed in another

Figure 6.7 *Offerings as part of the Javanese* tedak siten *ceremony are visualised in microscopic details in* Sang Pencerah

Figure 6.8 Rantaian sedap malam *(strings of tuberoses) on the rooster's cage provides an essential layer of microscopic detail in* Sang Pencerah

Figure 6.9 *A hard-boiled egg with hand-painted graphic illustrations displaying a* wayang *character in* Soekarno: Indonesia Merdeka

biopic from Hanung, *Soekarno: Indonesia Merdeka* (2013) – also production designed by Allan. In *Soekarno,* the hard-boiled egg as a component of the offerings is rendered in more detail with a hand-painted graphic illustration displaying a *wayang* character (see Figure 6.9).

Other than these elements of ritual, another element of set dressing that is important to the patterning of a certain visual motif in *Sang Pencerah* is the use of a thin white muslin curtain. These curtains are common to Javanese houses because of their use in place of doors to separate different domestic spaces. On top of these layers, there are also props that are designed especially for the film, such as a copy of the Cairo-based Islamic political magazine *Al Manār*, the official charter of Muhammadiyah written in Dutch, the Javanese and Malay language newspaper *Retnodhoemilah*, a vintage world map and, most important of all, the old prints of the Holy Qur'an (see Figure 6.10). All these small-scale items particularise the diegetic environment of *Sang Pencerah* to a tremendous scale.

What aesthetic functions emerge from this elaborate rendering of visual detail? Besides creating a plausible physical environment for the film, such microscopic details also have an important role in 'switching on' the reality effect. In this case, they work to enhance the period verisimilitude. Shooting on location in Yogyakarta certainly lays down a basic layer of authenticity. But, as I have indicated earlier, Hanung and Allan exploited the mode of multiple-locations-shooting to construct the authentic colonial Yogyakarta demanded by the film's period identity. Because Yogyakarta has changed so much since 1868, they had to go to the Botanical Garden in Bogor to simulate Malioboro Street and to the Ambarawa Railway Museum to simulate two train stations in Yogyakarta in the late 1800s. Moreover, Allan and his artistic team had to transform existing locations for interior shots, such as the

Figure 6.10 *A copy of the Cairo-based Islamic political magazine* Al Manār *in* Sang Pencerah

Great Mosque of Kauman, the Kota Gede area and the Sultan's Palace, to look more like they did in that period.³⁰ They also needed to build the *langgar*, which will become more important in the film after it is destroyed by the followers of Kamaludiningrat, the leader of the Great Mosque. This on-screen authenticity is enhanced by the little details supplied by the props mentioned above. The magazine *Al Manār* written in Arabic, the Dutch language publication, and the Javanese and Malay language newspaper *Retnodhoemilah* all contribute to a pictorially convincing presentation of the era.

But these details also evoke the atmosphere of the *tempo doeloe* in Java (a specific historical timeline in the late colonial era between 1870 and 1914), which is characterised by a culturally mixed composition, comprising Javanese syncretic Muslim, Chinese, Dutch and Arabic elements. The *tedak siten* ceremony vividly indicates this syncretic culture, as the details bring out the local colour of the story's setting. The Dutch *kweekschool* where Dahlan is seen teaching Islam to the *priyai* students is also reflective of this culturally diverse Java, as they use Javanese, Indonesian, Dutch and Arabic at school (see Figure 6.11). By enhancing these minute details, the spirit of the age is captured in many of the scenes.

Similar to *Laskar Pelangi*'s main setting, the *langgar*'s frugal design is contrasted with the opulent décor of the Great Mosque. The latter's fully flamboyant design, with gold ornament and an elegant chandelier featured in the mosque's interior, is a testament to the Great Mosque's position as the

Figure 6.11 Javanese, Indonesian, Dutch and Arabic taught by Ahmad Dahlan at the kweekschool *in* Sang Pencerah

supreme authority in Yogyakarta's religious life. Dahlan's *langgar*, on the other hand, with its modest wooden construction and lit only by a few bamboo-based oil lamps, characterises the position of minority groups in the constellation of Islamic communities in Yogyakarta. Again, Barnwell's polarisation function comes into play here.

Besides all these functions, which are comparable to those activated in *Laskar Pelangi*, the achievement of visual impact through compositional means is also prioritised in *Sang Pencerah*. If we look at how the details of interior decoration and dressing affect the ways in which the film's frames are composed, a certain set of recurrent visual motifs can be discerned. The first compositional motif is the placement of *batik* cloth on a bamboo support. The first shot in which this visual appears projects a kind of abstract composition. After the destruction of Dahlan's *langgar*, this shot reappears, although this time, the batik cloth is all torn up and drenched in rainwater (see Figure 6.12). Clearly, the composition accentuates the shape of the *batik* cloth

Figure 6.12 *A piece of* batik *cloth hunged on a bamboo structure as a visual motif with symbolic significance in* Sang Pencerah

itself: straight-lined in the first shot and disfigured in the second shot. In this way, there is a symbolic significance to this patterning: it represents Dahlan's morale before his *langgar* was destroyed.

The second compositional motif is the foregrounding of window frames. This visual motif serves the film's storytelling pattern: it usually appears whenever a third party is eavesdropping on Dahlan or his wife. This visual motif reinforces the idea that Dahlan is constantly being watched and monitored by those suspicious of his teaching. Additionally, there is a compositional motif that works to create a frame within the frame, exemplifying what Bordwell has called *aperture framing*.[31] In this technique, an element of set dressing is used to further frame the characters inside the encompassing frame of the film. In *Sang Pencerah*, curtains are also used for aperture framing, which usually occurs when the image is rendered in deep-focus cinematography. Typically, in the foreground, we see characters grouped together, listening to another set of characters conversing in another room (see Figure 6.13). The half-opened curtains then frame the characters discussing business, staged in depth in the far background. While the visual motif involving windows serves a narrational objective, the aperture framing, I contend, performs a decorative function – patterned for maximising visual interest in the shots. These frame-within-the-frame compositions don't necessarily channel narrative information required to advance the plot, nor do they enhance our understanding of the characters. As a crucial element of location designing, the curtain's patterning in the images rather contributes to the film's compositional force.

Figure 6.13 *Window frames and steel bars function as* aperture framing *devices in the cinematography of* Sang Pencerah

Finally, the fine-grained details in the film's production design also help delineate thematic meaning. In this regard, the *langgar*, as the base for Dahlan's reform efforts, becomes the centrepiece in the film's elaboration of its theme. Most telling of all the scenes involving the *langgar* is the dramatic moment when an angry mob – provoked by the leaders of the Great Mosque – is depicted harassing Dahlan's family and eventually destroying the *langgar* while he is away (see Figure 6.14). This destruction of the heart of Dahlan's spiritual teaching has a symbolic significance, considering the context of religious life in post-Suharto Indonesia. Minority groups have faced social prosecutions and threats when it comes to practising their religious beliefs, even in this period of democracy. For example, in the mid to late 2000s, the minority Muslim group Ahmadiyah endured physical attacks, including the destruction of their mosques, because many dominant religious organisations believed that they had deviated from mainstream Islam.[32] Ahmadiyah followers believe that there was another prophet after Muhammad, and this belief became the greatest contributing factor to the rejection of Ahmadiyah among the Muslim majority in Indonesia. So, a cogent reading of this destruction of Dahlan's *langgar* in the film is that it expresses a veiled criticism of mainstream Islamic groups in Indonesia for allowing or even provoking such an intolerance.[33]

Viewed this way, Dahlan's *langgar* and his followers stand in as the minority, and the destruction carried out by the angry mob represents mainstream Indonesian Muslims' discrimination against Ahmadiyah and other religious minorities. Hanung has been vocal about his views on these issues and has said many times that the reason he wants to make this film is to introduce

Figure 6.14 *An angry mob destroys Ahmad Dahlan's* langgar *in* Sang Pencerah

Ahmad Dahlan to the new generation who may not know who this figure is.[34] However, a stronger reason, he claims, is to promote tolerance and to show that Islam is a peaceful religion – far from terrorism as it is often portrayed.[35] Of course, his intention does not always come about quite clearly; hence, the film became caught up in controversy.

Later in the film, the *langgar* is rebuilt, and Dahlan is able to continue his teaching, spreading his modernist views of Islam, which includes cooperating with both nationalist leaders and Dutch bureaucrats. It is doubtful whether the destruction of the *langgar* actually happened in the history of Muhammadiyah. In this view, Hanung's decision to have the *langgar* demolished in the film becomes an essential part of his mythologising of Ahmad Dahlan as an agent of change whose spirit of resilience was reinforced by the repression of his beliefs by the status quo, none other than his fellow Javanese Muslim compatriots.

Comparing and contrasting the potential functions of microscopic detail in the production design of these two feature films has bolstered my argument for a bounded multifunctionalism; that is, even though several functions are activated, not all of these functions emerge equally. Contingent upon the genre of the film, the mode of filmmaking, the context of the scenes and the theme that the film deals with, some functions will be prioritised, while others are deemphasised. There are competing demands that the production designer, cinematographer and director have to resolve throughout the film; some scenes require the prioritisation of atmospheric over compositional goals, while others put narrational clarity or plot advancement at the forefront of their objective. *Laskar Pelangi* and *Sang Pencerah* are both period dramas whose production design is geared toward achieving fidelity through microscopic details; nevertheless, despite their similar emphasis on achieving an authentic period atmosphere, presenting social contrast, and communicating theme, there is a notable difference in that *Laskar Pelangi* suppresses compositional impact so that its storytelling can unfold while *Sang Pencerah*'s emphasis on composition sometimes puts storytelling imperatives temporarily to the side, in order to foreground decorative images. In either case, these films showcase the process of visual stylistic transformation in Indonesian cinema through a creative bolstering of production design and art direction.

THE DEVIL IS IN THE MICROSCOPIC DETAILS

As in the previous chapter on lighting, at this point, we need to look into the circumstances that have facilitated these changes in production design in post-New Order Indonesian cinema and the motivations that have driven contemporary Indonesian filmmakers to intensify their use of detail.

Structurally, the Indonesian film industry has become an open field in the post-Suharto period. In the Suharto era, as I have described in Chapter 1 and Chapter 5, those who wanted to work in the industry as art directors were required to be a member of the government-controlled workers' league KFT. For any creative personnel – from director to cinematographer – to advance his or her career, it was necessary to go through years of apprenticeship. But the senior members of KFT were so powerful that younger filmmakers could not pursue their own film projects or assume higher-level roles in the film industry. This also applies to the art directors who had to work in more junior roles in art departments for many years. Furthermore, there was a certain insularity to the film industry, in the sense that it had a high barrier to entry; those who were related in some way to the film crew, talent or producers or who went to IKJ – the only film school in Indonesia at the time – had a much higher chance of being employed. After the collapse of Suharto's New Order regime, KFT was dissolved, and this structural change gradually opened up opportunities for people without such existing connections to other film industry professionals. Directors, cinematographers and art directors who have never gone to film school or who have worked in advertising, music video production and other fields outside of film are now able to enter the industry.[36] There are also those who have gone abroad for their filmmaking education.[37] Many directors also have their own production companies, even though the majority of them still rely on the old major production companies for funding or exhibition. Nevertheless, these shifting institutional conditions have brought in a creative environment that's more open and fluid.

This openness and fluidity have facilitated a myriad of artistic influences to enter the realm of contemporary production design practices. The directors and art directors of the Sukarno and Suharto periods mostly had a background in the theatrical arts, whether folk or modern.[38] For example, Usmar Ismail was a playwright and theatre director for the theatre group Maya before he became a filmmaker;[39] Djajakusuma was also actively writing stage plays before transitioning to become a film director;[40] and Teguh Karya was the founder and director of the modern theatre collective in Jakarta, Teater Populer.[41] More importantly, structural reform has affected the working relationship between directors and production designers. In the old system, art directors and cinematographers were more or less considered technicians, so their creative input was ostensibly very limited. In the new climate of filmmaking, production designers and cinematographers are considered creative collaborators – at least from the perspective of directors like Riri Riza and Hanung Bramantyo.[42] This collaborative working relationship has often spawned long-term collaborations on numerous films, as we can see from the multifilm collaborations between these directors and their production designers (Riri with Eros and Hanung with Allan) instead of merely engaging in a one-off project.

More significantly, what drives this creative transformation – particularly in regards to the intensification of period film design – is a desire to reclaim history as a powerful platform for pictorial storytelling. During Suharto's New Order era, the narrative of Indonesia's history was dominated and fabricated by the supporters of the regime, who made period films to tell stories filled with images that amplified the myth of Suharto and his role as the saviour of the Republic of Indonesia. Period films were, in a lot of ways, a government-controlled cultural vehicle for maintaining dictatorial supremacy and sustaining the regime's cultural hegemony. Since the fall of this authoritarian regime, the historical narration – to a certain degree – has become an open field. In this context, period film as a mode of cinematic narration provides a compelling opportunity for contemporary filmmakers to offer their alternative renderings or, re-readings, of the nation's complicated history. Perhaps this can explain why period dramas – especially biopics – have become one of the most explored genres in post-Suharto Indonesian cinema.

CONCRETISING THE MULTILAYERED AND MULTIFACETED INDONESIA

This creative transformation vis-à-vis production design has a broader significance to the ways in which Indonesia as a pluralistic nation is being imagined in the post-Suharto era. While the Suharto era cinema tended to be Jakarta-centric, underrepresenting the rich diversity of local-regional cultures, the post-Suharto era cinema embraces the specificities of these local-regional cultures to a certain degree. This move toward a more inclusive form of filmmaking is also imperative because even in the post-Suharto era, which is characterised by decentralisation, the ways in which these local-regional cultures are represented in national media are still demonstrably superficial. Indonesian national television, for instance, tends to present these sub-national cultures primarily in terms of their traditional 'performance forms'.[43] What's at stake in this presentational symptom is the oversimplification of these communities that have long-held beliefs, values, social organising systems, non-verbal communication practices and non-performative artistic traditions into a set of clichés. Post-Suharto filmmakers, through production design, in this respect, attempt to demonstrate that it is not only performance forms that are central to these local-regional communities. By doing so, they cinematically envisage a much more multilayered and multifaceted Indonesia, which they consider to be *authentically* Indonesia – one whose face is no longer 'Jakarta-centric'.[44]

The fine-grained details articulated by the exploration of production design in post-Suharto films, particularly by heightening the exploration of location shooting coupled with location designing, furnish the visual style of contemporary Indonesian films with multilayered textural depth and compositional nuances. But the role of production design in Indonesian film has proven to be even more significant than I had initially expected. In addition to supporting the narrative, theme and visual style, production design conveys the local-regional cultural specificities of Indonesia. Consequently, this has complicated the notion of *Indonesian cinema* as a fixed concept because filmmakers in the different eras of Indonesian film history have explored production design in different ways to bring out the particularities of the diverse local cultures within this vast and pluralistic archipelago. As David Hanan argues, before we can ask 'What is Indonesian national cinema?' – a question that many scholars in the field have been grappling with – we need to ask 'What kinds of films have Indonesian filmmakers made that are unique to world cinema, which add to the dimensions of human experience?'[45] This chapter has helped in answering the latter question, as I have envisioned it. One important insight provided by my analysis here is that, through production design, the specifically Indonesian 'dimensions of human experience' in the context of local cultural practices are articulated more tangibly. Cultural artefacts in the forms of rituals and objects have their own meanings beyond serving the narrative. In the case of post-Suharto Indonesian films, this means that through concretising these local, regionally-specific human experiences via the art of production design, the concept of Indonesia itself as a nation is being re-evaluated, reimagined and contested.

But the revamping of visual style in post-Suharto cinema would not be as dynamic as it is without the foregrounded stylisation of the cinematic images by means of camera movement, which is the topic for the next chapter.

Notes

1. Roland Barthes, 'The Reality Effect', in *French Literary Theory Today*, trans. Tzvetan Todorov (New York: Cambridge University Press, 1982), pp. 11–17.
2. Riri Riza has made seven *period films* while Hanung Bramantyo has made eight in the 2000s and 2010s. Riri's filmography is available on the *Film Indonesia* website: http://filmindonesia.or.id/movie/name/nmp4b9bad6b2124b_riri-riza/filmography#.VjXnNryFElY.
   Hanung's filmography is available on the *Film Indonesia* website as well: http://filmindonesia.or.id/movie/name/nmp4b84ed860c823_hanung-bramantyo/filmography#.VjXomLyFElY.
3. I primarily use the label *period film* to cover a wide range of feature films that are set in the past, because it is more inclusive than the label *historical film*. The latter usually refers to dramatic feature films in which the main plot is based on actual historical occurrences or in which a dramatisation of the events unfold in such a

way that it becomes very central to the story, according to the definition offered by Natalie Zemon Davies. For the purpose of my analysis, I will use *period film* as an umbrella term. See Natalie Zemon Davis, *Slaves on Screen: Film and Historical Vision* (Cambridge, MA: Harvard University Press, 2000).
4. 'Sekuel "Laskar Pelangi" Dirilis 17 Desember', *Kompas.com*, accessed 11 October 2015, http://entertainment.kompas.com/read/2009/03/18/e174849/sekuel.laskar.pelangi.dirilis.17.desember.
5. Up until mid-2016, *Laskar Pelangi* enjoyed the prime status as the most viewed local film in Indonesia since its release in 2008. But its position has been superseded by *Warkop DKI: Reborn* (Anggy Umbara, 2016) in September 2016 as the film attracted 5 million viewers. Agniya Khoiri, 'Jumlah Penonton "Warkop DKI Reborn" Salip "Laskar Pelangi"', *CNN Indonesia*, 22 September 2016, https://www.cnnindonesia.com/hiburan/20160922122216-220-160247/jumlah-penonton-warkop-dki-reborn-salip-laskar-pelangi.
6. According to the *Film Indonesia* database, since *Kuldesak*, Riri Riza and Mira Lesmana have worked collaborated on twenty-seven film projects as of 2021 – including on films directed by other filmmakers. See 'Filmografi Untuk Riri Riza', accessed 31 August 2022, http://filmindonesia.or.id/movie/name/nmp4b9bad6b2124b_riri-riza/filmography.
7. Ekky Imanjaya, 'Idealism versus Commercialism in Indonesian Cinema: A Neverending Battle?', *Indonesian Cinematheque* (blog), 8 November 2009, https://indonesiancinematheque.blogspot.com/2009/11/idealism-versus-commercialism-in.html.
8. 'Sekolah Dasar Muhammadiyah – Laskar Pelangi (Belitung Island, Indonesia): Address, Point of Interest & Landmark Reviews', TripAdvisor, accessed 1 September 2022, http://www.tripadvisor.com/Attraction_Review-g668845-d4972215-Reviews-Sekolah_Dasar_Muhammadiyah_Laskar_Pelangi-Belitung_Island_Bangka_Belitung_Islands.html.
9. 'Paket Tour Laskar Pelangi Belitung 3D/2N', Bangkatour.com, accessed 1 September 2022, http://bangkatour.com/paket-tour-laskar-pelangi-belitung/.
10. Ekky Imanjaya and Indra Kusumawardhana, 'Film Tourism Indonesian Style: The Cases of Laskar Pelangi and Eat Pray Love', *Communicare: Journal of Communication Studies* 3, no. 2 (2018), pp. 9–28.
11. Rita Triana Budiarti and Salman Faridi, *Di Balik Layar Laskar Pelangi* (Yogyakarta: Bentang, 2008), p. 108.
12. Rheumason is a well-known brand of balm in Indonesia, used for relieving muscular injury and *kerokan* (drawing an oiled coin over the skin repeatedly until the skin turns bright red) to cure a symptom called *masuk angin,* which is a culturally specific belief about flu-related conditions caused by the entering of 'bad' wind into the body.
13. Budiarti and Faridi, *Di Balik Layar Laskar Pelangi*, p. 110.
14. Ibid.
15. Ibid., p. 111.
16. Ibid., p. 113.

17. Ibid.
18. This newly built replica of the school is currently one of the most visited sites in Belitong for tourism. See, 'Sekolah Dasar Muhammadiyah – Laskar Pelangi (Belitung Island, Indonesia)', TripAdvisor, accessed 1 September 2022, http://www.tripadvisor.com/Attraction_Review-g668845-d4972215-Reviews-Sekolah_Dasar_Muhammadiyah_Laskar_Pelangi-Belitung_Island_Bangka_Belitung_Islands.html#photos.
19. Barthes, 'The Reality Effect'.
20. The white sand also appears on the school's yard of Sekolah Muhammadiyah.
21. Jane Barnwell, *Production Design: Architects of the Screen* (London: Wallflower, 2004), p. 58.
22. Annette Kuhn and Guy Westwell, 'Production Design', *Oxford Dictionary of Film Studies* (Oxford: Oxford University Press, 2012), http://www.oxfordreference.com/view/10.1093/acref/9780199587261.001.0001/acref-9780199587261.
23. Naval Yazid, 'Year of the Flop for Indonesian Filmmaking', *Jakarta Globe*, 28 December 2010, https://web.archive.org/web/20110106035814/ or http://www.thejakartaglobe.com/entertainment/year-of-the-flop-for-indonesian-film-making/413989.
24. Adrian Jonathan Pasaribu of *Film Indonesia* explains that when the film was released, Muhammadiyah sympathisers – consisting mainly of Muslim clerics and *santri* (students at Islamic boarding schools) – flocked to the cinemas to watch the film. Some of them even came in rented pick-up trucks resembling bands of football supporters. Adrian Jonathan Pasaribu, e-mail interview, 5 November 2013.
25. A circulating rumour suggests that the film was rejected because of Hanung Bramantyo's allegiance to the organisation Muhammadiyah, hence the film's veneration of Ahmad Dahlan. This could have stirred conflict among different groups of Indonesian Muslims if the film had received the nominations. Added to this assumption is the notion that because the President of Indonesia at the time, Susilo Bambang Yudhoyono, was a supporter of rival Islamic organisation Nadhlatul Ulama, the nomination of *Sang Pencerah* could have created some political backlash for the FFI (Festival Film Indonesia). In the official explanation given by the FFI, however, they claimed that they had to reject the film due to its historical inaccuracy and dramatised portrayal of Ahmad Dahlan. Yet, it is widely believed that what has been presented as a purely content-related decision is ostensibly a case of politically-motivated sabotage, for reasons that are still unclear to this day. Nevertheless, the Bandung Film Festival awarded *Sang Pencerah* in seven categories, namely Best Picture, Best Cinematography, Best Art Direction, Best Director, Best Actor, Best Poster Design and Best Music. For a detailed discussion about this whole affair see Eric Sasono, 'Islamic Revivalism and Religious Piety in Indonesian Cinema', in *Performance, Popular Culture, and Piety in Muslim Southeast Asia*, ed. Timothy P. Daniels (New York, NY: Palgrave Macmillan, 2013), pp. 65–9.
26. Bagus Kurniawan, 'Di Balik Layar "Sang Pencerah" Bersama Hanung', *Detikhot*,

16 June 2010, http://hot.detik.com/movie/read/2010/06/16/155935/1379558/619/di-balik-layar-sang-pencerah-bersama-hanung.
27. This particular scene along with other scenes that depict Yogyakarta's train stations were in fact shot in Ambarawa – not Yogyakarta – at the Railway Museum. Cinematographer Faozan Rizal shot different parts of the museum from various camera angles to construct the illusion that the multiple scenes take place at Yogyakarta's Tugu Station and Lempuyangan Station.
28. Barnwell, *Production Design*, p. 80.
29. Fakhmi Kurniawan, 'Syuting Film K.H. Ahmad Dahlan Dimulai 21 Mei', *Detikhot*, 18 May 2010, http://hot.detik.com/movie/read/2010/05/18/174606/1359459/619/syuting-film-kh-ahmad-dahlan-dimulai-21-mei.
30. The accuracy of this recreation is certainly up for debate and subject to further investigation. Architectural historians of Java are more equipped to examine the exactness of the onscreen representations of these places.
31. David Bordwell, 'Visual Style in Japanese Cinema, 1925–1945', *Film History* 7, no. 1 (1995), p. 12.
32. See the following news reports: 'Indonesia Ahmadiyah Attack: Outrage over Victim Jailing', *BBC News*, 15 August 2011, http://www.bbc.com/news/world-asia-pacific-14526299; and 'Lagi, Masjid Ahmadiyah Dirusak Massa – Kompas. Com Megapolitan,' accessed 31 October 2015, http://megapolitan.kompas.com/read/2010/12/03/15534561/Lagi.Masjid.Ahmadiyah.Dirusak.Massa.
33. Sasono, 'Islamic Revivalism and Religious Piety in Indonesian Cinema', pp. 67–9.
34. 'Sang Pencerah (Behind the Scene)', Agus Taufik, 3 June 2011, video, 7:29, https://www.youtube.com/watch?v=dF6BsOApc3w.
35. Ibid.
36. Thomas Barker, 'A Cultural Economy of the Contemporary Indonesian Film Industry' (PhD Thesis, National University of Singapore, 2011), pp. 79–116.
37. Eric Sasono et al., *Menjegal Film Indonesia: Pemetaan Ekonomi Politik Industri Film Indonesia* (Jakarta: Rumah Film, 2011), pp. 128–30.
38. This topic is discussed in the following publications: Salim Said, *Shadows on the Silver Screen: A Social History of Indonesian Film* (Jakarta: Lontar Foundation, 1991); Gaston Soehadi, 'Teguh Karya: A Film Auteur Working Within a Collective' (PhD Thesis, Monash University, 2015); Satyagraha Hoerip, *Dua Dunia Dalam Djadoeg Djajakoesoema* (Jakarta: Dinas Kebudayaan DKI Jakarta & Institut Kesenian Jakarta, 1995); and Usmar Ismail, *Usmar Ismail Mengupas Film* (Jakarta: Penerbit Sinar Harapan, 1983).
39. Said, *Shadows on the Silver Screen*, p. 33.
40. Hoerip, *Dua Dunia Dalam Djadoeg Djajakoesoema*, p. 10.
41. Soehadi, 'Teguh Karya', p. 6.
42. Sasono et al., *Menjegal Film Indonesia*, p. 139.
43. David Hanan, *Cultural Specificity in Indonesian Film: Diversity in Unity* (Cham: Palgrave Macmillan Imprint, Springer International Publishing, 2017), p. 349.

44. 'Menggenjot Film Nasional Bermuatan Budaya Lokal', *Kompasiana.com*, 14 May 2017, https://www.kompasiana.com/irwanrinaldi/59068676ff22bde22c6cca38/menggenjot-film-nasional-bermuatan-budaya-lokal.
45. David Hanan, 'Moments of Renewal–Alternative Ways of Viewing Indonesian Cinema', *Jurnal Skrin Malaysia* 5, no. 2 (2008), p. 122.

CHAPTER 7

Camera Movement and Textural Reflexivity

How have filmmakers in the post-Suharto era explored the possibilities that camera movement as a stylistic device offers to revamp the look of Indonesian film? And how is this different from the way it was pursued in the earlier periods of Indonesian cinema history? We'll explore these questions in this chapter.

Contemporary Indonesian filmmakers have leveraged camera movement to dynamise the look of Indonesian films by intensifying the use of a wide range of mobile camera techniques. In particular, prowling or free-ranging camerawork has become a principal strategy among the variety of camera movement conventions explored by contemporary Indonesian filmmakers. Whether utilising a single technique or several techniques combined, free-ranging mobile shots are those with a vantage point that roams around, goes in/out and through the spaces, objects and other elements of the mise en scène fluidly and seamlessly. The free-ranging camerawork is often achieved by combining several techniques such as *circling/arcing shots, tracking shots (push-in and pull-back), handheld shots, booming and aerial shots* (including *drone shots*), *follow shots* (whether created on a dolly, Steadicam, Fig Rig[1] or other camera stabilisation gadgets) and *autonomous moves*.[2]

The exploration of this kind of prowling camerawork cuts across different genres and domains of Indonesian filmmaking. It can be found in horror, comedy and action films as well as independent art-house dramas. Films that explore this free-ranging camerawork include (but are not limited to) the following:

- *Kuldesak* (*Cul-de-sac*, Riri Riza/Nan Achnas/Mira Lesmana/Rizal Mantovani, d.p. Yadi Sugandi/Yudi Datau/Roy Lolang/Nur Hidayat, 1998);
- *Puisi Tak Terkuburkan* (*A Poet: Unconcealed Poetry*, Garin Nugroho, d.p. Winaldha E. Melalatoa, 1999);
- *Eliana, Eliana* (Riri Riza, d.p. Yadi Sugandi, 2002);
- *Beth* (Aria Kusumadewa, d.p. Enggong Supardi, 2000);
- *Janji Joni* (*Joni's Promise*, Joko Anwar, d.p. Ipung Rachmat Syaiful, 2005);

- *Catatan Akhir Sekolah* (*High School Diary*, Hanung Bramantyo, d.p. Suadi Utama, 2005);
- *Lentera Merah* (*Red Lantern*, Hanung Bramantyo, d.p. Roby Herby, 2006);
- *Quickie Express* (Dimas Djajadiningrat, d.p. Roy Lolang, 2007);
- *Maaf, Saya Menghamili Istri Anda* (*Sorry, I Got Your Wife Pregnant*, Monty Tiwa, d.p. Otoy Witoyo, 2007);
- *Perempuan Berkalung Sorban* (*Woman with a Turban*, Hanung Bramantyo, d.p. Faozan Rizal, 2009);
- *Keramat* (*Sacrosanct*, Monty Tiwa, d.p. Ucup Supena, 2009);
- *Madame X* (Lucky Kuswandi, d.p. Roni Arnold, 2010);
- *Lovely Man* (Teddy Soeriaatmadja, d.p. Ical Tanjung, 2011);
- *Sang Penari* (*The Dancer*, Ifa Isfansyah, d.p. Yadi Sugandi, 2011);
- *The Raid: Redemption* (Gareth Evans, d.p. Matt Flannery, 2011);
- *Something in the Way* (Teddy Soeriaatmadja, d.p. Ical Tanjung, 2013);
- *The Raid 2: Berandal* (Gareth Evans, d.p. Matt Flannery and Dimas Imam Subhono, 2014);
- *Cahaya Dari Timur: Beta Maluku* (*We Are Moluccans*, Angga Dwimas Sasongko, d.p. Robie Taswin, 2014) and
- *Siti* (Eddie Cahyono, d.p. Ujel Bausad, 2014).

The rigorous employment of free-ranging camerawork demonstrates the functional complexity of camera movement in post-Suharto cinema. Like any other type of camera movement, it serves multiple purposes. When employed, free-ranging camera movement can work to: orient the viewer in the diegetic space of the film; contribute to the film's visual rhythm; focalise the perspective of a character or an entity in the scene; produce a particular atmosphere; express the feelingful qualities of the space, character or event; imply an action or object and elicit viewer's imagination; facilitate meaning-making; enhance the authenticity of recording mechanisms as in found footage or fly-on-the-wall filming; and foreground the artifice of the mobile frame in its own right. As I have discussed in Chapter 3, Jakob Isak Nielsen, in his functional taxonomy of camera movement, refers to this last function as the *reflexive function*. With this function, camera movement can elicit a different type of engagement from the spectator, in addition to being plunged into the unfolding story.[3]

One of the features of this reflexive function, I argue, is the active valorisation of the *processual effects* of camera movement, which has emerged as a salient function in post-Suharto cinematography. As Tom Gunning argues, it is these processual effects that grant camera movement a unique set of functions as a distinctive stylistic device precisely because of its capacity to transform filmic space and time in a continuously progressing way, rather than chopping them up into several pieces through editing.[4] Because of this, camera movement contributes to making the post-1998 cinematic images replete with reflexive texture, which is one of the features of Indonesian contemporary cinema's stylistic complexity to reiterate my overall argument in this book.

To explore these claims, we will examine key scenes from three films: *The Raid: Redemption* (2011), *The Raid 2: Berandal* (2014) and *Janji Joni* (2005). But first, like in Chapters 5 and 6, let's survey the broad continuities and changes of camera movement in the post-Suharto era.

The Pluralistic Mobile Frame Forms and the Emergence of Free-Ranging Camerawork in the Post-Suharto Era

Post-Suharto cinema exhibits a pluralistic range of camera movement techniques. In addition to the usual palette of mobile frame techniques like the pan, tilt, push-in and pull-back, we can also detect other forms of camera mobility such as the arcing shot, the handheld shot, booming and aerial shot, active/passive follow shot and autonomous moves. The technology utilised to produce these mobile camera shots is also wide-ranging; we can find moving camera shots achieved by the Steadicam, dolly track, jib, crane and drone, as well as computer-generated imaging software. To get an immediate impression of a computer-generated camera movement stylising the visuals of post-Suharto cinema, let's consider this shot from *Kala* (*Dead Time*, Joko Anwar, d.p. Gunnar Nimpono, 2007). In a suspenseful scene, a mafia boss (Arswendi Nasution) intimidates the narcoleptic crime journalist (Fahri Achbar) during an interrogation scene. To get him to speak, the crime lord throws a burning cigarette in his direction. Instead of cutting from the shot of the boss throwing the lit cigarette to the shot of the journalist attempting to avoid it, we get a moving shot of the cigarette flying in the air in an extreme close-up (see Figure 7.1). This is a visual effect shot, where the movement of the camera is accomplished during filming, but the flying cigarette itself is accomplished in post-production through the digital intermediate (DI) process.[5] Alluding to the 'bullet time'[6] shot popularised by the science fiction film *The Matrix* (Lana and Lilly Wachowski, d.p. Bill Pope, 1999), this flying cigarette shot exemplifies the flourishing invigoration of camera movement in post-Suharto-era cinematography.

When applied in a lengthy shot, the free-ranging mode roams around the diegetic space, taking us to numerous areas in the setting, including the little pockets of the mise en scène that we couldn't identify had the camera stayed in one vantage point. A prime example of this is the opening scene's one-shot presentation (totalling six minutes and twenty-eight seconds) in

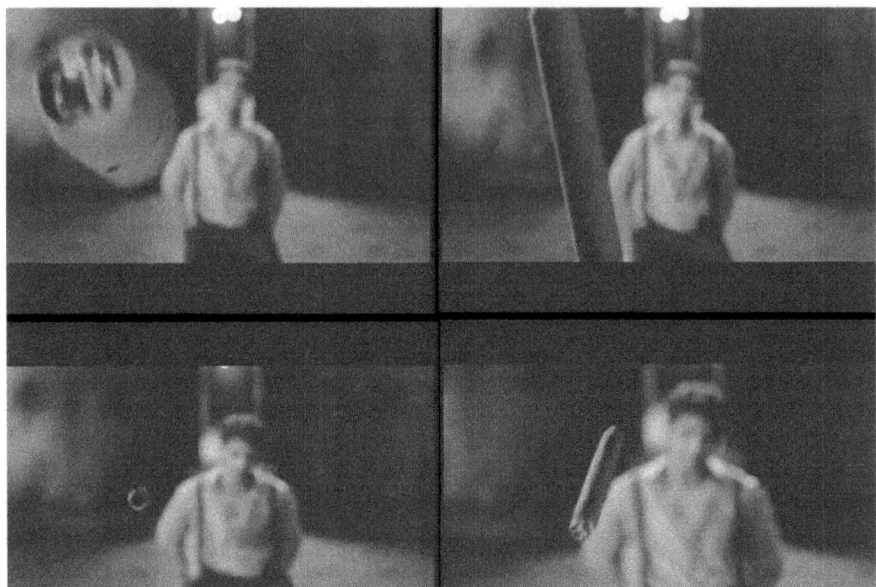

Figure 7.1 *A highly stylised shot involving a camera movement that follows a flying cigarette in* Kala

Hanung Bramantyo's *Catatan Akhir Sekolah* (2005), which I have described in Chapter 3. As a brief reminder: this one unbroken shot is accompanied by handheld camerawork that takes us to the different locales in the high school where the story is set. The free-ranging camera follows characters interacting with their classmates and pulling pranks on their teachers. It introduces us not only to the main characters but also to numerous sections of the school where narratively crucial events take place (see Figure 7.2).

To understand in more depth the aesthetic possibilities of the free-ranging camerawork as a salient stylistic strategy in post-Suharto-era cinematography, let's examine two mobile shots from *The Raid: Redemption* (which I will refer to as *The Raid 1*) and *The Raid 2: Berandal*, and one mobile shot from *Janji Joni*.

EXAMINING THE CONSTANTLY MOVING FRAMES: CASE STUDIES

The Raid: Redemption (Gareth Evans, d.p. Matt Flannery, 2011) and *The Raid 2: Berandal* (Gareth Evans, d.p. Matt Flannery and Dimas Imam Subhono, 2014)

The plot of *The Raid 1* revolves around an Indonesian elite police squad (SWAT) trapped inside a dilapidated apartment building belonging to the

Figure 7.2 *A free-ranging camera movement takes viewers into the interior and exterior spaces of the setting in one unbroken shot in* Catatan Akhir Sekolah

criminal mastermind Tama Riyadi (Ray Sahetapy). Ambushed and cornered on the fifth floor, the SWAT team decides to hide in one of the vacant rooms. But it doesn't take long for the gang members to find them. As the armed gangsters are trying to break in, the police officers must find an escape route. Rama (Iko Kuwais) comes up with an idea: make a hole in the apartment's floor so they can escape to the apartment one level below. So, he axes the floor until a hole is created wide enough for them to go through. The leader, Sergeant Jaka (Joe Taslim), jumps into the hole, but a group of armed thugs is already flooding the room below. Finding their sergeant in danger, Rama quickly drops himself through the hole to save Jaka. The camera then follows him immediately; it goes in and through the hole, plummeting into the other apartment room below, where Tama's criminal cronies are prepared to assault him from every corner. *The Raid*'s film crew calls this shot 'the Hole Drop shot' (see Figure 7.3).[7]

In the sequel, entitled *The Raid 2: Berandal*, Rama is now caught in the midst of a gang war. He's an undercover police agent who is trying to avenge his brother's death, and he's convinced that one of the leaders of these conflicting gangs is the murderer. But his real identity as a cop is on the brink of getting revealed. Suspected as a traitor, Rama is taken away by the gang members to be killed in a scrapyard outside Jakarta. On the way, however, Rama fights

Figure 7.3 The Hole Drop shot in The Raid: Redemption *in which the camera descends into and travels through a hole*

to wrestle himself free from captivity. Meanwhile, Eka (Oka Antara), who up to this point, functions as the right-hand man for the mafia boss, turns out to be an undercover police officer, too. Knowing that Rama is in trouble, he goes out of his way to rescue him. From this moment, a long sequence involving a complex set piece begins: a car chase through one of the busiest cities in the world, Jakarta.

This scene mainly uses a handheld camera style. The camera can move within the tight spaces of the car as Rama throws punches, kicks, and other stunts to defend himself. But the most memorable of all the mobile shots in this sequence, and in the whole film for that matter, is when the camera moves between cars in a smoothly flowing fashion. At the peak of the action, the camera gets behind Rama's position, exits out of the window, and pivots to the reverse direction of the moving car, providing a view of Eka's car coming toward it. Now, the camera floats on the highway for a couple of seconds before it enters Eka's car through the front seat and onto the back seat as it travels outside through the back-right window, supplying us with a view of a gang member sniping at Eka from the rear. To differentiate this shot from the one mentioned above, we can call it 'the car-to-car flyover shot' (see Figure 7.4).

These two cases demonstrate the free-ranging camerawork I described at the beginning of this chapter perfectly. When the filmmakers go through all the trouble to explore the continuously flowing shot, facilitated by the camera hand-over technique, taking the resources of more than two camera operators and a few gadgets, while they could have opted for exploit-

Figure 7.4 *The car-to-car flyover shot in* The Raid 2: Berandal *in which the camera exits the first car, floats on the highway and then enters the second car*

ing the resource of editing, one wonders what these camera moves are intended to accomplish. Put differently, what range of functions do they play?

Let me begin by pointing out which functions these mobile shots clearly do *not* activate. These shots obviously do not work as optical or affected POV shots, using Nielsen's focalising functional categories, outlined in Chapter 3. In the first scene – also known as the Hole Drop scene – the move inside the hole may slightly tease the focalising function without necessarily taking over the character's point-of-view. This is because the main character Rama, whose perspective of the action is central to the film's plot, has already jumped inside the hole. Could it be that this is the POV shot mediating another character behind him? I argue that the invoked POV function doesn't get switched on here because there are no lurking characters or entities whose presence requires invocation.

In the car-to-car flyover shot, the moving frames do not represent any character's point-of-view either because the flyover quality of the shot is non-anthropomorphic. That is to say that the floating camera moment is not a visual representation of any character's action. None of the characters have the superpowered ability to elevate above the highway or fly into another moving vehicle, despite the fact that they can leap into the air and kick.

The other function that isn't activated here is the *abstract* function. According to Nielsen's theory, the *abstract* function of camera movement is at play when the camera moves 'suggest abstract ideas and concepts'.[8] For instance, when a mobile shot acts as a visual metaphor. Although these films are replete with cues to facilitate meaning-making in relation to the theme of institutional corruption in post-Suharto Indonesia, these cues are conveyed mostly through dialogue and acting. In these action-driven scenes, there's hardly any dialogue, and acting is mostly concentrated on the *pencak silat* acrobatics.

Arguably, the baseline function that is activated by the two cases is pacing. In this case, these carefully executed mobile shots contribute to the film's visual rhythm. The set pieces and fighting scenes in both of *The Raid* films are handled exclusively in handheld shots accomplished on the Fig Rig system. Working together with the hard-edged up-tempo electronic music composed by Linkin Park's Mike Shinoda, these handheld shots give us a sense of urgency and franticness. The film's Indonesian title, *Serbuan Maut*, connotes a sudden rushing, fast-paced rhythm of action, which is forcefully enhanced by the prowling handheld camerawork. The Hole Drop shot and the car-to-car flyover shot only support this hyperkinetic rhythmic pattern.

These free-ranging camera moves are also reflexive. Firstly, in the Hole Drop shot, in which the camera goes inside the hole, there is a sense in which the unique attribute of the moving camera is being foregrounded. As I've noted earlier in this chapter, this unique attribute has to do with the capacity of camera movement to transform the filmic space and time in a continuously progressing fashion. Tom Gunning points out this distinctive aspect of camera movement:

> Editing can analyze space, but it cannot progressively explore it; it can reveal new spatial aspects through change of angles, but does not show the continuous temporal process of transformation. Thus I would define the uniqueness of camera movement as *precisely this temporal and spatial process of exploration and transformation that occurs continuously on the screen, without being broken into discrete units*.[9]

The progressing journey into the deep hole in the set design of the Hole Drop shot is arguably something that the technique of editing cannot achieve because, as Gunning points out, editing would break the temporality and space into fragmented 'discrete units'.[10] Not only does this dropping camera move accentuate the craft of set design, it also offers a different kind of visual experience where the unfolding, unbroken process thereof becomes exactly its most central attraction.

Secondly, these shots are reflexive in the sense that they embrace the 'virtuosity of transport' quality of the mobile frame.[11] The camera in these shots clearly doesn't penetrate through a wall or any solid barrier. As such, these shots don't embody the 'impact aesthetics' that Geoff King has pointed out as one modality within the virtuosity of transport function.[12] Nevertheless, they still put on display the camera's ability to traverse distances and locations, and seamlessly go in and out of static and moving objects. These shots, in many ways, are aligned with the *single shot cinema* aesthetics that the Dutch documentary cinematographer and filmmaker Leonard Retel Helmrich has conceptualised and demonstrated in his body of works in which the hand-over camera technique is a prominent method that pushes film as a visual medium to its limit.[13] But they also have antecedents in older forms of mobile camera technique that hark back to the European silent cinema of the 1910s and 1920s. The fly-over and journey-through quality of these shots echo the riveting spirit of the virtuosic transport shots popularised by films like Benjamin Christensen's *Hævnens nat* (*Blind Justice*, d.p. Johan Ankerstjerne, 1916) or F. W. Murnau's *Der letzte Mann* (*The Last Laugh*, d.p. Karl Freund, 1924). As my historical stylistics of the mobile frame in Indonesian cinema has shown (Chapter 4), these types of mobile shots were barely present in Indonesian films before the 2000s. So, it isn't too outlandish to claim that with their innovative exploration of the free-ranging camera movement, the reflexive function figures significantly in action-driven films like *The Raid: Redemption* and *The Raid 2: Berandal*.

In sum, these mobile camera shots demonstrate my notion of bounded multifunctionalism at work in the complex visual style of contemporary Indonesian film. That is to say that not every possible function gets equal treatment when a stylistic parameter is employed. The free-ranging camera movement in the cases examined above fulfils certain tasks such as pacing, orientation and reflexivity, but deprioritises other functions like POV and abstract functions.

Janji Joni (*Joni's Promise*, Joko Anwar, d.p. Ipung Rahmat Syaiful, 2005)

Janji Joni is a romantic comedy about Joni (Nicholas Saputra), a film reel delivery guy working for a movie theatre in Jakarta. Joni is responsible for delivering the film reels to cinemas in Jakarta, safely and on time. But this job comes with challenges, including the daily fight with the heavy traffic congestion that plagues Jakarta. In one memorable lengthy sequence handled with the *long take* technique, Joni discusses the variety of moviegoers in Indonesia

Figure 7.5 *A roaming camera hovers over the different types of moviegoers in* Janji Joni: *the sexually aroused couple; the movie pirate; the film critics; and the 'perfectionist'*

(see Figure 7.5). Using first-person voice-over narration, Joni classifies ten types of *penonton film* (moviegoer):

1. *Penonton cari perhatian* (the attention-getter)
2. *Penonton piknik* (the excessive 'snacker')
3. *Penonton pacaran* (the sexually aroused couple)
4. *Penonton pembajak* (the movie pirate)
5. *Penonton spoiler* (the plot spoiler)
6. *Kritikus film* (the film critics)
7. *Penonton ponsel* (the cell phone user)
8. *Penonton tidur* (the sleeper)
9. *Penonton telmi* (the 'slow' on the uptake)
10. *Penonton perfeksionis* (the perfectionist)

This scene comes eighteen minutes into the film. The segment on the ten types of movie audiences is captured in one shot, and it runs for two minutes and fifty seconds. By employing the crane shooting technique, the camera hovers over exemplars of each of these moviegoer types who are watching a film inside the cinema where Joni works. It starts with the first type of viewer, the attention-getter, and then moves to single out an example of each of the abovementioned types of film viewers. By the time it gets to moviegoer type 10, 'the perfectionist', the camera tracks this viewer as he gets up from his seat and walks up the stairs to the projection box. He then confronts the projectionist, claiming that the images on the cinema screen are out of focus. Subsequently, he scorns the projectionist in a condescending manner, telling him that he's doing a terrible job while in fact the film projected is in complete focus. The two get into an argument, and 'the perfectionist' viewer demands a refund from the projectionist because he feels that his cinematic experience has been ruined by the allegedly out-of-focus projection.

The camera movement in this segment does several things at once. First, it *directs our attention* to each type of viewer according to Joni's categorisation. It *orients us in the space* of the cinema, but it also *points to the subjects* being discussed, i.e., the different types of audience members. This move-and-stop characteristic of the shot acts like a museum guide, showing and explaining the exhibits displayed in various areas of the museum. In this case, the exhibits are the members of the movie audience, and the museum is the *bioskop* (movie theatre).

A second purpose that the camera movement in this sequence serves is the *reflexive* function. The camera movement in this particular segment is reflexive in the sense that it foregrounds the *processual* dimension of the mobile frame – just like the mobile shots in the two scenes from *The Raid*. Working in tandem with the long take technique – through which the scene is captured and presented in one unbroken shot – the moving crane shot emphasises the journey of the vantage point from A to Z, uninterrupted. Why? For one thing, if it was purely for directing our attention, then the director *Joko* Anwar and the cinematographer *Ipung* Rahmat Syaiful, could have presented this segment in a series of cuts to single out each type of audience member. But choosing to use editing would have created a different visual effect, which might have taken away that processual prowess, and instead yielded a more dissecting or analytical impression. For another, employing camera movement in this entire shot demonstrates a degree of technical virtuosity. To achieve this shot in one uninterrupted lengthy take required a great deal of necessary preparation, from preparing the choreography of the camera operation to the rehearsal. When something didn't go well in the first take of filming the sequence, they needed to start from the beginning. Had they used the *coverage* method, whereby the scene could have been captured shot-by-shot – relying on the convenience of editing afterwards – it would have been much more readily controllable and efficient because if something went wrong, they would not have had to restart the shoot from the beginning.[14] This virtuosic dimension of reflexive mobile shots demonstrated by this segment from *Janji Joni* and the two scenes from *The Raid* activates a particular kind of viewer's engagement that Neil Harris has conceptualised as an *operational aesthetic*,[15] which I have elucidated in Chapter 3 and will elaborate at the end of this chapter.

The camera movement in this segment from *Janji Joni* is also reflexive in another sense: it signifies the intervention of the director's commentary. We can ask, again, why did Joko and Ipung bother to go through this hassle when they could have simply opted for editing? I contend that by employing an unbroken moving camera shot, Joko and Ipung foreground the artifice of camera mobility as a way to playfully articulate a commentary on the contemporary cinema culture of Indonesia. One piece of evidence that substantiates my claim for this authorial commentary comes during the moment in the segment when the camera stops at the moviegoer type number six: film critics. Curiously, this is the only time that the narrator-protagonist, Joni, elaborates on this type of moviegoer: 'Type number six: film critics. Now, I don't know if these are the film critics that genuinely want to review films or just to prove their point. For all I know, I'd never trust the words of film critics!' There's a degree of self-referentiality alluded to here: Joko was a professional film critic before he became a filmmaker. In fact, he was writing film reviews for the English-language national newspaper *The Jakarta Post* at the same time as he was developing the script for this film. When asked in an interview whether he was anxious that critics would dismiss *Janji Joni* – considering this is his first film and the fact that he was always a harsh critic of Indonesian filmmakers – his response was wryly similar to Joni's commentary in the shot: 'I never trust the words of film critics.'[16] We can take Joko's response as ironic or disingenuous. However, it shows how his state of mind seeps into the shots, and the camera movement visually enhances this intervention of the filmmaker's hand.

This shot also alludes to the kinds of films that address movie-going culture or film fandom (aka cinephilia). We can cite hundreds of films in world cinema that depict moments inside the movie theatre. But one particular example stands out: in Jean-Luc Godard's *Masculin Féminin* (d.p. Willy Kurant, 1966), the main character Paul (Jean-Pierre Léaud) is watching a film, but he gets upset about the film projection because, according to him, it is shown in the wrong aspect ratio. So, he walks up to the projection box and tells the projectionist to correct this mistake. In *Janji Joni*, the last audience type in Joni's list, i.e., 'the perfectionist', thinks that the projected film is out of focus; so, he gets up from his seat, leaves his girlfriend sitting next to him, and walks up to the projection box, too. Curiously, Joko admits that he has personally experienced this episode in his life. When he was an undergraduate student in Bandung, he went to a cinema, and during the screening, the projection stopped for ten minutes. He walked up to the projection box and confronted the projectionist. As it turned out, the film reel delivery boy had gotten into an accident, so he couldn't deliver the rest of the film reels on time.[17] That 'perfectionist' audience member in Joni's list of moviegoer types is based on Joko's own persona. It is this first-hand experience that actually inspired him to write the script for *Janji Joni* in 1999.

This reflexive engagement with camera movement and the authorial commentary isn't too farfetched if we consider Joko's trajectory as a self-taught filmmaker who has openly identified himself as a cinephile or, more precisely, a cinéaste – a film enthusiast who also makes films. Joko is passionate about film history – both Indonesian and international film history. As a testament to this passion, he has made films that allude to popular cinematic genres from horror to film noir. Joko also exhibits sheer enthusiasm for local film history, which is often neglected. His film *Pengabdi Setan* (2017), which we discussed in Chapter 5, is a reboot of a 1980 horror film of the same title and a manifestation of his passion for the locally-made exploitation films that were popular in the 1970s and '80s, but had been forgotten in the 2000s. As a final note, *Janji Joni* has been instrumental in setting off the proliferation of metafilms (films about filmmaking or the film world) in the late 2000s and 2010s. Some of these films include those that tackle behind-the-scenes stories, the hardship of film production or cinema culture in post-Suharto Indonesia at large. Some examples of these post-Suharto metafilms include: *Maaf, Saya Menghamili Istri Anda* (*Sorry, I Got Your Wife Pregnant*, 2007); *Keramat* (*Sacrosanct*, 2009); *Jakarta Maghrib* (*Jakarta at Dusk*, 2010); *Cinta Brontosaurus* (*Brontosaurus Love*, Fajar Nugros, d.p. Yadi Sugandi, 2013); and *Melancholy is a Movement* (Richard Oh, d.p. Yunus Pasolang and Halfian, 2015).

The Moving Parts of the Moving Frames

Now, we need to consider the pertinent factors that have permitted these changes in the development of camera movement in post-1998 cinematographic style. In general, the enabling circumstances that have facilitated the changes in other stylistic domains discussed in the study – production design and art direction, as well as lighting – have also played a role in enabling the transformations in the use of camera movement. These overarching factors would have to include technology, production culture, structural formation of the film industry, transnational trends, and socio-cultural dynamics. But the exact contours of each of these enabling factors are unique to camera movement. I will highlight two factors here: technology and transnational trends.

The proliferation of compact and lightweight consumer digital cameras in the 2000s has had an impact on filmmaking globally.[18] In Indonesia, these cameras have allowed filmmakers to incorporate camera movements, such as the handheld shot, that would have been too impractical to do on bulky 35mm film cameras. Eric Sasono and his co-researchers explain that many cinematographers relied on digital cameras like the Sony Digital Betacam, Panasonic Varicam, Sony CineAlta F900, Canon XLH1, Sony EX3, Sony F 32 and, the most popular of them all, the Panasonic P2HD in the early to mid-2000s.[19] By relying on these compact cameras, filmmakers have been able to go out shooting in a run-and-gun fashion, whether inside a cramped prison in Garin Nugroho's *Puisi Tak Terkuburkan* (*A Poet: Unconcealed Poetry*, d.p. Winalda E. Melalatoa, 1999) or through the deep slums of inner Jakarta in *Riri* Riza's *Eliana, Eliana* (d.p. Yadi Sugandi, 2002). These films also pioneered the adoption of the cine-transfer process whereby the video footage captured by the digital cameras is transferred to 35mm films for exhibition purposes.[20] But by the time high-end digital cinema cameras became accessible to Indonesian filmmakers to emulate the 'film look' – for instance, the Panasonic AG-AF100A or Arri Alexa – filmmakers bypassed this cine-transfer process by going digital entirely.[21] When cinema exhibitors converted to digital projection systems in the late 2000s – replacing film projectors with DCP (Digital Cinema Package) systems – shooting exclusively with digital cameras became the norm for Indonesian film production.[22] As these 'film look' digital cameras became the standard in the industry, mobility-support gadgets for these cameras came along as well. These stabilisation gadgets, namely the Fig Rig or the DSLR (Digital Single Lens Reflex) camera shoulder rig, have provided more opportunities for hyperactive mobile shooting, but with more pristine and stabilised images.[23] Unlike the shaky and jittery images produced by unsupported handheld techniques, shooting with these stabilisation instruments enables cinematographers to produce similar mobile images to those the Steadicam normally generates. As such, these gadgets provide Indonesian filmmakers with a more economical alternative to the cost-prohibitive Steadicam rig.

In addition to such economic and practical contingencies, shooting with digital cameras was also driven by aesthetic trends in transnational cinema. The influence of the Danish film movement Dogme 95, which advocated an unpolished aesthetic supported by the deliberate incorporation of Hi8 home video cameras, spread to Indonesia as well. The formation of iSinema by the new generation of filmmakers like Riri, Mira Lesmana, Nan T. Achnas, Yato Fio Nuala and others in 1999 reflected the non-conformist attitude of these filmmakers in the vein of Dogme 95. Their 1999 manifesto suggests that the do-it-yourself spirit of their Danish counterparts was highly relevant to the Indonesian context. The video aesthetic that Thomas Vinterberg and Lars von Trier had embraced in their influential Dogme films inspired Riri to shoot *Eliana, Eliana* (2002) with a Sony DV camera, just like Aria Kusumadewa in

Beth (d.p. Enggong Supardi, 2000) and Rudi Soedjarwo in *Rumah Ketujuh* (*The Seventh House*, d.p. Roy Lolang, 2002). Using the DV camera to their artistic advantage, these filmmakers were not only able to exploit the raw and unpolished look of video images produced by this prosumer camera, but also to capture the scenes in prowling handheld shots.

In commercial mainstream filmmaking, the influence of the *intensified continuity* paradigm is more palpable. Bordwell has argued that intensified continuity as a governing principle of contemporary filmmaking has an international baseline.[24] In other words, although initially developed in post-1960s Hollywood cinema, it has since become an international visual stylistic phenomenon. It's more than plausible that the free-ranging camerawork in post-Suharto cinematography has been influenced by the aesthetic of intensified continuity – of which the prowling mobile camera is one of the core traits.[25] Hollywood's presence in Indonesia has a long history; it stretches back to the 1900s when cinemagoing began to develop as a vibrant entertainment outlet.[26] In the early 1990s, the ubiquity of American films intensified due to the exhibition monopoly exercised by 21 Group, which catered to the interests of Hollywood movie distributors.[27] Future research should be dedicated to further investigating the degree to which the intensified continuity aesthetic is present in post-1998 cinematic visual style because one would have to take into account the other parameters of this stylistic paradigm as well: cutting pace, bi-polar use of lens length and the dominant use of 'singles' in conversation scenes.[28] Judging from the prevalence of free-ranging camerawork, at least a partial feature of the intensified continuity aesthetic is detectable in the visual style of post-1998 Indonesian films.

These two points obviously cannot capture the whole range of enabling circumstances that permit the flourishing development of camera mobility in post-Suharto Indonesian cinematography. Minimally, however, they explicate that these changes are historically situated, facilitated by the availability of technology, and driven by both economic and aesthetic objectives. In short, these developments are not simply the result of the filmmakers' artistic brilliance. As the historical poetics of cinema perspective has shown us, in the history of film style, a network of enabling factors intersects to drive changes and sustain some continuities of particular stylistic developments.

Reflexivity and the Foregrounding of the Operational Aesthetic

As a way to conclude this chapter, I wish to reflect on the development of reflexive camera movements in post-Suharto Indonesian cinema and connect them to a broader discussion on contemporary media aesthetics. Is stylistic reflexivity unique to our time? Film and media scholar Angela Ndalianis argues that it isn't. In *Neo-Baroque Aesthetics and Contemporary Entertainment*, Ndalianis seeks to unravel the aesthetic logic that governs the entertainment media of our current age. She argues that today's film, comic books, video games and even theme parks bear parallels with the seventeenth-century baroque arts. For this reason, she proposes that it is appropriate to frame these current entertainment forms as compelling manifestations of neo-baroque aesthetics.

What are the parallels? To begin with, the baroque artists used spectacle to delight and astonish, and so do the creators of these contemporary entertainment products, according to Ndalianis. She claims that contemporary cinema and other entertainment media depend upon several basic features of Baroque art: seriality, polycentrism, virtuosity and hypertextuality.[29] Virtuosity as a salient feature of the neo-baroque aesthetic, she argues, is 'revealed through stylistic flourish and allusion'.[30] But, more importantly, it relies on a self-reflexivity that requires the 'active engagement of audience members, who are invited to *participate in a self-reflexive game involving the work's artifice*'.[31] The pursuit and display of technical and artistic virtuosity through the 'game of self-reflexivity' ultimately reveals '*a desire of the makers to be recognized for taking an entertainment form to new limits*'.[32]

If the seventeenth-century baroque arts and contemporary media are similar in this regard, what is so neo about the neo-baroque media? Ndalianis contends that what's different is that neo-baroque media exhibit an excessive fixation with technological advancement and scientific principles; that is, the virtuoso display of technical handling reflects a quasi-religious devotion to technology itself.[33]

As much as Ndalianis's concept of neo-baroque aesthetics is helpful in elucidating the implication of the foregrounded camera movement artifice as a form of stylistic virtuosity, I wouldn't immediately jump to the conclusion that contemporary Indonesian cinema is neo-baroque. For one thing, although we can detect some use of reflexive camera movement in contemporary Indonesian films, this finding is too small-scale to be used as the primary indicator for the whole aesthetics of contemporary Indonesian cinema. One would have to investigate whether virtuosity and self-reflexivity, as well as the other features of the neo-baroque aesthetic she mentions (seriality, polycentrism and hypertextuality), also operate in the other formal and stylistic aspects of Indonesian cinema. For another, neo-baroque virtuosity, as Ndalianis conceives it, relies heavily on self-reflexivity. But as my case analysis has shown, the reflexive function of camera mobility isn't always activated by a *self-reflexive* exploration of the film medium. For instance, in the cases we studied earlier, only the example from *Janji Joni* appropriately displays self-reflexive engagement as the scene and the whole film in fact reflect on the world of filmmaking and cinemagoing. The two examples from *The Raid* films, by contrast, are not self-reflexive in the sense that they reflect on the world of film in their plots. The foregrounding of the camera movement artifice in its own right, thus activating the reflexive function, doesn't always need to be self-reflexive in its function.

A competing concept germane to this discussion is Harris's *operational aesthetic*. Through this concept, Harris argues that there are forms of entertainment that revel in the display of artifice. In contrast to Ndalianis, Harris claims that this operational aesthetic doesn't rely solely on self-reflexivity. In *The Operational Aesthetic in the Performance of Professional Wrestling*, William P. Lipscomb III shows that an operational aesthetic can be used as a lens to understand why fans of professional wrestling engage with wrestling programmes – whether live or televised – week in, week out. He has found that these wrestling programmes, which have been characterised as a fraudulent sport of scams, expose rather than veil their operations and thereby invite the audience to scrutinise how they work.[34] As such, fans are invited and compelled to take part in the production of the meanings of these 'phoney' wrestling matches, which in turn becomes the exact reward and pleasure that audiences reap. But Lipscomb's analyses of these 'exposures of operations' do not demonstrate that these are self-reflexive forms of wrestling.[35] Consequently, this finding supports Harris' idea that in order for an artwork or entertainment form to foreground its medium's artifice and, as such, to activate an operational aesthetic, it isn't necessary for it to be self-reflexive.

From that perspective, the reflexive mobile shots in contemporary Indonesian films activate an operational aesthetic in which the salient question becomes, 'How did the makers of *The Raid* achieve that car-to-car flyover shot?' As evidence of this type of engagement, viewers on YouTube react to the behind-the-scenes documentary on the making of *The Raid 2* by leaving comments and questions, some of them related to the construction of the reflexive mobile shot.[36] One viewer, John Navarro, writes: 'Are you telling me there was a hidden guy in that chair in the car the whole time? Just to pass off a camera?'[37] Another commentator, named PalmDesertRock, remarks: 'Saw this movie yesterday and kept asking myself how they did that shot where the camera moves through the car. Now I know, and I would never have come up with the idea that it's a guy disguised as a seat. Brilliant stuff.'[38] Just to cite one last reaction here, a commenter named CrawlingDust specifically points out the flyover quality of the moving shot by saying: 'When I saw that in the cinema – it blew my mind. Big kudos to the crew for going that insane. Others would go with CGI.'[39] What these comments tell us is that audiences do pay attention to the *constructional aspect* of this shot, and they laud the filmmakers of *The Raid 2* for being able to achieve that, especially without the use of computer-generated imaging technology. Of course, not all of the 316 comments posted on this YouTube page are about the mobile shot. Nevertheless, these reactions powerfully show that thanks in part to the advent of social media, filmmakers' virtuosic handling of stylistic techniques is subject to scrutiny, and viewers can make use of the social media affordances to express their evaluations of this virtuosic technique. For film and media researchers, a further affordance that a social media platform like YouTube offers is the fact that audiences' embrace of this operational aesthetic can be readily observed and documented.

In conclusion, the use of free-ranging camerawork has dynamised the look of post-New Order Indonesian films in general. Acting as more than just visual embellishment, these free-ranging mobile shots can activate a multitude of functions that may not always serve to transmit story information or advance the plot. Although these mobile shots may appear gratuitous at first, examined more closely, they can be seen as an attempt to reinvigorate one of the fundamental powers of the mobile frame as a pre-narrative cinematic technique: *the processual exploration of time and space*.

This exhilarating, onscreen foregrounding of processual composition is aimed at inviting the viewer to engage in an operational aesthetic. In this case, these carefully executed mobile shots beckon the spectator to join in a forensic appreciation of the craft put into the formal and stylistic technics of the work. When engaged in an operational aesthetic, the viewer not only revels in the story and action but also in the creative mechanics of the presentational style. To deny the significance of this mode of textual engagement in contemporary Indonesian cinematic culture would be to deny the pleasure of appreciating the technological design of filmic artworks at large. As film philosopher Barys Gaut argues, appreciating a cinematic artwork depends partly on appreciating its technological incorporation – technology, in his understanding, is the know-how harnessed to put together a riveting shot, a sequence or a whole film that appears to be notably difficult to accomplish from the perspective of a non-trained moviegoer.[40] Having examined the cases in this chapter, I agree with Gaut's contention completely.

Notes

1. A *Fig Rig* is a camera stabilisation system designed by filmmaker Mike Figgis, which was intended for smaller video cameras.
2. I adopt these labels from Jakob Isak Nielsen's categories of camera movement. He defines these techniques as follows. An *arcing shot* is a shot in which

the camera arcs around the motive (regardless of camera support). A *push-in* is a type of mobile frame in which there's a movement onscreen achieved by physically pushing the camera on a dolly or by zooming in toward a subject or object in the frame. The *pull-back* is the opposite of push-in: there's a movement on the screen away from the subject or object. *Booming and aerial shots* are those shots in which onscreen movement is achieved from a perspective that 'appears disconnected from the ground level, for instance booming through space, flying over a scenery', according to Nielsen. These shots include those that are created by drones. *Follow shots* are shots in which the camera appears to follow the characters whether in the form of a Steadicam shot, dolly shot, pan, tilt or handheld shot. *Autonomous moves* are those mobile shots in which the camera moves independently of moving action or subject, for instance, by panning off of a character or tracking sideways to diverge from a character or action. See Jakob Isak Nielsen, 'Camera Movement in Narrative Cinema: Towards a Taxonomy of Functions' (PhD Thesis, University of Aarhus, 2007), p. 309.
3. See Jakob Isak Nielsen, 'Five Functions of Camera Movement in Narrative Cinema', in *Transnational Cinematography Studies*, eds Lindsay Coleman, Daisuke Miyao, and Roberto Schaefer (Lanham, MD: Lexington Books, 2017), 40; Nielsen, 'Camera Movement in Narrative Cinema', p. 248.
4. Tom Gunning, 'Rounding out the Moving Image: Camera Movement and Volumetric Space' (paper presented at the Society of Cinema and Media Studies Conference, Montreal, 26 March 2015), p. 3.
5. Joko Anwar, 'Dead Time: Kala, a Film by Joko Anwar: The Director's Blog: Fear of the Unknowns', *Dead Time the Movie* (blog), accessed 1 May 2016, http://deadtimethemovie.blogspot.com/2006/09/fear-of-unknowns.html.
6. *Bullet Time* (sometimes referred to as time-slice photography) is a visual effect seen in films and computer games through which the passage of time is slowed down so that an observer can see the individual bullets or any other fast-moving object flying throughout the shot at a conceivable rate, sometimes with streaks and trails made visible. See 'Bullet Time', TV Tropes, accessed 1 May 2016, http://tvtropes.org/pmwiki/pmwiki.php/Main/BulletTime.
7. 'The Raid Production Blog #3: The Courtyard and Hole Drop (ID)', Merantau Films, 3 March 2012, video, 5:51, https://www.youtube.com/watch?v=-reavq1wQCs.
8. Nielsen, 'Five Functions of Camera Movement in Narrative Cinema', p. 45.
9. Gunning, 'Rounding out the Moving Image', p. 3 (emphasis added).
10. Ibid.
11. Nielsen, 'Camera Movement in Narrative Cinema', p. 248.
12. Geoff King, 'Spectacle and Narrative in the Contemporary Blockbuster', in *Contemporary American Cinema*, eds Linda Ruth Williams and Michael Hammond (New York, NY: McGraw Hill, 2006), 340, cited in Nielsen, 'Camera Movement in Narrative Cinema', p. 249.
13. Leonard Retel Helmrich and Anton Retel Helmrich, 'Single Shot Cinema: A Different Approach to Film Language', *Avanca* Cinema 2013 (2013), pp. 1–9.

14. On the affordances of the *uninterrupted long-take shooting approach* as opposed to the *coverage shooting method* in film production, see my article: Ari Purnama, 'Syndromes of Indirect Communication: A Functional Analysis of the Static Long-Take Technique in Apichatpong Weerasethakul's Feature Films', *Asian Cinema* 26, no. 2 (2015), pp. 205–22.
15. Neil Harris, *Humbug: The Art of P. T. Barnum* (Chicago, IL; London: University of Chicago Press, 1981).
16. Ekky Imanjaya, interview with Joko Anwar, 11 April 2005, www.layarperak.com, cited in Erwan Juhara, Eriyadi Budiman, and Rita Rohayati, *Cendekia Berbahasa: Bahasa Dan Sastra Indonesia Untuk Kelas XI Sekolah Menengah Atas /Madrasah Aliyah Program Bahasa*, 1st edn (Jakarta Selatan: PT Setia Purna Inves, 2005), p. 57.
17. Ibid.
18. Christopher Lucas, 'The Modern Entertainment Marketplace: 2000–present', in *Cinematography*, ed. Patrick Keating (New Brunswick, NJ: Rutgers University Press, 2014), pp. 132–58.
19. Eric Sasono et al., *Menjegal Film Indonesia: Pemetaan Ekonomi Politik Industri Film Indonesia* (Jakarta: Rumah Film, 2011), p. 183.
20. Ibid., p. 182.
21. Riri Riza has pointed out this fact during a discussion on the development of digital cinema in Indonesia at Komunitas Salihara Jakarta, 5 March 2013. See Riri Riza, 'Diskusi: Sejumlah Masalah Sinema Digital Indonesia', Salihara Arts Center, 25 April 2013, video, 2:17:48, https://www.youtube.com/watch?v=r23P9r-Ey-0.
22. Ibid.
23. 'Tips Membuat Film Pendek Dengan DSLR Yang Wajib Kamu Ketahui', *SocialTextJournal.Com*, accessed 2 May 2016, http://socialtextjournal.com/tips-membuat-film-pendek-dengan-dslr-yang-wajib-kamu-ketahui/.
24. David Bordwell, 'Intensified Continuity Visual Style in Contemporary American Film', *Film Quarterly* 55, no. 3 (March 2002), pp. 21–2.
25. Ibid.
26. See Chapter 1 of Dafna Ruppin, 'The Komedi Bioscoop: The Emergence of Movie-Going in Colonial Indonesia (1896–1914)' (PhD Thesis, Utrecht University, 2015).
27. Thomas Barker, 'A Cultural Economy of the Contemporary Indonesian Film Industry' (PhD Thesis, Singapore, National University of Singapore, 2011), pp. 258–61.
28. These parameters of the intensified continuity style have been outlined by Bordwell in these accounts: Bordwell, 'Intensified Continuity'; and David Bordwell, *The Way Hollywood Tells It: Story and Style in Modern Movies* (Berkeley, CA: University of California Press, 2006).
29. Angela Ndalianis, *Neo-Baroque Aesthetics and Contemporary Entertainment* (Cambridge, MA: The MIT Press, 2004).
30. Ibid., p. 15.
31. Ibid., p. 25 (emphasis added).

32. Ibid.
33. Ibid., pp. 209–56.
34. William P. Lipscomb III, 'The Operational Aesthetic in the Performance of Professional Wrestling' (PhD Dissertation, Louisiana State University, 2005).
35. Ibid., pp. 125–92.
36. As of 1 September 2022, this behind-the-scene documentary has garnered 726,919 views and 370 comments since its publication on 11 March 2014 on YouTube. See 'The Raid 2 – Behind the Scenes – Part 1', Madman Anime, video, 10:22, https://www.youtube.com/watch?v=puoPsmepZDk&t=550s (the segment on the reflexive camerawork in the film begins at minute 8:46).
37. Ibid.
38. Ibid.
39. Ibid.
40. Barys Gaut, 'Cinematic Art and Technology', in *Current Controversies in Philosophy of Film*, ed. Katherine Thomson-Jones (New York, NY: Routledge, 2016), p. 17.

Part 4: Resolution

Wrapping Up and Looking Ahead

CHAPTER 8

Concluding Notes: All The Stylistic Pieces Matter

Visual anthropologist Karl G. Heider wrote the following passage in the concluding chapter of his book *Indonesian Cinema: National Culture on Screen* – published in 1991: 'Eventually, perhaps, we can even hope for a close cinematographic reading of Indonesian films along the lines which Donald Richie, David Bordwell and others have laid out for Japanese film.'[1] If we take Heider's idea of a 'close cinematographic reading of Indonesian films' to mean the systematic analysis of Indonesian cinematic visual style, this book is the first scholarly step toward fulfilling his hope – thirty-two years later. The book's chief purpose has been to build a stylistics of Indonesian film by examining three components of cinematic visual style through the lens of functional theories of film style: lighting, production design and camera movement. My concluding remarks articulated in the following pages will look to answer the question: what do all these findings mean?

I began the book by explaining that my motivation to conduct this study was prompted by the paucity of aesthetic inquiry in Indonesian cinema scholarship. So, this book is written in the conviction that Indonesian films can be treated as worthy aesthetic objects, just as other Indonesian arts have been in fields such as musicology (*gamelan*), theatre studies (*ludruk* and *wayang*), textile studies (*batik*) and art history (Javanese-Buddhist wall reliefs, sculptures and paintings). My intention has been to show that Indonesian fiction films can be dissected and analysed based on their aesthetic features through the lens of the functional theories of film style, grounded in the poetics of cinema research programme. By doing so, I have shown that Indonesian cinema is not just an ideological battleground – a site for competing ideologies from within and outside Indonesia to wage the war of representation – rather, it is a cultural-creative product, created with a sense of design and artistry. Of course, as each chapter in this book has shown, extratextual factors (politics, cultural shift, technology and commerce) have played an enormous role in enabling the transformations that have taken place in post-Suharto Indonesian cinema. Nevertheless, to assume that extratextual forces such as commerce and the state 'define the film texts produced'[2] would be to deny the conscious efforts and the ingenuity of the filmmakers themselves (cinematographers, production designers, producers and directors), who have leveraged visual stylisation not merely as a cosmetic veneer covering their films' story material, but as an indispensable means to create particular cinematic experiences that attract, move, provoke, compel and impact Indonesian movie viewers affectively.

Moreover, examining visual style in Indonesian cinema doesn't simply tell us about film style itself, but reveals further insights into the culture at large. Pertinent to post-Suharto cinematic storytellers is the exploration of the Indonesian archipelago's cultural diversity. Visual style puts on display the various dimensions of human experience, which entails delineating the specific traits and features of Indonesia's regional cultures through production design techniques such as location choice, props, set design and so on. In previous eras of Indonesian cinema history, the representation of these regional cultures was suppressed – in mass media and especially in cinema. Visual stylisation, then, contributes immensely to this shift toward representing the 'true faces' of Indonesia, which is diverse and rich in traditions, beliefs, artefacts and customs.

Therefore, as I see it, the pop culture thesis as an explanation proposed by contemporary scholars on Indonesian cinema such as Thomas Barker, is insufficient. As we have seen in Chapter 1, Barker has argued that because Indonesian films in the post-Suharto era have become part of pop culture (or follow a pop culture logic), Indonesian cinema has become more accepted domestically.[3] On the level of visual aesthetics, the results of my analyses have shown that filmmakers have explored and reinvigorated techniques that belong specifically to the realm of film art. If anything, post-Suharto filmmakers have tapped into the artistic resources provided by the film medium (cinematography and mise en scène) rather than pop culture in general.

On a theoretical level, having examined the roles of key stylistic devices in transforming the look of contemporary Indonesian film, I conclude that the functional theories of film style are currently limited. Although they are helpful conceptual lenses to examine a range of effects that film style can generate in a filmic artwork, they tend to look inward in the sense that they decipher the functions of style mainly in relation to the films' narrative dynamics. With the exception of Noël Carroll's theory, which proposes that film style also functions in some cases to 'communicate ideas about life, society or even about film',[4] these theories don't dare to look outward by analysing how film style can do something else besides helping tell stories or producing filmic atmospheres. For this reason, in relation to my previous point, perhaps we can add to this range of film style functions the capacity of film style to *delineate specific cultural features*. Film style, in this case, has a *cultural specifying function*, which particularises local cultural textures through fine-grained details.

Of course, as with any scholarly endeavour, this book can't tackle everything. Firstly, I have not compared and contrasted the stylistic devices I analyse – lighting, production design and camera movement – with other potentially pertinent elements such as sound, music and performance. Secondly, I have dealt with the stylistic devices used in the previous eras of Indonesian cinema rather cursorily. Ideally, the functions of the stylistic elements employed in the films made in those previous eras of Indonesian film history should be examined in more detail. More fruitfully, the analysis of cases should also incorporate examples of the stylistic application found in older films so that we can ascertain the extent to which the range of functions activated by the same stylistic technique differs in each period. Thirdly, this study has relied on theories that, in some cases, assume the effects of style on the audience. For instance, on the issue of reflexivity, the theorists I refer to assume that this type of stylistic exploration requires active engagement. However, no empirical proof has been provided that this is, in fact, the case. Viewers may engage rhetorically in a reception discourse about a certain film, as in the case of the YouTube comments on *The Raid 2* I discussed in the previous chapter. But we can't establish with a high degree of certainty that this foregrounding of artifice affects viewers psychologically.

This is where future research can help. Research into the spectatorship of Indonesian film aesthetics, especially the relationship between film style and audience engagement, could bring us more insights into this problem. A phenomenological approach, on the one side, and a cognitive approach, on the other, could fruitfully shed further light on this issue. Next to this, a dedicated study of the relationship between visual style in Indonesian cinema and style in the other arts of Indonesia shall provide us with compelling findings regarding whether there are some specific features of Indonesian filmic visual style that are modelled or inspired by the traditional visual arts or performing arts. Through that research effort, we can hopefully discover aesthetic theories specific to the Indonesian artistic realm that can apply to the study of cinematic visual style. Lastly, concerning specific cultural traits delineated by film style, future studies can also systematically investigate the use of regional languages and their relation to screen performance in contemporary Indonesian cinema. Perhaps, by pursuing that inquiry, we would discover unique elements of Indonesian cinema that might not be found in other world cinema traditions.

What I propose all along is that Indonesian films are worth examining as artistic artefacts, and with that, this book contributes to enriching the field of study that, up until this point, has treated Indonesian film primarily as a social phenomenon – a fertile research ground for unravelling the dynamics of cultural politics in the world's third-biggest democratic (developing) nation.

The value of stylistic analysis for Indonesian cinema scholarship cannot be underestimated, for it discloses aspects of the artefacts that have been taken for granted or even deemed insignificant (i.e., lighting, production design and camera movement). In this respect, it highlights the relevance of this research activity as a form of connoisseurship – to evoke Richard Neer's idea – whose primary objective involves making others see the aspects. Alluding to Wittgenstein's notion of 'aspect-dawning', on this point, Neer contends: 'The recognition of a style involves a shift in what one does when one sees, in a way that is identical to that of the shift from duck to rabbit. For connoisseurs and archaeologists alike, style is an aspect.'[5] This 'aspect-dawning' nature of stylistic inquiry ties in perfectly with the fundamental objective of poetics, which is 'active-making'. 'Aspect-dawning' or 'active-making' is hopefully what I have accomplished in this book, which is sorely needed for advancing Indonesian cinema scholarship, on the one hand, and for eliciting a deeper 'design appreciation'[6] of contemporary Indonesian films, on the other.

My final point: visual style in post-1998 Indonesian cinema is not simply a surface phenomenon or window-dressing arranged to present 'content'. In many cases, the content is the style itself, as when a particular stylistic artifice is foregrounded. Thus, the notion that style is an insignificant surface feature that contrasts with the more imperative, supreme 'substance' should be questioned, reassessed, and, dare I say, rejected. Throughout this book, I have shown the veracity of Francis-Noël Thomas and Mark Turner's contention that 'any concept of style that treats it as optional is inadequate',[7] because style is a set of *fundamental decisions* taken by the agent of creative-cultural activity, be it the artist, the writer, the designer, the cinematographer, the art director or any other individual working in a creative-cultural domain. As such, 'Nothing we do can be done "simply" and in no style, because style is something inherent in action, not something added to it.'[8] In light of all this, we can no longer accept the saying 'All style, no substance'.

Notes

1. Karl G. Heider, *Indonesian Cinema: National Culture on Screen* (Honolulu: University of Hawaii Press, 1991), p. 139.
2. Katinka van Heeren, *Contemporary Indonesian Film: Spirits of Reform and Ghosts from the Past* (Leiden: KITLV Press, 2012), p. 2.
3. Thomas Barker, *Indonesian Cinema After the New Order: Going Mainstream* (Hong Kong: Hong Kong University Press, 2019).
4. Noël Carroll, 'Film Form: An Argument for a Functional Theory of Style in the Individual Film', *Style*, Literature Online, 32, no. 3 (1998), p. 275.

5. Richard Neer, 'Connoisseurship and the Stakes of Style', *Critical Inquiry* 32, no. 1 (Autumn 2005), p. 17.
6. Noël Carroll, *Philosophy of Art: A Contemporary Introduction*, Routledge Contemporary Introductions to Philosophy (London: Routledge, 1999), p. 151.
7. Francis-Noël Thomas and Mark Turner, *Clear and Simple as the Truth: Writing Classic Prose* (Baltimore, MD: Princeton University Press, 1996), p. 142.
8. Ibid. (emphasis added).

Bibliography

Alton, John. *Painting with Light*. With a New Foreword by John Bailey edition. Berkeley and Los Angeles, CA: University of California Press, 2013.

Ardan, S. M. *Jejak Seorang Aktor: Sukarno M. Noor Dalam Film Indonesia*. Jakarta: Aksara Karunia, 2004.

Asyari, Suaidi. *Traditionalist vs. Modernist Islam in Indonesian Politics: Muhammadiyah & Nahdlatul Ulama (NU) in the Contemporary Indonesian Democratic and Political Landscape*. Saarbrücken, Germany: VDM Verlag Dr. Müller, 2010.

Barker, Thomas. *Indonesian Cinema After the New Order: Going Mainstream*. Hong Kong: Hong Kong University Press, 2019.

———. 'A Cultural Economy of the Contemporary Indonesian Film Industry'. PhD Thesis, National University of Singapore, 2011.

Barnwell, Jane. *Production Design: Architects of the Screen*. London: Wallflower, 2004.

Barsacq, Léon. *Caligari's Cabinet and Other Grand Illusions: A History of Film Design*. 1st English language edn. New York, NY: New York Graphic Society, 1976.

Barthes, Roland. 'The Reality Effect'. In *French Literary Theory Today*, translated by Tzvetan Todorov, pp. 11–17. New York, NY: Cambridge University Press, 1982.

Beach, Christopher. *A Hidden History of Film Style: Cinematographers, Directors and the Collaborative Process*. Oakland, CA: University of California Press, 2015.

'Behind the Scene Film Pengabdi Setan', Rapi Films. 28 September 2017. Video, 20:14. https://www.youtube.com/watch?v=C2_D0-GNdYI.

Bhaskar, Ira. 'On "Historical Poetics," Narrative and Interpretation'. In *A Companion to Film Theory*, edited by Robert Stam and Toby Miller, pp. 387–412. London: Blackwell, 1999.

Biran, Misbach Yusa. *Sejarah Film 1900–1950: Bikin Film Di Jawa*. 2nd edn. Jakarta: Komunitas Bambu dan Dewan Kesenian Jakarta, 2009.

Böhme, Gernot. 'Atmosphere as the Fundamental Concept of a New Aesthetics'. *Thesis Eleven* 36, no. 1 (1993), pp. 113–26.

Bordwell, David. *Figures Traced in Light: On Cinematic Staging*. Berkeley, CA: University of California Press, 2005.

———. 'Historical Poetics of Cinema'. In *The Cinematic Text: Methods and Approaches*, edited by R. Barton Palmer, pp. 369–98. New York, NY: AMS Press, 1989.

———. 'Intensified Continuity Visual Style in Contemporary American Film'. *Film Quarterly* 55, no. 3 (March 2002), pp. 16–28.

———. *Making Meaning: Inference and Rhetoric in the Interpretation of Cinema*. Cambridge, MA: Harvard University Press, 1989.

———. *Narration in the Fiction Film*. Madison, WI: The University of Wisconsin Press, 1985.

———. *On the History of Film Style*. Cambridge, MA: Harvard University Press, 1997.

———. *Planet Hong Kong: Popular Cinema and the Art of Entertainment*. Second edition. Madison, WI: Irvington Way Institute Press, 2011.

———. *Poetics of Cinema*. New York, NY: Routledge, 2008.

———. *The Way Hollywood Tells It: Story and Style in Modern Movies*. Berkeley, CA: University of California Press, 2006.

———. *Visual Style in Cinema*. Frankfurt am Main: Verlag der Autoren, 2001.

———. 'Visual Style in Japanese Cinema'. *Film History* 7, no. 1 (Spring 1995), pp. 5–31.

Bordwell, David, and Noël Carroll, eds *Post-Theory: Reconstructing Film Studies*. Madison, WI: University of Wisconsin Press, 1996.

Bordwell, David, and Kristin Thompson. *Film Art: An Introduction*. 8th Edition. Boston, MA: McGraw Hill, 2008.

Bosley, Rachael. 'Better Call Saul: Darkness Gains Dimension'. *American Cinematographer*, 26 June 2017. https://ascmag.com/articles/better-call-saul-darkness-gains-dimension.

Branigan, Edward. *Projecting a Camera: Language-Games in Film Theory*. New York, NY; Abingdon: Routledge, 2006.

Brown, Blain. *Cinematography: Theory and Practice*. Oxford: Focal Press/Elsevier, 2012.

Budiarti, Rita Triana, and Salman Faridi. *Di Balik Layar Laskar Pelangi*. Yogyakarta: Bentang, 2008.

'Bullet Time'. TV Tropes. Accessed 1 May 2016. http://tvtropes.org/pmwiki/pmwiki.php/Main/BulletTime.

Butler, Jeremy G. *Television Style*. New York, NY: Routledge, 2010.

———. *Toward a Theory of Cinematic Style: The Remake*. Electronic edition. Morrisville, NC: Lulu, 2003.

Cahyana, Ludhy, and Muhlis Suhaeri. *Benyamin S: Muka Kampung Rezeki Kota*. Jakarta: Yayasan H. Benjamin Sueb, 2005.

Caldwell, John Thornton. *Production Culture: Industrial Reflexivity and Critical Practice in Film and Television*. Durham, NC: Duke University Press, 2008.

Carroll, Noël. 'Film Form: An Argument for a Functional Theory of Style in the Individual Film.' *Style* 32, no. 3 (1998), pp. 385–401.

———. 'Film Form: An Argument for a Functional Theory of Style in the Individual Film'. In *Engaging the Moving Image*, pp. 127–46 New Haven, CT: Yale University Press, 2003.

———. *Philosophy of Art: A Contemporary Introduction*. Routledge Contemporary Introductions to Philosophy. London: Routledge, 1999.

———. 'Style'. In *The Routledge Companion to Philosophy and Film*, edited by Paisley Livingston and Carl Plantinga, pp. 268–78. London; New York, NY: Routledge, 2009.

Chion, Michel. *Film, a Sound Art*. New York, NY: Columbia University Press, 2009.

Clark, Marshall. *Maskulinitas: Culture, Gender and Politics in Indonesia*. Melbourne: Monash University Publishing, 2010.

Coleman, Lindsay, Daisuke Miyao, and Roberto Schaefer, eds *Transnational Cinematography Studies*. Lanham, MD: Lexington Books, 2017.

Coppens, Laura. 'Films of Desire: Queer(ing) Indonesian Cinema'. In *Asian Hot Shots: Indonesian Cinema*, edited by Yvonne Michalik and Laura Coppens, pp. 177–99. Marburg: Schüren, 2009.

Cribb, R. B. *The Late Colonial State in Indonesia: Political and Economic Foundations of the Netherlands Indies, 1880–1942*. Leiden: KITLV Press, 1994.

Cutting, James E., Kaitlin L. Brunick, Jordan E. DeLong, Catalina Iricinschi, and Ayse Candan. 'Quicker, Faster, Darker: Changes in Hollywood Film over 75 Years'. *i-Perception* 2, no. 6 (2011), pp. 569–76.

'Daftar Judul Film Indonesia Berdasarkan Tahun "2010"'. *Film Indonesia*. Accessed 3 October 2018. http://filmindonesia.or.id/movie/title/list/year/2010.

Davis, Natalie Zemon. *Slaves on Screen: Film and Historical Vision*. Cambridge, MA: Harvard University Press, 2000.

Dessem, Matthew. 'Why TV Shows Are (Literally) Darker Than They've Ever Been'. *Slate Magazine*, 29 June 2016. https://slate.com/culture/2016/06/cinematographers-from-game-of-thrones-jessica-jones-and-better-call-saul-on-why-tv-shows-are-darker-than-theyve-ever-been.html.

Dewan Perwakilan Rakyat Republik Indonesia. *Undang Undang Republik Indonesia No. 44 Tahun 2008 Tentang Pornografi*, 2008. Accessed 4 January 2019. www.bpkp.go.id/uu/filedownload/2/33/151.bpkp.

Dinata, Nia, dir. *Perempuan Punya Cerita (Chants of Lotus)*. Jakarta: Kalyana Shira Films, 2007. DVD.

Edensor, Tim. 'Reconnecting with Darkness: Gloomy Landscapes, Lightless Places'. *Social & Cultural Geography* 14, no. 4 (June 2013), pp. 446–65.

Ekman, Paul, and Wallace V. Friesen. *Unmasking the Face*. Englewood Cliffs, NJ: Prentice-Hall, 1975.

Ettedgui, Peter. *Production Design & Art Direction*. Hove: RotoVision, 1999.

Fischer, Lucy, ed. *Art Direction and Production Design: A Modern History of Filmmaking*. Behind the Silver Screen. London; New York, NY: IB Tauris, 2015.

'Film "The Raid" Tayang di Indonesia'. *Viva.co.id*. November 2 2011. https://www.viva.co.id/showbiz/260949-film-the-raid-tayang-di-indonesia.

Foley, Kathy. 'The Sundanese Wayang Golek, the Rod Puppet Theatre of West Java'. PhD Thesis, University of Hawaii, 1979.

Fraser-Lu, Sylvia. *Indonesian Batik: Processes, Patterns, and Places*. Singapore: Oxford University Press, 1986.

Frayling, Christopher. *Ken Adam and the Art of Production Design*. London: Faber and Faber, 2005.

———. 'Perspectives on Production Design'. LICA-Lancaster University. 12 June 2013. Video, 1:24:39. https://www.youtube.com/watch?v=HFZSuNdT5vo.

Frederick, William H. 'Rhoma Irama and the Dangdut Style: Aspects of Contemporary Indonesian Popular Culture'. *Indonesia* 34 (October 1982), pp. 103–30.

Frith, Simon. 'Popular Culture'. In *A Dictionary of Cultural and Critical Theory*, edited by Michael Payne and Jessica Rae Barbera, pp. 553–5. Chichester, West Sussex: Wiley-Blackwell, 2010.

Galinier, J., A. M. Becquelin, G. Bordin, L. Fontaine, F. Fourmaux, J. R. Ponce, P. Salzarulo, P. Simonnot, M. Therrien, and I. Zilli. 'Anthropology of the Night: Cross-Disciplinary Investigations'. *Current Anthropology* 51, no. 6 (2010), pp. 819–47.

Gaut, Barys. 'Cinematic Art and Technology'. In *Current Controversies in Philosophy of Film*, edited by Katherine Thomson-Jones, pp. 17–35. New York, NY: Routledge, 2016.

Geertz, Clifford. *The Religion of Java*. Glencoe, IL: Free Press, 1960.

Geertz, Hildred. *The Javanese Family a Study of Kinship and Socialization*. Prospect Heights, IL: Waveland Press, 1989.

Gibbs, John. *Mise-En-Scène: Film Style and Interpretation*. London; New York, NY: Wallflower, 2002.

Gibbs, John, and Douglas Pye, eds *Style and Meaning: Studies in the Detailed Analysis of Film*. Manchester: Manchester University Press, 2005.

Giovacchini, Saverio, and Robert Sklar, eds *Global Neorealism: The Transnational History of a Film Style*. Jackson, MS: University Press of Mississippi, 2013.

Griffero, Tonino. *Atmospheres: Aesthetics of Emotional Spaces*. English Edition. Surrey: Ashgate Publishing Limited, 2014.

Gunning, Tom. 'Crazy Machines in the Garden of Forking Paths'. In *Classical Hollywood Comedy*, edited by Kristine Brunovska Karnick and Henry Jenkins, pp. 87–105. New York, NY: Routledge, 1995.

———. 'Rounding out the Moving Image: Camera Movement and Volumetric Space'. Paper presented at the Society of Cinema and Media Studies Conference, Montreal, March 2015.

Hadimaja, Ramadhan K. H., and Nina Pane Budiarto. *Pengusaha, Politikus, Pelopor Industri Film: Djamaludin Malik, Melekat di Hati Banyak Orang*. Jakarta: Kata Hasta Pustaka, 2006.

Hadiz, Vedi. 'Indonesia: Order and Terror in a Time of Empire'. In *Empire and Neoliberalism in Asia*, edited by Vedi Hadiz, pp. 123–38. London and New York: Routledge, 2006.

Hafil, Muhammad. 'Film Impor Masih Mendominasi'. *Republika Online*, 21 February 2017. https://republika.co.id/berita/senggang/film/17/02/21/olpu5w326-film-impor-masih-mendominasi.

Hanan, David. 'A Tradition of Political Allegory and Political Satire in Indonesian Cinema'. In *Asian Hot Shots: Indonesian Cinema*, edited by Yvonne Michalik and Laura Coppens, pp. 14–45. Marburg: Schüren, 2009.

———. *Cultural Specificity in Indonesian Film: Diversity in Unity*. Cham: Palgrave Macmillan Imprint, Springer International Publishing, 2017.

———. 'Gotot Prakosa and Independent Indonesian Cinema'. *Cantrills Filmnotes* 63/64 (1990), pp. 23–4.

———. 'Innovation and Tradition in Indonesian Cinema'. *Third Text* 24, no. 1 (2010), pp. 107–21.

———. *Moments in Indonesian Film History: Film and Popular Culture in a Developing Society 1950–2020*. Cham: Springer International Publishing AG, 2021.

———. 'Moments of Renewal–Alternative Ways of Viewing Indonesian Cinema'. *Jurnal Skrin Malaysia* 5, no. 2 (2008), pp. 1–15.

Hanich, Julian. *Cinematic Emotion in Horror Films and Thrillers: The Aesthetic Paradox of Pleasurable Fear*. New York, NY: Routledge, 2010.

———. 'Omission, Suggestion, Completion: Film and the Imagination of the Spectator'. *Screening the Past*, no. 43 (April 2018). Accessed 24 September 2018. http://www.screeningthepast.com/2018/02/omission-suggestion-completion-film-and-the-imagination-of-the-spectator/.

Harris, Neil. *Humbug: The Art of P. T. Barnum*. Chicago, IL; London: University of Chicago Press, 1981.

Hartley, Barbara. *Javanese Performances on an Indonesian Stage*. Honolulu: University of Hawaii Press, 2008.

Heeren, Katinka van. *Contemporary Indonesian Film: Spirits of Reform and Ghosts from the Past*. Leiden: KITLV Press, 2012.

———. 'Indonesian Side-Stream Film'. In *Asian Hot Shots: Indonesian Cinema*, pp. 71–97. Marburg: Schüren, 2009.

Heider, Karl G. *Indonesian Cinema: National Culture on Screen*. Honolulu: University of Hawaii Press, 1991.

———. *Landscapes of Emotion: Three Maps of Emotion Terms in Indonesia*. New York, NY: Cambridge University Press, 1991.

Helmrich, Leonard Retel, and Anton Retel Helmrich. 'Single Shot Cinema: A Different Approach to Film Language'. *Avanca* Cinema 2013 (2013), pp. 1–9.

Heryanto, Ariel, and Vedi Hadiz. 'Post-Authoritarian Indonesia'. *Critical Asian Studies* 37, no. 2 (2005), pp. 251–75.

Heusden, Barend van. 'Dealing with Difference: From Cognition to Semiotic Cognition'. *Cognitive Semiotics*, no. 4 (Spring 2009), pp. 116–32.

Hoerip, Satyagraha. *Dua Dunia Dalam Djadoeg Djajakoesoema*. Jakarta: Dinas Kebudayaan DKI Jakarta & Institut Kesenian Jakarta, 1995.

Højbjerg, Lennard. 'The Circular Camera Movement: Style, Narration, and Embodiment', *Projections* 8, no. 2 (1 December 2014), pp. 71–88.

Holt, Claire. *Art in Indonesia: Continuities and Change*. Ithaca, NY: Cornell University Press, 1967.

Horton, Sarah. 'The Craft of Art Direction'. *Pushing Pixels*. Last modified 16 August 2011. http://www.pushing-pixels.org/2011/08/16/the-craft-of-art-direction-conversation-with-sarah-horton.html.

Imanjaya, Ekky. 'Idealism versus Commercialism in Indonesian Cinema: A Neverending Battle?' *Indonesian Cinematheque/Cinemantique*, 8 November 2009. https://indonesiancinema theque.blogspot.com/2009/11/idealism-versus-commercialism-in.html.

———. 'Revisiting Italian Neorealism: Its Influence toward Indonesia and Asian Cinema or There's No Such Thing Like Pure Neorealist Films'. *Journal of European Studies* IV, no. 3 (2008), pp. 57–66.

Imanjaya, Ekky, and Diani Citra. 'Dissecting the Female Roles in Indonesia's Post-Authoritarian Cinema: A Study of Sammaria Simanjuntak's Demi Ucok'. In *Indonesian Women Filmmakers*, edited by Yvonne Michalik, pp. 95–114. Berlin: RegioSpectra, 2013.

Imanjaya, Ekky, and Indra Kusumawardhana. 'Film Tourism Indonesian Style: The Cases of Laskar Pelangi and Eat Pray Love'. *Communicare: Journal of Communication Studies* 3, no. 2 (2018), pp. 9–28.

'Indonesia Ahmadiyah Attack: Outrage over Victim Jailing'. *BBC News*, 15 August 2011. http://www.bbc.com/news/world-asia-pacific-14526299.

'Islamic Sect Ahmadiyah Faces Ban in Indonesia'. *BBC News*, 21 April 2011. http://www.bbc.com/news/world-asia-pacific-13155924.

Ismail, Usmar. *Usmar Ismail Mengupas Film*. Jakarta: Penerbit Sinar Harapan, 1983.

Izharuddin, Alicia. *Gender and Islam in Indonesian Cinema*. Singapore: Palgrave-Macmillan, 2017.

Jakobson, Roman. 'Closing Statement: Linguistics and Poetics'. In *Style in Language*, edited by Thomas A. Sebeok, pp. 350–77. Cambridge, MA: The Technology Press of Massachusetts Institute of Technology and John Wiley & Sons, Inc., 1960.

Jones, Tod. 'Indonesian Cultural Policy in the Reform Era'. *Indonesia* 93, no. April (2012), pp. 147–76.

Juhara, Erwan, Eriyadi Budiman and Rita Rohayati. *Cendekia Berbahasa: Bahasa Dan Sastra Indonesia Untuk Kelas XI Sekolah Menengah Atas/Madrasah Aliyah Program Bahasa*. 1st edn. Jakarta Selatan: PT Setia Purna Inves, 2005.

Karno, Rano. *Rano Karno: Si Doel*. Edited by Mirna Yulistianti. Cetakan ketiga. Jakarta PT Gramedia Pustaka Utama, 2016.

Keating, Patrick, ed. *Cinematography*. New Brunswick, NJ: Rutgers University Press, 2014.

———. *The Dynamic Frame: Camera Movement in Classical Hollywood*. New York, NY: Columbia University Press, 2019.

———. *Hollywood Lighting from the Silent Era to Film Noir*. New York, NY: Columbia University Press, 2010.

Keeler, Ward. *Javanese Shadow Plays, Javanese Selves*. Princeton Legacy Library Edition 2017. Baltimore, MD: Princeton University Press, 1987.

Keil, Charlie, and Kristen Whissel, eds *Editing and Special/Visual Effects*. Behind the Silver Screen. New Brunswick, NJ: Rutgers University Press, 2016.

Kessler, Frank. *Mise en scène*. Montréal: caboose, 2014.

Khoiri, Agniya. 'Jumlah Penonton "Warkop DKI Reborn" Salip "Laskar Pelangi"'. *CNN Indonesia*, 22 September 2016. https://www.cnnindonesia.com/hiburan/20160922122216-220-160247/jumlah-penonton-warkop-dki-reborn-salip-laskar-pelangi.

King, Geoff. 'Spectacle and Narrative in the Contemporary Blockbuster'. In *Contemporary American Cinema*, edited by Linda Ruth Williams and Michael Hammond, pp. 334–52. New York, NY: McGraw Hill, 2006.

Koslofsky, Craig. *Evening's Empire: A History of the Night in Early Modern Europe*. Cambridge [etc.]: Cambridge University Press, 2011.

Kristanto, J. B. 'Sepuluh Tahun Terakhir Perfilman Indonesia'. In *Katalog Film Indonesia 1926–2007*, pp. xxi–xxix. Jakarta: Nalar, 2007.

Kristanto, J. B., and Adrian Jonathan Pasaribu. 'Catatan 2011: Menonton Penonton'. *Film Indonesia*, 30 December 2011. http://filmindonesia.or.id/article/catatan-2011-menonton-penonton.

Kuhn, Annette, and Guy Westwell. 'Production Design'. *Oxford Dictionary of Film Studies*. Oxford: Oxford University Press, 2012. Accessed 7 September 2015. http://www.oxfordreference.com/view/10.1093/acref/9780199587261.001.0001/acref-9780199587261.

Kurniawan, Bagus. 'Di Balik Layar "Sang Pencerah" Bersama Hanung'. *Detikhot*, 16 June 2010. http://hot.detik.com/movie/read/2010/06/16/155935/1379558/619/di-balik-layar-sang-pencerah-bersama-hanung.

Kurniawan, Fakhmi. 'Syuting Film K.H. Ahmad Dahlan Dimulai 21 Mei'. *Detikhot*, 18 May 2010. http://hot.detik.com/movie/read/2010/05/18/174606/1359459/619/syuting-film-kh-ahmad-dahlan-dimulai-21-mei.

Lallo, Michael. 'Will Someone Please Turn on the Lights: Why Have TV Dramas Literally Become So Dark?'. *The Sydney Morning Herald*, last modified 9 September 2016. https://www.smh.com.au/entertainment/tv-and-radio/will-someone-please-turn-on-the-lights-why-have-tv-dramas-literally-become-so-dark-20160909-grchcu.html.

Lebo, Harlan. *The Godfather Legacy*. New York, NY: Fireside, 1997.

Lestari, Umi. 'Basuki Resobowo as a Jack of All Trades: The Intersectionality of Arts and Film in Perfini Films and Resobowo's Legacy in Indonesian Cinema'. *Southeast of Now: Directions in Contemporary and Modern Art in Asia* 4, no. 2 (2020), pp. 313–45. https://doi.org/10.1353/sen.2020.0014.

Lipscomb III, William P. 'The Operational Aesthetic in the Performance of Professional Wrestling'. PhD Dissertation, Louisiana State University, 2005.

LoBrutto, Vincent. *The Filmmaker's Guide to Production Design*. New York, NY: Allworth Press, 2002.

Lucas, Christopher. 'The Modern Entertainment Marketplace: 2000–Present'. In *Cinematography*, edited by Patrick Keating, pp. 132–57. New Brunswick, NJ: Rutgers University Press, 2014.

Mamer, Bruce. *Film Production Technique: Creating the Accomplished Image*. Sixth edition. Boston, MA: Cengage Learning, 2014.

Martin, Adrian. *Mise En Scène and Film Style: From Classical Hollywood to New Media Art*. Basingstoke [etc.]: Palgrave Macmillan, 2014.

McCarthy, Todd, Stuart Samuels, and Arnold Glassman. *Visions of Light: The Art of Cinematography*. Kino International, 1992.

McLean, Adrienne L. *Costume, Makeup, and Hair*. Behind the Silver Screen. New Brunswick, NJ: Rutgers University Press, 2016.

'Menggenjot Film Nasional Bermuatan Budaya Lokal', *Kompasiana.com*, 14 May 2017, https://www.kompasiana.com/irwanrinaldi/59068676ff22bde22c6cca38/menggenjot-film-nasional-bermuatan-budaya-lokal.

Metallinos, Nikos. *Television Aesthetics: Perceptual, Cognitive, and Compositional Bases*. Mahwah, NJ: Lawrence Erlbaum Associates, Inc., 2009.

Michalik, Yvonne L., ed. *Indonesian Women Filmmakers*. Berlin: RegioSpectra, 2013.

Mittell, Jason. 'Narrative Complexity in Contemporary American Television'. *The Velvet Light Trap* 58, no. 1 (2006), pp. 29–40.

Miyao, Daisuke. *The Aesthetics of Shadow: Lighting and Japanese Cinema*. Durham, NC; London: Duke University Press, 2013.

Morgan, Stephanie, and Laurie Jo Sears, eds *Aesthetic Tradition and Cultural Transition in Java and Bali*. Madison, WI: University of Wisconsin, Center for Southeast Asian Studies, 1984.

Morrison, Miriam J. 'The Bedaya Serimpi Dances of Java'. *Dance Chronicle* 2, no. 3 (January 1978), pp. 188–212.

Mrázek, Jan. *Phenomenology of a Puppet Theatre: Contemplations on the Art of Javanese Wayang Kulit*. Leiden: KITLV Press, 2005.

Munir, Maimunah. 'Challenging the New Order's Gender Ideology in Benyamin Sueb's Betty Bencong Slebor: A Queer Reading'. *Plaridel: A Philippine Journal of Communication, Media and Society* 11, no. 2 (August 2014), pp. 95–116.

Murtagh, Ben. 'Double Identities in Dorce's Comedies: Negotiating Gender and Class in New Order Indonesian Cinema'. *Bijdragen tot de Taal-, Land- en Volkenkunde* 173, no. 2/3 (2017), pp. 181–207.

———. *Genders and Sexualities in Indonesian Cinema: Constructing Gay, Lesbi and Waria Identities on Screen*. New York, NY: Routledge, 2013.

Muttaqin, Ahmad. 'Spirit of Progressive and Moderation in "Sang Pencerah"'. *The Jakarta Post*, 23 October 2010.

Ndalianis, Angela. *Neo-Baroque Aesthetics and Contemporary Entertainment*. Cambridge, MA: The MIT Press, 2004.

Neer, Richard. 'Connoisseurship and the Stakes of Style'. *Critical Inquiry* 32, no. 1 (Autumn 2005), pp. 1–26.

Nielsen, Jakob Isak. 'Bordwell on Bordwell: Part II – Functions of Film Style'. *16:9*. September 2004. http://www.16-9.dk/2004-09/side11_inenglish.htm.

———. 'Camera Movement in Narrative Cinema'. *16:9*. 2 February 2015. http://www.16-9.dk/2015/02/camera-movement-in-narrative-cinema/.

———. 'Camera Movement in Narrative Cinema: Towards a Taxonomy of Functions'. PhD Thesis, University of Aarhus, 2007.

———. 'Five Functions of Camera Movement in Narrative Cinema'. In *Transnational Cinematography Studies*, edited by Lindsay Coleman, Daisuke Miyao, and Roberto Schaefer, pp. 25–53. Lanham, MD: Lexington Books, 2017.

Niogret, Hubert, dir. *Le cinéma indonésien entre censures et espoirs*. Paris: Les Films du Tamarin/Magnolias Films/Filmoblic, 2015.

'Paket Tour Laskar Pelangi Belitung 3D/2N'. Bangkatour.com. Accessed 1 September 2022. http://bangkatour.com/paket-tour-laskar-pelangi-belitung/.

Palmier, Leslie H. 'Modern Islam in Indonesia: The Muhammadiyah After Independence'. *Pacific Affairs* 27, no. 3 (September 1954), pp. 255–63.

Paramaditha, Intan. 'Cinema, Sexuality and Censorship in Post-Soeharto Indonesia'. In *Southeast Asian Independent Cinema: Essays, Documents, Interviews*, edited by Tilman Baumgärtel, pp. 69–87. Singapore: NUS Press, 2012.

———. 'Contesting Indonesian Nationalism and Masculinity in Cinema'. *Asian Cinema* 18, no. 2 (1 September 2007), pp. 41–61.

———. 'Film Studies in Indonesia: An Experiment of a New Generation'. *Bijdragen tot de taal-, land- en volkenkunde / Journal of the Humanities and Social Sciences of Southeast Asia* 173, nos 2–3 (1 January 2017), pp. 357–75.

Pasaribu, Adrian Jonathan. 'Box Office Terus Menurun, Waktunya Mengambil Risiko?'. *Film Indonesia*, 26 July 2012. http://filmindonesia.or.id/article/box-office-terus-menurun-waktunya-mengambil-risiko.

Pasaribu, Adrian Jonathan, Shadia Pradsmadji, and Julita Pratiwi. 'Bersinema Bersama di Temu Komunitas Film Indonesia 2018'. *Cinema Poetica*. Last modified April 14, 2018. Accessed 4 January 2019. https://cinemapoetica.com/bersinema-bersama-di-temu-komunitas-film-indonesia-2018/.

Pausacker, Helen. 'Hot Debates'. *Inside Indonesia*. Last modified 14 December, 2008. Accessed 4 January 2019. https://www.insideindonesia.org/hot-debates.

'Penghargaan Bagi R.A. Kartini (1982)'. *Film Indonesia*. Accessed 29 October 2015. http://filmindonesia.or.id/movie/title/lf-r011-82-655427_ra-kartini/award#.VjKNKqLATBM.

'Penghargaan Bagi SunanKalijaga (1983)'. *Film Indonesia*. Accessed 29 October 2015. http://filmindonesia.or.id/movie/title/lf-s013-83-072357_sunan-kalijaga/award#.VjKNQ6LATBM.

Plantinga, Carl. 'Art Moods and Human Moods in Narrative Cinema'. *New Literary History* 43, no. 3 (2012), pp. 455–75.

———. 'The Scene of Empathy and the Human Face on Film'. In *Passionate Views: Film, Cognition, and Emotion*, edited by Carl Plantinga and Greg M. Smith, pp. 239–55. Baltimore, MD: Johns Hopkins University Press, 1999.

'Police Arrest Punks in Indonesia – in Pictures'. *The Guardian*, 14 December 2011. http://www.theguardian.com/world/gallery/2011/dec/14/police-arrest-punks-indonesia.

Prakosa, Gotot. *Film Pinggiran*. Jakarta: FFTV-IKJ and YLP Fatma Press, 1997.

Prince, Stephen. 'Hollywood's Digital Backlot: 2000–Present'. In *Art Direction and Production Design*, edited by Lucy Fischer, pp. 139–56. Behind the Silver Screen. London; New York, NY: IB Tauris, 2015.

Purnama, Ari. *A Conversation with David Bordwell: Poetics of Cinema, Film Stylistics and Research Valorization*. Vimeo. 23 October 2013. Video, 53:28. https://vimeo.com/77626940.

———. 'Syndromes of Indirect Communication: A Functional Analysis of the Static Long-Take Technique in Apichatpong Weerasethakul's Feature Films'. *Asian Cinema* 26, no. 2 (2015), pp. 205–22.

———. 'The Video Compact Disc and the Digital Preservation of Indonesian Cinema'. In *Exposing the Film Apparatus: The Film Archive as a Research Laboratory*, edited by Giovanna Fossati and Annie Van den Oever, pp. 141–50. Framing Film. Amsterdam: EYE Filmmuseum/ Amsterdam University Press, 2016.

Rahman, Lisabona. 'Apa Kabar Film Impor?'. *Film Indonesia*, 8 May 2011. http://filmindonesia.or.id/article/apa-kabar-film-impor.

'The Raid 2 – Behind the Scenes – Part 1'. Madman Anime. Video, 10:22. https://www.youtube.com/watch?v=puoPsmepZDk&t=550s.

'The Raid Production Blog #3: The Courtyard and Hole Drop (ID)'. Merantau Films. 3 March 2012. Video, 5:51. https://www.youtube.com/watch?v=-reavq1wQCs.

Riantiarno, Nano. *Teguh Karya Dan Teater Populer 1968–1993*. Jakarta: Penerbit Sinar Harapan, 1993.

Ricklefs, Merle Calvin. *A History of Modern Indonesia Since C. 1200*. Stanford, CA: Stanford University Press, 2001.

Riza, Riri. 'Diskusi: Sejumlah Masalah Sinema Digital Indonesia'. Salihara Arts Center. 25 April 2013. Video, 2:17:48. https://www.youtube.com/watch?v=r23P9r-Ey-0.

Ruppin, Dafna. 'The Komedi Bioscoop: The Emergence of Movie-Going in Colonial Indonesia (1896–1914)'. PhD Thesis, Utrecht University, 2015.

Rushton, Richard, and Gary Bettinson. *What Is Film Theory? An Introduction to Contemporary Debates*. Maidenhead: McGraw Hill Open Univ. Press, 2010.

Rzepińska, Maria, and Krystyna Malcharek. 'Tenebrism in Baroque Painting and Its Ideological Background'. *Artibus et Historiae* 7, no. 13 (1986), pp. 91–112.

Renika, Sabina. 'Di Balik Layar: Membingkai'. Cinesurya. 17 November 2017. Video, 6:15. https://www.youtube.com/watch?v=TPVJH9mDKQE.

Said, Salim. *Shadows on the Silver Screen: A Social History of Indonesian Film*. Jakarta: Lontar Foundation, 1991.

'Sang Pencerah (Behind the Scene)'. Agus Taufik. 3 June 2011. Video, 7:29. https://www.youtube.com/watch?v=dF6BsOApc3w.

Sasono, Eric. 'Islamic Revivalism and Religious Piety in Indonesian Cinema'. In *Performance, Popular Culture, and Piety in Muslim Southeast Asia*, edited by Timothy P. Daniels, pp. 45–75. New York, NY: Palgrave Macmillan, 2013.

Sasono, Eric, Ekky Imanjaya, Ifan Adriansyah Ismail, and Hikmat Darmawan. *Menjegal Film Indonesia: Pemetaan Ekonomi Politik Industri Film Indonesia*. Jakarta: Rumah Film, 2011.

Sawyer, R. Keith. *Group Creativity: Music, Theater, Collaboration*. New York, NY; London: Routledge, 2003.

Schleier, Merrill. 'Postwar Hollywood, 1947–1967.' In *Art Direction and Production Design*, edited by Lucy Fischer, pp. 73–96. Behind the Silver Screen. London; New York, NY: IB Tauris, 2015.

'Sekolah Dasar Muhammadiyah – Laskar Pelangi (Belitung Island, Indonesia): Address, Point of Interest & Landmark Reviews'. TripAdvisor. Accessed 1 September 2022. http://www.tripadvisor.com/Attraction_Review-g668845-d4972215-Reviews-Sekolah_Dasar_Muhammadiyah_Laskar_Pelangi-Belitung_Island_Bangka_Belitung_Islands.html.

'Sekolah Dasar Muhammadiyah – Laskar Pelangi (Belitung Island, Indonesia)'. TripAdvisor. Accessed 1 September 2022. http://www.tripadvisor.com/Attraction_Review-g668845-d4972215-Reviews-Sekolah_Dasar_Muhammadiyah_Laskar_Pelangi-Belitung_Island_Bangka_Belitung_Islands.html#photos.

'Sekuel "Laskar Pelangi" Dirilis 17 Desember'. *Kompas.com*. Accessed 11 October 2015, http://entertainment.kompas.com/read/2009/03/18/e174849/sekuel.laskar.pelangi.dirilis.17.desember.

Sellors, C. Paul. *Film Authorship: Auteurs and Other Myths*. London: Wallflower, 2010.

Sen, Krishna. *Indonesian Cinema: Framing the New Order*. London; Atlantic Highlands, NJ: Zed Books, 1994.

Sen, Krishna, and David Hill. *Politics and the Media in 21st Century Indonesia: Decade of Democracy*. London: Routledge, 2011.

Sen, Krishna, and David T. Hill. *Media, Culture and Politics in Indonesia*. Melbourne; Oxford: Oxford University Press, 2000.

Setijadi-Dunn, Charlotte, and Thomas Barker. 'Imagining "Indonesia": Ethnic Chinese Film Producers in Pre-Independence Cinema'. *Asian Cinema* 21, no. 2 (2010), pp. 25–47.

'Siti – Production & Contact Info'. IMDbPro. Accessed 8 August 2022, https://pro.imdb.com/title/tt4186170/.
Soebijoto, Hertanto. 'Lagi, Masjid Ahmadiyah Dirusak Massa'. *Kompas.com*, 3 December 2010. http://megapolitan.kompas.com/read/2010/12/03/15534561/Lagi..Masjid.Ahmadiyah.Dirusak.Massa.
Soehadi, Gaston. 'Teguh Karya: A Film Auteur Working Within a Collective'. Ph.D. Thesis, Monash University, 2015.
Sontag, Susan. *Against Interpretation and Other Essays*. New York, NY: Farrar, Straus & Giroux, 1966.
———. *Against Interpretation and Other Essays*. Reprint. London: Penguin, 2009.
Springer, Claudia, and Julie Levinson, eds *Acting*. New Brunswick, NJ: Rutgers University Press, 2015.
Sugandi, Yadi. 'Yadi Sugandi: Mengapa Tidak Digital?'. Interview by Arie Kartikasari. *Film Indonesia*, 10 November 2011. http://filmindonesia.or.id/article/yadi-sugandi-mengapa-tidak-digital#.VyMdDmaA_ow.
Surya, Mouly. 'Mouly Surya: Mencintai Film, Memfilmkan Cinta'. Interview by Adrian Jonathan Pasaribu. *Film Indonesia*, 6 May 2013. http://filmindonesia.or.id/article/mouly-surya-mencintai-film-memfilmkan-cinta#.YwBXbC-cZ-U.
Sutton, R. Anderson. *Traditions of Gamelan Music in Java: Musical Pluralism and Regional Identity*. Cambridge: Cambridge University Press, 1991.
Tanjung, Ical. 'Belajar Jadi Penata Kamera Ulung Seperti Ical Tanjung'. Cine Crib. 16 December 2019. Video, 9:42. https://www.youtube.com/watch?v=Qdh7riZtHz0.
Tashiro, C. S. *Pretty Pictures: Production Design and the History Film*. 1st edn. Austin, TX: University of Texas Press, 1998.
Tatyzo, Claire. 'Nia Dinata and Indonesia's Post-New Order Film Culture'. *AsiaOnline* Flinders Asia Centre Occasional Paper, no. 3 (May 2011), pp. 1–42.
Teo, Stephen. *The Asian Cinema Experience: Styles, Spaces, Theory*. 1st edition. Abingdon; New York, NY: Routledge, 2012.
Thomas, Francis-Noël, and Mark Turner. *Clear and Simple as the Truth: Writing Classic Prose*. Baltimore, MD: Princeton University Press, 1996.
'Tips Membuat Film Pendek Dengan DSLR Yang Wajib Kamu Ketahui.' *SocialTextJournal.com*. Accessed 2 May 2016. http://socialtextjournal.com/tips-membuat-film-pendek-dengan-dslr-yang-wajib-kamu-ketahui/.
VanArendonk, Kathryn. 'TV Dramas Are (Literally) Too Dark'. *Vulture*, 31 August 2016. https://www.vulture.com/2016/08/tv-dramas-are-literally-too-dark.html.
Waal, Frans de. *The Ape and the Sushi Master: Cultural Reflections by a Primatologist*. New York, NY: Basic Books, 2001.
Weintraub, Andrew N. *Power Plays: Wayang Golek Puppet Theater of West Java*. Athens, OH: Ohio University Press, 2004.
Whitlock, Cathy. *Designs on Film: A Century of Hollywood Art Direction*. 1st edition. New York, NY: HarperCollins, 2010.
Wilson, George. 'Interpretation'. In *The Routledge Companion to Philosophy and Film*, edited by Paisley Livingston and Carl Plantinga, pp. 162–72. London; New York, NY: Routledge, 2009.
———. 'On Film Narrative and Narrative Meaning'. In *Film Theory and Philosophy*, edited by Richard Allen and Murray Smith, pp. 221–38. Oxford: Clarendon Press, 1997.
Woodrich, Christopher. 'Ekranisasi Awal: Bringing Novels to the Silver Screen in the Dutch East Indies'. MA Thesis, University of Gadjah Mada, 2014.

Yazid, Naval. 'Year of the Flop for Indonesian Filmmaking'. *Jakarta Globe*, 28 December 2010. https://web.archive.org/web/20110106035814/http://www.thejakartaglobe.com/entertainment/year-of-the-flop-for-indonesian-film-making/413989.

Yngvesson, Dag. 'Non-Aligned Features: The Coincidence of Modernity and the Screen in Indonesia'. PhD Thesis, University of Minnesota, 2016.

Filmography

#TemanTapiMenikah/#FriendsButMarried (2018)
3 Hari Untuk Selamanya/Three Days to Forever (2007)
3 Nafas Likas/Likas' Three Breaths (2014)
7 Hati 7 Cinta 7 Wanita/7 Hearts 7 Loves 7 Women (2010)
9 Naga/9 Dragons (2006)
Ada Apa Dengan Cinta?/What's Up with Cinta? (2002)
Ada Apa Dengan Cinta? 2/What's Up with Cinta? 2 (2016)
Ai Lop Yu Pul/I Love You Full (2009)
Air Mata Kekasih/Lover's Tears (1971)
Akibat Pergaulan Bebas/The Effects of Free Sex (1977)
Akibat Pergaulan Bebas/The Effects of Free Sex (2010)
Alone in the Dark (2005)
Ambisi/Ambition (1973)
Anak Perawan di Sarang Penyamun/The Virgin and the Bandits (1962)
Anak-anak Gass dalam Elegi Buat Nana/Elegy for Nana (1988)
Antara Bumi dan Langit/Between the Earth and the Sky (1950)
Apa Ini Apa Itu/What's This? What's That? (1981)
Apa Yang Kau Tjari, Palupi?/What Are You Looking For, Palupi? (1969)
Arie Hanggara (1985)
Arisan!/The Gathering (2003)
Aruna dan Lidahnya/Aruna & Her Palate (2018)
Asal Tahu Saja/Just So You Know (1984)
Asrama Dara/Girl's Dormitory (1958)
Atambua 39 Derajat Celcius/Atambua 39° Celcius (2012)
Ave Maryam (2018)
Babi Buta Yang Ingin Terbang/Blind Pig Who Wants to Fly (2008)
Bangkitnya Si Mata Malaikat/The Rise of the Angels' Eye (1988)
Bayi Ajaib/The Diabolical Child (1982)
Bebas Bercinta/Free to Make Love (1995)
Benyamin Biang Kerok/The Trouble Maker (1972)
Benyamin Koboi Ngungsi/Benyamin the Refugee Cowboy (1975)
Benyamin Raja Lenong/Benyamin: The Lenong King (1975)
Benyamin Brengsek/Benyamin the Contemptible (1973)
Benyamin Spion 025/Benyamin the Spy 025 (1974)
Berbagi Suami/Love for Share (2005)
Bernapas dalam Lumpur/The Longest Dark (1970)
Bernapas dalam Lumpur/The Longest Dark (1991)

Beth (2000)
Betty Bencong Selebor/Betty the Eccentric 'Bencong' (1978)
Bing Slamet Koboi Cengeng/The Weeping Cowboy (1974)
Buaye Gile/The Crazy Playboy (1974)
Buffalo Boys (2018)
Bumi Makin Panas/The Earth Gets Hotter (1973)
Bumi Manusia/This Earth of Mankind (2019)
Buruan Cium Gue!/Kiss Me Quick! (2004)
Ca Bau Kan/The Courtesan (2002)
Cahaya Dari Timur: Beta Maluku/We Are Moluccans (2014)
Catatan Akhir Sekolah/High School Diary (2005)
Catatan Dodol Calon Dokter/Cado Cado: Doctor 101 (2016)
Catatan Si Boy/Boy's Diary (1987)
Catatan Si Boy 2/Boy's Diary 2 (1988)
Catatan Si Boy 3/Boy's Diary 3 (1990)
Cerita Cibinong/Story from a Village (2007)
Cerita Jakarta/Story from the Capital City (2007)
Cerita Pulau/Story from an Island (2007)
Cincin Berdarah/The Bloody Ring (1973)
Cinta Brontosaurus/Brontosaurus Love (2013)
Cinta di Balik Noda/There's Love Underneath the Pain (1984)
Cinta Pertama/First Love (1973)
Cobra (1977)
Coklat Stroberi/Chocolate Strawberry (2007)
Darah dan Doa/The Long March (1950)
Darah Garuda (aka *Merah Putih II)/Blood of Eagles* (2010)
Darah Muda/Young Blood (1977)
Daun Diatas Bantal/Leaf on a Pillow (1998)
Demi Ucok/For Ucok's Sake (2010)
Der letzte Mann/The Last Laugh (1924)
Dilan 1990 (2018)
Diskotik DJ/The Disc Jockey (1990)
Djakarta-Hongkong-Macao (1968)
Doea Tanda Mata/Mementos (1985)
Duyung Ajaib/The Magical Mermaid (1978)
Ecstacy & Pengaruh Sex/Ecstasy and Sexual Influence (1996)
Eliana, Eliana (2002)
Embun/Dewdrop (1951)
Enam Djam di Djogja/Six Hours in Djogja (1951)
Fatahillah (1997)
Filosofi Kopi/Coffee Philosophy (2015)
Gadis Desa/Village Girl (1949)
Gagak Item/Black Raven/De Zwarte Raaf (1939)
Gara-Gara Bola/Soccer Fever (2008)
Garuda Didadaku/Garuda in My Heart (2009)
Gending Sriwijaya/The Robbers (2013)
Gie (2005)
Gitar Tua Oma Irama/Oma Irama's Old Guitar (1977)

Golok Setan/ The Devil's Sword (1983)
Gundala Putra Petir/Gundala the Lightning's Son (1981)
Guru Bangsa Tjokroaminoto/Tjokroaminoto: Teacher of the Nation (2015)
Habibie dan Ainun/Habibie and Ainun (2012)
Hævnens nat/Blind Justice (1916)
Harimau Tjampa/Tiger from Tjampa (1953)
Harry Potter and the Deathly Hallows: Part 1 (2010)
Harta Karun/The Treasure (1949)
Hati Merdeka/Hearts of Freedom (2011)
Headshot (2016)
Hijab (2015)
Hippies Lokal/Local Hippies (1976)
Hulahoop Soundings (2008)
Hunger Games, The (2012)
Ibunda/Mother (1986)
Il Grido/The Cry (1957)
Intan Berduri (1972)
IQ Jongkok/The Skewed IQ (1981)
Istana Kecantika/Palace of Beauty (1988)
Jagal/The Act of Killing (2012)
Jakarta Maghrib/Jakarta at Dusk (2010)
Jalanan (2014)
Janji Joni/Joni's Promise (2005)
Jelangkung (2001)
Jenderal Soedirman/General Soedirman (2015)
Kala/Dead Time (2007)
Kartini/Kartini: Princess of Java (2017)
Kejarlah Daku Kau Kutangkap/Chase Me, I'll Catch You (1985)
Keluarga Cemara/Cemara's Family (2018)
Kenikmatan Tabu/Taboo Pleasure (1994)
Keramat/Sacrosanct (2009)
King (2009)
Kipas Kipas Cari Angin/Running Free (1989)
Koper/The Lost Briefcase (2006)
KTP/Identity Card (2017)
Kuldesak/Cul-de-sac (1998)
Kuntilanak (2018)
Lagi-lagi Krisis/Crisis, Once More (1955)
Lahirnja Gatotkatja/The Birth of Gatotkatja (1960)
Langitku Rumahku/My Sky, My Home (1990)
Laskar Pelangi/The Rainbow Troops (2008)
Laut Bercermin/The Mirror Never Lies (2011)
L'Avventura/The Adventure (1960)
Legenda Sundel Bolong/The Legend of Sundel Bolong (2007)
Lentera Merah/Red Lantern (2006)
Lewat Djam Malam/After the Curfew (1954)
Le cinéma indonésien entre censures et espoirs (2015)
Loetoeng Kasaroeng/The Lost Lutung (1926)

Lovely Man (2011)
Luka di Atas Luka/Wounds (1987)
Maaf, Saya Menghamili Istri Anda/Sorry, I Got Your Wife Pregnant (2007)
Madame X (2010)
Magyar rapszódia/Hungarian Rhapsody (1979)
Maju Kena Mundur Kena/Damned If You Do, Damned If You Don't (1983)
Malam Jumat Kliwon/Night of Jumat Kliwon (1986)
Malam Satu Suro/Night of Satu Suro (1988)
Malam Suro di Rumah Darmo/Night of Suro at Darmo's House (2014)
Malin Kundang Anak Durhaka/Malin Kundang the Ungrateful Son (1971)
Marlina Si Pembunuh dalam Empat Babak/Marlina the Murderer in Four Acts (2017)
Marsinah/Cry Justice (2002)
Masculin Féminin (1966)
Maskot (2006)
Matjan Kemajoran/The Tiger of Kemayoran (1965)
Matrix, The (1999)
Matt Dower (1969)
May (2008)
Melancholy is a Movement (2015)
Menerjang Badai/Weathering the Storm (1984)
Menggapai Matahari/Reaching for the Sun (1986)
Merah Putih/Red and White (2009)
Meta Ekologi (1979)
Mistik: Punahnya Rahasia Ilmu Iblis Leak/Mystics in Bali (1981)
Modus Anomali/Ritual (2012)
Musuh Bebuyutan/Arch Enemy (1974)
My Stupid Boss (2016)
Nagabonar (1986)
Napsu Gila/Crazy Lust (1973)
Night Comes for Us, The (2018)
Night of the Living Dead (1968)
November 1828 (1979)
Nji Ronggeng/The Ronggeng Dancer (1969)
Opera Jawa/Requiem from Java (2006)
Pagar Kawat Berduri/Barbed Wire Fence (1961)
Pareh/Pareh, Song of the Rice (1936)
Pasir Berbisik/Whispering Sands (2001)
Pembalasan Rambu/Rambu (aka *The Intruder*) (1985)
Pembalasan Ratu Laut Selatan/Lady Terminator (1988)
Pendekar Tongkat Emas/The Golden Cane Warrior (2014)
Pengabdi Setan/Satan's Slave (1980)
Pengabdi Setan/Satan's Slaves (2017)
Pengkhianatan G-30-S-PKI/The Betrayal of the 30th September Movement (1984)
Perempuan Berkalung Sorban/The Girl with the Turban (2009)
Perempuan di Sarang Sindikat/Virgins from Hell (1986)
Perempuan Punya Cerita/Chants of Lotus (2007)
Perempuan Tanah Jahanam/Impetigore (2019)
Peronika (2004)

Petualangan Sherina/Sherina's Adventure (2000)
Pintu Terlarang/The Forbidden Door (2009)
Pocong 2 (2006)
Posesif/Possessive (2017)
Psycho (1960)
Puisi Tak Terkuburkan/A Poet: Unconcealed Poetry (1999)
Quickie Express (2007)
R.A. Kartini (1982)
Rahasia Seorang Ibu/A Mother's Secret (1977)
Raid 2: Berandal, The (2014)
Raja Copet/The Pickpockets' King (1977)
Rashomon (1950)
Ratu Ular/The Snake Queen (1972)
Realita Cinta dan Rock 'n' Roll/The Reality of Love and Rock 'n' Roll (2006)
Red Psalm (1972)
RepublikTwitter/The Twitter Republic (2012)
Rhoma Irama Berkelana I (1978)
Ricky: Nakalnya Anak Muda/Ricky: The Restless Youth (1990)
Road to Perdition (2002)
Roro Mendut/The Rebellious Woman (1982)
Rumah Dara/Macabre (2009)
Rumah Ketujuh/The Seventh House (2002)
Salawaku (2017)
Samson Betawi/The Strong Man (1975)
Sang Kiai/The Clerics (2013)
Sang Pemimpi/The Dreamer (2009)
Sang Penari/The Dancer (2011)
Sang Pencerah/The Enlightener (2010)
Saur Sepuh: Satria Madangkara/Saur Sepuh: The Madangkara Warrior (1988)
Se7en (1995)
Secangkir Kopi Pahit/Bitter Coffee (1985)
Sekala Niskala/The Seen and Unseen (2017)
Sentuhan Erotik/Erotic Touch (1997)
Senyap/The Look of Silence (2014)
Serbuan Maut/The Raid: Redemption (2011)
Si Bongkok/The Hunchback (1972)
Si Buta Dari Gua Hantu/The Blindman from the Haunted Cave (1970)
Si Buta Lawan Jaka Sembung/Si Buta Versus Jaka Sembung (1983)
Si Doel Anak Betawi/Doel: The Betawi Kid (1973)
Si Doel Anak Modern/Doel: The Modern Kid (1975)
Si Doel the Movie (2018)
Si Mamad (1973)
Si Pintjang (1951)
Singa Laoet/The Sea Lion (1941)
Siti (2014)
Skandal Terlarang/The Forbidden Scandal (1995)
Soegija (2012)
Soekarno: Indonesia Merdeka (2013)

Something in the Way (2013)
Srigala Item/Black Wolf/De Zwarte Wolf (1941)
Suci Sang Primadona/Suci the Prima Donna (1977)
Sultan Agung: Tahta, Perjuangan, Cinta/Sultan Agung: Power, Struggle, Love (2018)
Sunan Kalijaga (1983)
Sunan Kalijaga dan Syech Siti Jenar/Sunan Kalijaga and Syech Siti Jenar (1985)
Sundel Bolong (1981)
Surat Untuk Bidadari/Letter to An Angel (1994)
Suzanna: Bernapas Dalam Kubur/Suzanna: Buried Alive (2018)
Tabula Rasa (2014)
Tak Seindah Kasih Mama/Nothing Beats a Mother's Love (1985)
Tamu Agung/The Exalted Guest (1955)
Tanda Tanya/Question Mark (2011)
Tarsan Kota/The City Tarzan (1974)
Tengkorak Hidoep/The Living Skeleton (1941)
Tengkorak Hitam/Black Skull (1978)
Terang Boelan/Full Moon (1937)
Tiga Buronan/Three Fugitives (1957)
Tiga Janggo/Three Cowboys (1976)
Tilik/Ladies on Top (2018)
Titian Serambut Dibelah Tujuh/The Narrow Bridge (1983)
Tjambuk Api/The Whip of Fire (1958)
Tjitra/Image (1949)
Tjoet Nja Dhien (1989)
Tutur Tinular II: Naga Puspa Kresna (1991)
Uang Panai' = Maha(r)l (2016)
Vakansi yang Janggal dan Penyakit Lainnya/Peculiar Vacation and Other Illnesses (2012)
Violetta (1962)
Visions of Light: The Art of Cinematography (1992)
Wait Until Dark (1967)
Wajah Seorang Laki-Laki/Ballad of a Man (1970)
Walet Merah/The Red Swallow (1993)
Warkop DKI Reborn: Jangkrik Boss Part 1 (2016)
Warkop DKI Reborn: Jangkrik Boss Part 2 (2017)
Warung Pojok/The Corner Shop (1977)

Index

Note: *italicised* page numbers indicate illustrations. 'n' indicates a note.

3 Nafas Likas/Likas' Three Breaths (2014), 151
9 Naga/9 Dragons (2006), 125
21 Group, 193

abstract function of camera movement, 59, 186, 187
Achnas, Nan, 49, 192
acting style, 38, 63, 64
Ada Apa Dengan Cinta?/What's Up with Cinta? (2002), 5, 17, 30
Ada Apa Dengan Cinta? 2/What's Up with Cinta? 2 (2016), 5
Adobe Lightroom software, 41, *42*
aerial shots, 179, 181
aesthetics, 3, 8, 9, 11, 13, 21, 203, 204, 205
 aesthetic functions, 3, 9, 47, 50, 145, 150, 157–8, 166
 bounded multifunctionalism, 21, 127, 150, 171, 187
 'impact aesthetics', 187
 of intensified continuity, 193
 neo-baroque, 194
 operational aesthetic, 70, 189–90, 195–6
 recent scholarship on, 13–20
 single shot cinema, 187
 of suggested and direct horror, 12–13, 67–8, 139
 of visual clarity and opacity, 127
 of world cinema, 10, 192–3
 see also style
affected point-of-view, 60, 108
Ahmadiyah sect, 39, 134, 170
Algemeen Nederlandsch Indische Film Syndicaat (ANIF), 93–4

allegory, 16, 134
Alone in the Dark (2005), 66
Althusser, Louis, 45n
Altman, Robert, 61
Alton, John, 147n
American Society of Cinematographers (ASC), 18
Anak Perawan di Sarang Penyamun/The Virgin and the Bandits (1962), 108
analytic stylistics, 10, 20, 39, 40–2, 47, 48, 206
anti-communist purge (1965–6), 14, 16, 48, 51
Antonioni, Michelangelo, 38–9
Anwar, Joko, 36, 66, 125, 189, 190–1
Apa Yang Kau Tjari, Palupi?/What Are You Looking For, Palupi? (1969), 109–10
aperture framing, 169, *169*
arcing shots, 179, 181, 196n
Arisan!/The Gathering (2003), 18
Aristo, Salman, 152
Arnheim, Rudolf, 34
art direction/art directors, 57, 69, 91–2, 150, 162, 171, 172
Atambua 39 Derajat Celcius/Atambua 39° Celcius (2012), 151
atmosphere, 10, 12, 55–6, 65–7, 69, 133, 156, 161, 162–3, 167, 180
 definition, 65
 lighting and, 12, 32, 35, 52, 53, 66, 86, 88, *88*, 89, 126–7, 132–3, 138, 141
 see also mood
audiences
 constructional aspect of shots, 195–6
 film reception, 70, 162
 types of moviegoers, 187–9, *188*, 190–1

Australia, 142
authenticity, 12, 54, 57, 68–70, 99, 132–3, 140, 167, 171, 173, 180
  location shooting and, 56, 94, 95, 96, 157–9, *159*, 161, 166, 167
authorial commentary, 190, 191
autonomous moves, 179, 181, 197n
available light shooting, 121, 124

backlight, 84, 124, 126, 133
Balink, Albert, 92, 93–4
Banda Aceh, Sumatra, 8
Bandung Film Festival, 176n
Bandung, West Java, 5–6, 12, 82, 92, 96, 190
Barker, Thomas, 14, 15, 16
Barnum, P. T., 70
Barnwell, Jane, 47, 55, 69–70, 161, 163, 168
baroque arts, 33, 52, 133, 142–3, 194
Barsacq, Léon, 55, 66
Barthes, Roland, 68–9, 150
Bazin, André, 34
beauty lighting, 126
Belitong (was Belitung), Southeastern Sumatra, 152–3, 155, 156, *157*, 158, 159, 161, 176n
Benyamin Koboi Ngungsi/Benyamin the Refugee Cowboy (1975), 111
Benyamin Raja Lenong/Benyamin: The Lenong King (1975), 111
Benyamin S (Benyamin Sueb), 6, 64, 97, 110, 111–12
Berbagi Suami/Love for Share (2005), 124
Bernapas dalam Lumpur/The Longest Dark (1970), 85, *86*, *87*
Betamax videocassettes, 6
Beth (2000), 179, 192–3
Bettinson, Gary, 36, 40
Bhaskar, Ira, 37
Bing Slamet Koboi Cengeng/The Weeping Cowboy (1974), 89
bioskop (movie theatre), 4, 6, 189
Biran, Misbach Yusa, 17, 80, 92, 116n
blurry swirl, 50, 63
body language, 29–31, *30*, *31*, 33, 38–9, 63; *see also* non-verbal communication
Böhme, Gernot, 66, 75n
booming and aerial shots, 179, 181, 197n

Bordwell, David, 11, 16, 33–4, 35, 36–7, 38, 39, 47, 50–2, 60, 62–4, 71, 169, 193
Borobudur, Central Java, 31, 94, 115n
bounded multifunctionalism, 21, 127, 150, 171, 187
Bramantyo, Hanung ('Hanung'), 53, 61, 150, 162, 163, 164–5, *165*, 170–1, 172–3, 176n, 181–2
Buaye Gile/The Crazy Playboy (1974), 111
Buddhism, 29, 31
'bullet time' shots, 181
Bumi Makin Panas/The Earth Gets Hotter (1973), 85–6
Burch, Noël, 34, 51
Buruan Cium Gue!/Kiss Me Quick! (2004), 26n
Butler, Jeremy G., 40

Ca Bau Kan/The Courtesan (2002), 151
Cahaya Dari Timur: Beta Maluku/We Are Moluccans (2014), 151, 180
Cahyono, Eddie, 4
Caldwell, John Thornton, 18
camera movement, 3, 8, 10, 12, 21, 47, 62, 67, 70, 71, 79, 102–14
  abstract function, 59, 186, 187
  blurry swirl, 50, 63
  circular moving camera style, 39, 49
  close-ups, 68, 85, 99, 109, 110, 112, 113, 131, 181, *182*
  colonial era, 102–5, *103*, *104*
  definition, 11, 25n
  focalisation function, 59, 60–1, 185
  free-ranging (prowling) camerawork, 11, 21, 48, 79, 114, 179–96, *183*, *184*, *185*
  functions of, 58–62, 185
  inflection function, 59, 60, 62, 64, 65
  orientation function, 59–60, 187
  pacing function, 59, 186, 187
  panning and tilting, 102–5, *103*, *104*, 108, 113, 136, 137
  post-Suharto era, 20, 21, 71, 102, 114, 174, 179–96, *182*, *183*
  processual effects of, 180–1, 189, 196
  pull-back technique, 106, 107, 108, 109, 179, 197n
  push-in technique, 60, 106, 107, 108, 110, 179, 197n

Index

reflexivity, 21, 59, 61–2, 70, 179–96
Suharto era, 109–14, *111*
Sukarno era, 105–9, *107*, 113
tracking shots, 48–9, 54, 105, 106, 107–8, 110, 130, 179
zoom technique, 11, 61, 108, 109–14, *111*
car-to-car flyover shot (*The Raid 2: Berandal*), 184, 185, *185*, 186, 195–6
Carroll, Noël, 36, 47–8, 49, 71
Catatan Akhir Sekolah/High School Diary (2005), 61, 180, 181–2, *183*
Catatan Si Boy/Boy's Diary (1987), 17–18
censorship, 8, 14, 15, 16, 68, 140, 141
Cerita Cibinong/Story from a Village (2007), 124, 127, 135–41, *136*, *137*, *138*, 144
Cerita Pulau/Story from an Island (2007), 60
chiaroscuro, 33, 52, 80, *81*, 82, *83*, 133
Chion, Michel, 135
Christensen, Benjamin, 187
Cibinong, Java, 138
Cine Crib (YouTube channel), 5
cine-transfer process, 192
cinematography, 3, 8, 9–10, 11, 12–13, 18, 25n, 57–8, 72n, 102, 142–3, 163, 203; *see also* camera movement; lighting; production design
cinephilia (film fandom), 190–1
Cinta Brontosaurus/Brontosaurus Love (2013), 191
circular moving camera style, 39, 49
Citra Awards, 4
close-ups, 68, 85, 99, 109, 110, 112, 113, 131, 181, *182*
Coklat Stroberi/Chocolate Strawberry (2007), 18
colonial era, 6, 17, 22, 26n, 29–30, 33, 41–2, 66, 99–100, 105, 112–13, 128, 132, 155
camera movement, 102–5, *103*, *104*
exterior/interior scenes, 92
Java, 17, 26n, 66, 75n, 100, 163, 167
lighting, 79–81, *81*
location shooting, 92–4, *93*
low-key lighting, 20–1, 79–81, *81*
visual details connote, 155, 162–3, 166–7, *167*
comedy films, 81–2, 89–91, 110–12, *111*, 125
computer-generated imagery (CGI), 10–11, 57, 149, 163, 181, *182*, 195–6

costume design, 19, 20
coverage method, 189
crane shooting, 49, 60, 181, 188
cultural dominance, 30–1
cultural specificity, 17, 30, 174, 204
Cutting, James, 142
cutting pace, 193

Dahlan, Kiyai Haji Ahmad, 29, 32–3, 35, 39, 48, 134, 162, 170–1, 176n
Darah dan Doa/The Long March (1950), 17, 30, 81, 82–4, *83*, 94, 95, 96, 105–6, *107*
Darah Garuda (aka *Merah Putih II)/Blood of Eagles* (2010), 60, 121–2, *122*, 124, 151
darkness, 32, 52, 66, 80, 82
cultural meaning of, 143–5
see also intensified visual darkness; low-key lighting
Darmawan, Hikmat, 15
Daun Diatas Bantal/Leaf on a Pillow (1998), 56
de Waal, Frans, 42
decorative function of film style, 10, 51–2, *51*, 169
democracy, 8, 170, 205
Denmark, 192
Denninghoff-Stelling, A. A., 80
denotative function of film style, 10, 50, 52, 62, 63–4, 133–4, 161
Der letzte Mann/The Last Laugh (1924), 187
desainer produksi (production designer), 91
descriptive stylistics, 40, 48
Dewan Produksi Film Nasional (National Film Production Council), 109–10
dialogue, 9, 68, 69, 99, 100, 105, 186
diegesis, 21, 24n, 50, 59, 62, 101, 103, 149–78, 180, 181
differentiation, strategy of, 91, 128
digital cameras, 14, 124, 141–2, 191–3
digital intermediate (DI) process, 181
Dilan 1990 (2018), 12
Dinata, Nia, 60, 138–9, 140
direct horror, aesthetic of, 67
Djajakusuma, D., 94, 95, 106, 107, 108, 109, 172
Dogme 95, 192
dolly shots, 105, 106, 108, 110, 179, 181

drone shots, 179, 181
duduk bersila (type of body language), 29–31, *30*, 33
'dynamic synthesis', 31

Ecstacy & Pengaruh Sex/Ecstasy and Sexual Influence (1996), 7
Edensor, Tim, 144
editing, 68, 180–1, 185, 186, 189, 190
effect lighting, 53, 56, 88–9, 158
Eflin, Eros, 155, 156, 158, 173
Eisenstein, Sergei, 34
Eliana, Eliana (2002), 179, 192–3
Embun/Dewdrop (1951), 95, 96
emotions *see* feelings/emotions
Enam Djam di Djogja/Six Hours in Djogja (1951), 81
enlightenment, 32, 35, 48
'entrenched auteurism', 19
Europe
　Baroque art, 33, 52, 133, 143
　films from, 3, 19, 38, 56, 187
　medieval, 144
evaluative stylistics, 40
Evans, Gareth, 55–6
expressive function of film style, 10, 50–1, 52, 60, 62–5, 71, 133–4
exterior scenes, 149
　colonial era, 92
　post-Suharto era, 21, 57, 75n, 149, 153, 154
　Suharto era, 98, 110, 114
　Sukarno era, 82, 94–5, 96–7, 108, 149
external dynamics, 35

fantasy films, 142
feelings/emotions, 39, 48, 49, 50, 55, 60, 62–5, 80, 81, 85–6, 89–91, 112, 123–4, 127; *see also* mood
feminism, 19, 36
Festival Film Indonesia (FFI), 4, 100, 162, 176n
Fig Rigs, 179, 186, 192
fill light, 82, 124, 126
film nasional, 14
film noir, 36, 147n, 191
film percontohan (prototype for 'quality' films), 109, 110

film studies, 9, 19, 20, 33–40, 47
Fincher, David, 143
focalisation function of camera movement, 59, 60–1, 185
follow shots, 179, 181, 197n
Fourcolour Films, 4
Frayling, Christopher, 54, 95–6
free-ranging (prowling) camerawork, 11, 21, 48, 79, 114, 179–96, *183*, *184*, *185*

Gadis Desa/Village Girl (1949), 41
Gagak Item/Black Raven/De Zwarte Raaf (1939), 41, 102–3, *103*
gamelan (indigenous orchestra), 19, 203
Gaut, Barys, 196
Geertz, Hildred, 144
gender, 8, 17–18, 19
Gending Sriwijaya/The Robbers (2013), 151
genre lighting, 81–4, *83*, 85, 88–9, 91, 121, 158
Gentong, Southeastern Sumatra, 152, 153, 154, 155–6, 157, *157*
Gibbs, John, 38, 39
Gie (2005), 51, 124, 151
Godard, Jean-Luc, 190
Grand Theories, 36, 40
graphic effects of lighting, 52, 53, 127
　chiaroscuro, 33, 52, 80, *81*, 82, *83*, 133
　see also intensified visual darkness
green screen technique, 163
group body language, 29–31, *30*, *31*, 33
Gunning, Tom, 70, 180, 186
Guru Bangsa Tjokroaminoto/Tjokroaminoto: Teacher of the Nation (2015), 151

Habibie dan Ainun/Habibie and Ainun (2012), 124, 151
Hævnens nat/Blind Justice (1916), 187
Halim, Angela, 92
Hall, Conrad, 142–3, 145
Hanan, David, 16, 17, 18, 29, 30–1, 41, 94, 95, 174
handheld shots, 48, 49, 61, 179, 181, 182, 184, 186, 191–2, 193
Hanich, Julian, 12, 65, 66, 67, 68, 139
Harimau Tjampa/Tiger from Tjampa (1953), 94–5, 106–7, 108
Harris, Neil, 70, 189–90, 195

Harta Karun/The Treasure (1949), 41, 103–5, *104*
Hati Merdeka/Hearts of Freedom (2011), 124
Heider, Karl G., 17, 31, 64–5
hermeneutics, 36, 37, 39
Heuveldorp, L., 92
high-key lighting, 32, 84, 85, *87*, 88, *88*, 125–6, 128
Hinduism, 36, 51, 144
Hirata, Andrea, 152, 156
historical stylistics, 20, 40–1, 102, 187
Højbjerg, Lennard, 39, 49
Hole Drop shot (*The Raid: Redemption*), 183, *184*, 185, 186
Hollywood, 107, 108, 126, 193
  domination, 7, 152
  lighting, 52, 84, 142–3
Home and Away (Australian soap opera), 142
Hong Kong, 61, 113
horror, aesthetic of suggested, 12–13, 67–8, 139
horror/thriller films, 12, 49, 66, 67, 85, 125, 191
  lighting, 66, 68, 81–2, 86–91, *86*, *88*, *90*, 125–7, *126*
Horton, Sarah, 57
Hulahoop Soundings (2008), 49
The Hunger Games (2012), 4
hypertextuality, 194

identity politics, 19
Ikatan Karyawan Film dan Televisi Indonesia (KFT), 18, 141, 172
Il Grido/The Cry (1957), 38–9
illusion of roundness, 62
'illusion of wholeness', 56–7, 96, 163
imagination, 10, 12, 15, 67, 68, 127, 139, 140, 180; *see also* suggested horror, aesthetics of
Imanjaya, Ekky, 15, 152
'impact aesthetics', 187
independence, Indonesian, 6, 84, 105, 106, 121
independent (indie) films, 4, 14, 49, 91, 179
Indonesia Production Designer (IPD), 18
Indonesian Censorship Board (LSF), 140
Indonesian Cinematographers Society (ICS), 18

Indonesian Film Festival (2016), 5
industrial craft reflexivity, 18
inflection function of camera movement, 59, 60, 62, 64, 65
Institut Kesenian Jakarta/Jakarta Arts Institute (IKJ), 15, 172
intensified continuity paradigm, 193
intensified visual darkness, 11, 20, 68, 88, 121–45, *126*
  Cerita Cibinong/Story from the Village, 124, 135–41, *136*, *137*, *138*
  *Darah Garuda (*aka *Merah Putih II)/Blood of Eagles*, 121–3, *122*, 124
  definition, 124
  Pengabdi Setan/Satan's Slave (1980), 125–7, *126*
  Pengabdi Setan/Satan's Slaves (2017), 66, 126–7
  Sang Pencerah/The Enlightener, 32, 48, 124, 129–35, *129*, *130*, *131*, *132*, 140–1, 144
  Siti, 122–3, *123*
interior scenes, 149
  colonial era, 92
  post-Suharto era, 21, 166–7
  Suharto era, 97, 98, 149
  Sukarno era, 82, 95, 106, 108, 149
internal dynamics, 16, 34–5
intertextual dynamics, 35–6
invoked point-of-view, 60, 185
Irama, Rhoma, 6
Isfansyah, Ifa, 4
iSinema, 192
Islam, 15, 16, 19, 29, 30, 31–4, 35, 39, 84, 94, 98, 134, 162, 166, 170–1; *see also* Muhammadiyah (Islamic organisation)
Ismail, Ifan Adriansyah, 15
Ismail, Usmar ('Usmar'), 17, 79–89, 96, 108, 109, 117n, 172
  Anak Perawan di Sarang Penyamun/The Virgin and the Bandits, 108
  Darah dan Doa/The Long March, 17, 30, 81, 82–4, *83*, 94, 95, 96, 105–6, *107*
  Enam Djam di Djogja/Six Hours in Djogja, 81
  Harta Karun/The Treasure, 41, 103–5, *104*
  Lewat Djam Malam/After the Curfew, 79, 81
  Tjitra/Image, 41, 80, *81*, 92, 105–6

Istana Kecantikan/Palace of Beauty (1988), 17
Italy, 96, 108

Jakarta, 4, 22n, 25n, 115n, 116n, 172
   centre of film production, 4, 15, 173
   films set in, 85, 97–8, 110, 114, 184, 187, 192
   Sinematek Indonesia, 17, 41
Jakarta Maghrib/Jakarta at Dusk (2010), 191
Jakobson, Roman, 59
Janji Joni/Joni's Promise (2005), 179, 181, 187–91, *188*, 194–5
Jansco, Miklós, 38
Japan, 144
Java, 4, 14, 31–3, 92, 167
   colonial era, 17, 26n, 66, 75n, 100, 163, 167
   Darah dan Doa/The Long March, 82, 94, 95, 96
   Sang Pencerah/The Enlightener, 29, 35, 48, 129–35, 162–4, *164*, 166–7, *167*, 171
   Sunan Kalijaga, 98–9, *99*, 100, 164
   tedak siten ceremony, 98–100, *99*, *101*
   traditional arts, 19, 26n, 31, 36, 51, 135, 203
   see also individual locations
Java Industrial Film Company, 93
Jelangkung (2001), 125
Jepara, Central Java, 99–100

Kala/Dead Time (2007), 36, 151, 181, *182*
Karno, Rano, 6
Kartini/Kartini: Princess of Java (2017), 151
Kartini, Raden Ajeng, 99–100
Karya, Teguh ('Teguh'), 6, 112, 113, 172
Keating, Patrick, 47, 52, 54, 56, 57, 62, 84, 91, 132
Keramat/Sacrosanct (2009), 49, 60–1, 125, 180, 191
Kessler, Frank, 13, 24n
King (2009), 151
King, Geoff, 187
Kipas Kipas Cari Angin/Running Free (1989), 89–91
Koslofsky, Craig, 144
Kuhn, Anette, 54
Kuldesak/Cul-de-sac (1998), 48–9, 51, *51*, 54, 61, 152, 179

Kurosawa, Akira, 108
Kusumadewa, Aria, 192–3

Langitku Rumahku/My Sky, My Home (1990), 114
Laskar Pelangi/The Rainbow Troops (2008), 50–1, 57, 150, 152
   production design, 50–1, 150, 152–62, *154*, *155*, *157*, *158*, *159*, *160*
L'Avventura/The Adventure (1960), 38
layar tancap (mobile screens), 6
legenda films, 98
Legenda Sundel Bolong/The Legend of Sundel Bolong (2007), 125
Legok Bidara Cina (film studio), 93
Lentera Merah/Red Lantern (2006), 125, 180
Lesmana, Jack, 108
Lesmana, Mira, 49, 152, 192
Lewat Djam Malam/After the Curfew (1954), 79, 81
lighting, 3, 8, 10, 12, 47, 62, 63, 66, 71, 79–91, 125
   atmosphere and, 12, 32, 35, 52, 53, 66, 86, 88, *88*, 89, 126, 127, 132–3, 138, 141
   available light shooting, 121, 124
   beauty lighting, 126
   colonial era, 79–81, *81*
   effect lighting, 53, 56, 88–9, 158
   functions of, 32–3, 51, 52–4, 56
   genre lighting, 81–4, *83*, 85, 88–9, 91, 121, 158
   high-key lighting, 32, 84, 85, *87*, 88, *88*, 125–6, 128
   Hollywood, 52, 84, 142–3
   horror/thriller films, 66, 68, 81–2, 86–91, *86*, *88*, *90*, 125–7, *126*
   light-to-dark ratios, 32, 33, 80
   multifunctionalism of, 52–4, 121, 132, 144
   opacity, 21, 32, 121–48
   painterly effects, 32, 33, 35, 52–3, 54, 133
   post-Suharto era, 20–1, 54, 91, 121–48, *122*, *123*, *129*, *130*, *131*, *132*, *136*, *137*, *138*
   practical light sources, 32, 89, *90*, 124
   realism and, 35, 52, 54, 56, 132, 133–4, 139, 140–1

scene lighting, 80–1, 85, 88–9, 91, 121
selective lighting, 32
single-source lighting, 121, 124
storytelling and, 51, 52, 54, 132, 133, 135, 138
Suharto era, 85–91, *86, 87, 88, 90*
Sukarno era, 81–4, *83*
see also graphic effects of lighting; low-key lighting
Lipscomb III, William P., 195
LoBrutto, Vincent, 54
local and regional cultures, 10, 17, 58, 94–5, 106, 135, 150, 173–4, 204
local film (*filem lokal*), 4, 5, 6–7, 152, 175n, 191
location choice, 8, 10, 12, 66, 152, 153, 204
location designing, 11, 21, 58, 69–70, 79, 98–9, 149–74
location shooting, 11, 56–7, 69–70, 79, 92–101
 authenticity and, 56, 94, 95, 96, 157–9, *159*, 161, 166, 167
 colonial era, 92–4, *93*
 definition, 149
 Laskar Pelangi/The Rainbow Troops, 152–62, *154, 157*
 post-Suharto era, 21, 149–78
 Sang Pencerah/The Enlightener, 162–71
 Suharto era, 97–101, *99, 101, 102*, 149
 Sukarno era, 94–7, 108, 149
Loetoeng Kasaroeng/The Lost Lutung (1926), 92
long shots, 95, 97, 105, 110, 129, *129*, 130, 131
long-take technique, 4–5, 38, 45n, 61, 123, 181–2, *183*, 187–8, 189, 190, 198n
love, 39, 49
Lovely Man (2011), 180
low-key lighting, 11, 20–1, 48, 53, 79–89, 121, 144
 colonial era, 20–1, 79–81, *81*
 horror films, *88*, 89–90, 125
 post-Suharto era, 20–1, 51, 121, 124, 125, 128–45
 Sang Pencerah/The Enlightener, 32, 35, 48, 53, 129–35, *129, 130, 131, 132*
 Suharto era, 85–91, *86, 87, 88, 90*

Sukarno era, 81–4, *83*
see also intensified visual darkness
LSF (Lembaga Sensor Film), 14, 15, 140

Maaf, Saya Menghamili Istri Anda/Sorry, I Got Your Wife Pregnant (2007), 180, 191
macro functional theory of film style, 47–52, 71
macroscopic visual details, 54, 149
 Laskar Pelangi/The Rainbow Troops, 153, 161
 post-Suharto era, 21, 101, 149, 153, 161, 162
 Sang Pencerah/The Enlightener, 162
 Suharto era, 99, 100, 101, *102*, 149
Madame X (2010), 180
Magyar rapszódia/Hungarian Rhapsody (1979), 38
Malam Jumat Kliwon/Night of Jumat Kliwon (1986), 66, 89, *90*
Malam Satu Suro/Night of Satu Suro (1988), 66
Malam Suro di Rumah Darmo/Night of Suro at Darmo's House (2014), 66
Mantovani, Rizal, 49, 51
Marlina Si Pembunuh dalam Empat Babak/Marlina the Murderer in Four Acts (2017), 56–7
Marsinah/Cry Justice (2002), 151
Marxism, 36, 38, 45n
Masculin Féminin (1966), 190
Maskot (2006), 125
mati suri (coma), 7, 141
Matjan Kemayoran/The Tiger of Kemayoran (1965), 108–9
The Matrix, 181
May (2008), 151
meaning, 36–8
 interpretation of, 10, 36–9, 64–5
 and reality, 69
 thematic, 39, 134, 140, 170
meaning-making, 10, 39, 112, 134, 186
Mecca, Zaskia Adya, 162
medium shots, 98, 99, 136, 137
Melancholy is a Movement (2015), 191
melodrama, 85–6, 89, 124
Merah Putih/Red and White (2009), 124, 151
Meta Ekologi (1979), 17

metafilms, 191
micro functional theories of film style, 47, 52–62, 71
microscopic visual details, 54, 57, 95, 96, 155, 171
  definition, 149
  Laskar Pelangi/The Rainbow Troops, 155, 156, *158*, 161, 171
  post-Suharto era, 21, 101, 149, 150, 155, 156, *158*, 161, 163–4, 171–3
  Sang Pencerah/The Enlightener, 163–7, *164*, *165*, *166*, *167*, *168*, 171
  Suharto era, 99, 101, 149–50
  see also props
Miles Films, 152
Minangkabau community (West Sumatra), 65, 94–5
mise en scène, 3, 9–10, 12, 13, 24n, 181
Mittell, Jason, 70
Miyagawa, Kazuo, 108
mobile frame, 25n; *see also* camera movement
Modus Anomali/Ritual (2012), 125
mood, 10, 52, 65, 80, 81–2, 85, 91; *see also* atmosphere
Mrázek, Jan, 135
Muhammadiyah (Islamic organisation), 29, 33, 160, 162, 166, 176n
  school in *Laskar Pelangi*, 153, 155–6, *157*, 158–9, 160, 161
multifunctional lighting, 52–4, 121, 132, 144
multifunctionalism, bounded, 21, 127, 150, 171, 187
Münsterberg, Hugo, 34
Murnau, F. W., 187
Murtagh, Ben, 17–18
music, 8, 9, 12, 50, 54, 62–3, 64, 80, 106, 108, 153, 172, 186
musicals, 81–2, 125, 128
Musuh Bebuyutan/Arch Enemy (1974), 111
MVP Pictures, 35

Nahdlatul Ulama (NU) (Islamic organisation), 33, 43n, 176n
naming practices, 22
narrative films, 16, 24n, 31, 37, 41, 47–71
nationalism, 14, 95
Ndalianis, Angela, 193–4
Neer, Richard, 37–8
neorealism, 56, 96, 108
Netherlands Indies, 6, 41, 80, 92–3, 105, 132–3; *see also* colonial era
New Order era *see* Suharto/New Order era (1966–98)
Nidji, 153
Nielsen, Jakob Isak, 47, 58–61, 62–4, 70, 108, 180, 185, 186, 196n
Night of the Living Dead (1968), 66
Nji Ronggeng/The Ronggeng Dancer (1969), 110
non-verbal communication, 64–5; *see also* body language
November 1828 (1979), 17
Nuala, Yato Fio, 192
Nugroho, Garin, 48, 51, 56, 192

one-shot presentation *see* long-take technique
opacity, 21, 32, 121–48
Opera Jawa/Requiem from Java (2006), 36, 51
operational aesthetic, 70, 189–90, 195–6
optical point-of-view, 60–1, 108
orientation function of camera movement, 59–60, 187

pacing function of camera movement, 59, 186, 187
painterly effects of lighting, 32, 33, 35, 52–3, 54, 133
Pangalengan, West Java, 66, 67
panning, 102–5, *103*, *104*, 108, 113, 136, 137
Paramaditha, Intan, 10, 140
parametric narration, 51–2
Pareh/Pareh, Song of the Rice (1936), 92
Pasaribu, Adrian Jonathan, 7
Pasir Berbisik/Whispering Sands (2001), 151
penata artistik (art department head), 91–2
pencak silat (martial art), 4, 94, 113, 186
Pendekar Tongkat Emas/The Golden Cane Warrior (2014), 61, 151
Pengabdi Setan/Satan's Slave (1980), 125–7, *126*
Pengabdi Setan/Satan's Slaves (2017), 30, 61, 66, 67, 125, 126–7, 151, 191
penggiat sinema (cinema activists), 7, 41
Perempuan Berkalung Sorban/The Girl with the Turban (2009), 151, 180
Perempuan Punya Cerita/Chants of Lotus (2007), 60

Perfini (film company), 94, 95, 105, 106, 107, 108, 115n
period films, 57, 67, 98–101, 132–3, 150–71, 173; *see also individual films*
Persari (film company), 105
Petualangan Sherina/Sherina's Adventure (2000), 125, 128
pictorial function of lighting, 33, 54, 132, 133–4, 140, 141, 150, 161
Pintu Terlarang/The Forbidden Door (2009), 125
Plantinga, Carl, 65, 145n
The Player (1992), 61
PN Timah, 152, 158, 159, 160, 161
poetics of cinema, 8, 10, 20, 33–40, 42, 203
point-of-view (POV) shots, 60–1, 108–9, 187
  affected, 60, 108
  invoked, 60, 185
  optical, 60–1, 108
polarisation function of production design, 55, 161, 168
polycentrism, 194
pop culture, 14, 16, 204
pornographic films, 6–7
post-Suharto era (post-New Order or post-1998), 3, 7, 8, 14–15, 16, 18, 20, 22, 39, 79
  camera movement, 20, 21, 71, 102, 114, 174, 179–96, *182, 183*
  complexity, 3, 9, 10, 21, 71, 114, 143, 180–1, 187
  exterior scenes, 21, 57, 75n, 149, 153, 154
  fundamentalist cultural politics, 8, 14–15, 16
  interior scenes, 21, 166–7
  lighting, 20–1, 54, 91, 121–48, *122, 123, 129, 130, 131, 132, 136, 137, 138*
  location shooting, 21, 149–74
  low-key lighting, 20–1, 51, 121, 124, 125, 127, 128–45
  macroscopic visual details, 21, 101, 149, 153, 161, 162
  microscopic visual details, 21, 101, 149, 150, 155, 156, *158*, 161, 163–4, 171–3
  production design, 9, 11, 20, 21, 71, 101, 149–78
practical light sources, 32, 89, *90*, 124
Prakosa, Gotot, 17

Prince, Stephen, 56, 96, 163
processual effects of camera movement, 180–1, 189, 196
production design, 3, 8, 10, 11, 12, 13, 18–19, 22, 47, 62, 69–70, 71, 79, 91–101, 204
  computer-generated imagery (CGI), 10–11, 57, 149, 163, 181, *182*, 195–6
  definition, 10–11
  Dilan 1990, 12
  functions of, 54–8, 62, 67, 161, 168
  Laskar Pelangi/The Rainbow Troops, 50–1, 150, 152–62, *154, 155, 157, 158, 159, 160*
  location choice, 8, 10, 12, 66, 152, 153, 204
  location designing, 11, 21, 58, 69–70, 79, 98–9, 149–74
  polarisation function, 55, 161, 168
  post-Suharto era, 9, 11, 20, 21, 71, 101, 149–74
  Sang Pencerah/The Enlightener, 39, 58, *58*, 150, 162–71, *164, 165, 166, 167, 168, 169, 170*
  set design, 8, 10, 12, 39, 50–1, 54–5, 57, 58, 66, 67, 149, 186
  set dressing, 96, 149, 154, 156, 161, 163–4, 166, 169
  Suharto era, 97–102, 149
  Sukarno era, 94–7, 149
  visual compositional impact, 57–8, 168–9, *168, 169*
  visual shortcuts, 54–5
  see also props
production designers, 18, 22, 54, 57–8, 91–2, 172–3
Profilti (Dutch film company), 93–4
props, 8, 10, 54, 57, 100, 154, *154*, 156–7, *158*
  Kuldesak/Cul-de-sac, 54
  Laskar Pelangi/The Rainbow Troops, 50–1, 57, *159*, 160, *160*
  lighting, 32, 89, *90*, 96
  Malam Jumat Kliwon/Night of Jumat Kliwon, 90
  R.A. Kartini, 100
  Sang Pencerah/The Enlightener, 166, *166*, 167
  Sunan Kalijaga, 98–9, *99*

props (cont.)
    Sunan Kalijaga dan Syech Siti Jenar/Sunan Kalijaga and Syech Siti Jenar, 32
prostitute films, 85–6, *86*, *87*
prowling (free-ranging) camerawork, 11, 21, 48, 79, 114, 179–96, *183*, *184*, *185*
Psycho (1960), 44n
psychoanalysis, 36, 45n
PT Elang Perkasa (film equipment rental company), 49
Puisi Tak Terkuburkan/A Poet: Unconcealed Poetry (1999), 48, 179, 192
pull-back technique, 106, 107, 108, 109, 179, 197n
push-in technique, 60, 106, 107, 108, 110, 179, 197n
Pye, Douglas, 38, 39

queer theory, 19
Quickie Express (2007), 125, 180

R.A. Kartini (1982), 99–100, *101*, *102*
Rahardjo, Slamet, 114
The Raid: Redemption/Serbuan Maut (2011), 4, 55–6, 125, 180, 181, 182–7, 189–90, 195
    Hole Drop shot, 183, *184*, 185, 186
The Raid 2: Berandal (2014), 180, 181, 182–7, 189–90, 195–6
    car-to-car flyover shot, 184, 185, *185*, 186, 195–6
Rapi Films, 145n
Rashomon (1950), 108
Ratu Ular/The Snake Queen (1972), 86
realism, 56–7, 68–70, 157, 161
    lighting and, 35, 52, 54, 56, 132, 133–4, 139, 140–1
Realita Cinta dan Rock 'n' Roll/The Reality of Love and Rock 'n' Roll (2006), 18
the reality effect, 68–70, 150, 161, 166
Red Psalm (1972), 38
reflexivity, 10, 21, 70, 205
    camera movement, 21, 59, 61–2, 70, 179–96
    Catatan Akhir Sekolah/High School Diary, 142
    industrial craft reflexivity, 18
    Kuldesak/Cul-de-sac, 142

Pendekar Tongkat Emas/The Golden Cane Warrior, 142
self-reflexivity, 194–5
Reformasi era *see* post-Suharto era (post-New Order or post-1998)
regional cultures, 10, 17, 58, 94–5, 106, 135, 150, 173–4, 204
religion, 8, 15, 16, 29, 39, 144; *see also* Hinduism; Islam
Republik Twitter/The Twitter Republic (2012), 55
Resobowo, Basoeki, 94
Retel Helmrich, Leonard, 187
reverse engineering, 34–5
Rheumason box, 155, *155*
Ricklefs, Merle, 132
rituals, 29, 98–9, *99*, 100–1, *101*, 144, 164–5, *164*, *165*, 174
Riza, Riri ('Riri'), 4–5, 49, 142, 150, 152, 156, 172–3, 192–3, 198n
Rizal, Faozan, 32, 53, 133–5, 142–3
RKO Radio Pictures, 93–4
Road to Perdition (2002), 142–3
Roro Mendut/The Rebellious Woman (1982), 17
Rumah Ketujuh/The Seventh House (2002), 192–3
Rushton, Richard, 36, 40

Said, Salim, 17
Samson Betawi/The Strong Man (1975), 110–11, *111*
Sang Kiai/The Clerics (2013), 151
Sang Pemimpi/The Dreamer (2009), 151
Sang Penari/The Dancer (2011), 180
Sang Pencerah/The Enlightener (2010), 29, *30*, 31–3, 34–5
    intensified visual darkness, 32, 48, 124, 129–35, *129*, *130*, *131*, *132*, 140–1, 144
    low-key lighting, 32, 35, 48, 53, 129–35, *129*, *130*, *131*, *132*
    production design, 39, 58, *58*, 150, 162–71, *164*, *165*, *166*, *167*, *168*, *169*, *170*
Sasono, Eric, 15, 134, 192
satire, 16, 89
Saur Sepuh: Satria Madangkara/Saur Sepuh: The Madangkara Warrior (1988), 30
Sawyer, Keith, 13
scene lighting, 80–1, 85, 88–9, 91, 121
Se7en (1995), 143

Sebastian, Allan, 162–3, 165, 173
Sekala Niskala/The Seen and Unseen (2017), 17
Sellors, C. Paul, 19
semiotics, 17, 36, 44n
Sen, Krishna, 17
Sentuhan Erotik/Erotic Touch (1997), 7
Serbuan Maut/The Raid: Redemption (2011), 4, 55–6, 125, 180, 181, 182–7, 189–90, 195
   Hole Drop shot, 183, *184*, 185, 186
set design, 8, 10, 12, 39, 50–1, 54–5, 57, 58, 66, 67, 149, 186
set dressing, 96, 149, 154, 156, 161, 163–4, 166, 169; *see also* props
sex, 16, 36n, 49, 85, 139, 140–1
sex films (*film esek-esek*), 6–7
sexuality, 17–18, 19, 44n, 140
shadow, 52, 80, 82, 86, 121, 124, 128, 131, 137, 139, 144
   tenebrism, 33, 133–4
   wayang kulit (Javanese shadow puppetry), 19, 26n, 51, 135
Shinoda, Mike, 186
Si Bongkok/The Hunchback (1972), 113
Si Doel Anak Modern/Doel: The Modern Kid (1975), 97–8
'side-stream' filmmaking, 14
silat films, 4, 6, 30, 61, 94–5, 106–7, 108–9, 113
silent films, 29–30, 41, 187
sindiran (criticism), 16
Sinematek Indonesia, 17, 41
Sinematografi Indonesia (SI), 18
Singa Laoet/The Sea Lion (1941), 29–30, 41, 103
single shot cinema aesthetics, 187
single-source lighting, 121, 124
Siti (2015), 4–5, 122–3, *123*, 124, 180
Sjuman Djaya, 6, 99
social media, 3, 5, 55, 195–6; *see also* YouTube
Soedjarwo, Rudi, 192–3
Soegija (2012), 124, 128, 151
Soekarno: Indonesia Merdeka (2013), 53, *53*, 151, 165, *165*
Something in the Way (2013), 180
Sontag, Susan, 12
sound, 26n, 40, 67, 68, 126, 127, 137, 139

non-diegetic, 111, 126
soundtracks/scores, 108, 153
see also music
South Pacific Film, 106
space, 56, 65–7, 137, 180–1, 186
Srigala Item/Black Wolf/De Zwarte Wolf (1941), 41, 92–3, *93*
staging, 29–31, *30*, 68, 105, 108, 136, 137, 139
Steadicam, 179, 181, 192
storytelling, 9, 16, 49, 57, 62–5, 123–4, 135, 169, 171, 173
   lighting and, 51, 52, 54, 132, 133, 135, 138
studio filming, 57, 92–7, 105, 108, 149
style, 3, 8–12, 18–21, 203–6
   change in Indonesian film, 8, 20, 29, *30*, 31–2, *31*, 40–1, 79, 102, 109, 128, 181, 191, 193
   continuity in Indonesian film, 20, 29–31, *30*, *31*, 79, 102
   decorative function, 10, 51–2, *51*, 169
   definitions, 8–9, 11, 48
   denotative function, 10, 50, 52, 62, 63–4, 133–4, 161
   expressive function, 10, 50–1, 52, 60, 62–5, 71, 133–4
   Harimau Tjampa/Tiger from Tjampa, 94
   Kala/Dead Time, 36
   Laskar Pelangi/The Rainbow Troops, *158*
   macro functional theory, 47–52, 71
   Matjan Kemayoran/The Tiger of Kemayoran, 108
   micro functional theory, 47, 52–62, 71
   in narrative films, 47–71
   reflexive function, 10, 21, 70
   Sang Pencerah/The Enlightener, 35, 48, 162
   Siti, 4–5
   suggestive function, 10, 139
   symbolic function, 10, 51, 52, 99, 169, 170
   see also aesthetics; analytic stylistics; camera movement; lighting; production design
stylistics
   analytic, 10, 20, 39, 40–2, 47, 48, 206
   definition, 40
   descriptive, 40, 48
   evaluative, 40
   historical, 20, 40–1, 102, 187
Subang, West Java, 94, 96

Sugandi, Yadi, 156
suggested horror, aesthetics of, 12–13, 67–8, 139
suggestive function of film style, 10, 139
Suharto/New Order era (1966–98), 6, 8, 10, 14, 15, 17, 18, 22, 48, 172, 173
   camera movement, 109–14, *111*
   duduk bersila, 30
   exterior scenes, 98, 110, 114
   film industry, 141
   interior scenes, 97, 98, 149
   location shooting, 97–101, *99*, *101*, *102*, 149
   low-key lighting, 85–91, *86*, *87*, *88*, *90*
   macroscopic visual details, 99, 100, 101, *102*, 149
   microscopic visual details, 99, 101, 149–50
   production design, 97–102, 149
Suharto, President, 159, *159*
Sukarno era (1950–65), 15, 22, 172
   camera movement, 105–9, *107*, 113
   exterior scenes, 82, 94–5, 96–7, 108, 149
   interior scenes, 82, 95, 106, 108, 149
   location shooting, 94–7, 108, 149
   low-key lighting, 81–4, *83*
   production design, 94–7, 149
Sukarno, President, 6, 53
Sunan Kalijaga (1983), 98–9, *99*, 100, 164
Sunan Kalijaga dan Syech Siti Jenar/Sunan Kalijaga and Syech Siti Jenar (1985), 30, 31–2, *31*, 33
Sundel Bolong (1981), 88–9, *88*
Sutan Takdir Alisjahbana, 108
Syaiful, Ipung Rahmat, 189, 190
symbolic function of film style, 10, 51, 52, 99, 169, 170

taboos, 128, 134, 140, 145
Talbott, Albert, 6
Tan Khoen Yauw, 93
Tanissan, Djufri, 99
Tanizaki, Junichiro, 144
Tanjung, Ical, 139–40, 143
Tan's Film Co Studio, 93
Tarigan, F. E. S., 88, 91
Tashiro, Charles, 47, 69–70
tata artistik (production design and art direction), 91, 92, 95–6

tata kamera (cinematography), 102
Tavoularis, Dean, 57, 155
technology, 6, 9, 10, 11, 14, 35, 141–2, 144, 181, 194, 195, 196
   cameras, 141–2, 191–3
   CGI, 10–11, 57, 149, 163, 181, *182*, 195–6
tedak siten ceremony, 98–100, *99*, *101*
television, 6, 141, 142, 173
tenebrism, 33, 133–4
Tengkorak Hidoep/The Living Skeleton (1941), 41
Tera, Max, 84, 106
Terang Boelan/Full Moon (1937), 80
thematic meaning, 39, 134, 140, 170
Thomas, Francis-Noël, 12
thriller films *see* horror/thriller films
tilting, 102, 108, 113
Tjambuk Api/The Whip of Fire (1958), 94, 106, 107
Tjitra/Image (1949), 41, 80, *81*, 92, 105–6
tourism, 153
tracking shots, 48–9, 54, 105, 106, 107–8, 110, 130, 179; *see also* pull-back technique; push-in technique
transgender individuals, 17–18
transnational trends, 142, 191, 192–3
Trier, Lars von, 192
Turner, Mark, 12
Twitter, 55
two-shots, 97, 130, 131

Umboh, Wim, 109
underexposure, 21, 145
United States, 7, 18, 19, 36, 56, 142–3, 193
Utama, Suadi, 61

van Heeren, Katinka, 14–15, 16
van Heusden, Barend, 37
Vermeer, Johannes, 53–4
video compact discs (VCDs), 3, 14, 25n, 116n
Vinterberg, Thomas, 192
virtuosity, 61, 189–90, 194, 196
virtuosity of transport, 187
visual compositional impact, 57–8, 168–9, *168*, *169*
visual shortcuts, 54–5, 95–6

Wait Until Dark (1967), 66
Wajah Seorang Laki-Laki/Ballad of a Man (1970), 112–13
walk-and-talk shots, 106, *107*, 108
war films, 82, 121–2, *122*, 124
Warkop DKI, 6
wayang golek (Sundanese rod-puppet theatre), 19, 26n
wayang kulit (Javanese shadow puppetry), 19, 26n, 51, 135
Westwell, Guy, 54
Wilson, George, 37

Wiranatakusumah V (Regent of Bandung), 92
women filmmakers, 15, 17
Wong Brothers, 93
world cinema, 10, 108, 142, 191, 192–3
wuxia cinema (Hong Kong), 61

Yogyakarta, Central Java, 4, 39, 49, 56, 82, 96, 122, 162, 163, 166, 167–8
YouTube, 3, 5, 145n, 195–6, 199n

Zone System, 124
zoom technique, 11, 61, 108, 109–14, *111*

EU representative:
Easy Access System Europe
Mustamäe tee 50, 10621 Tallinn, Estonia
Gpsr.requests@easproject.com